MW00423963

She Said What?
Quotable Women
Talk Leadership

More than 3000 quotes
from women leaders on leadership

Ability

*In the field of sports you are more or less accepted
for what you do rather than what you are.*
Althea Gibson *(1927-2003)*
American tennis player

*More important than talent, strength, or knowledge is the ability
to laugh at yourself and enjoy the pursuit of your dreams.*
Amy Grant *(1960-)*
American singer, songwriter

*Luck? Sure. But only after long practice and only
with the ability to think under pressure.*
Babe Didrikson Zaharias *(1911-1956)*
American golfer

You never know what you can do until you have to do it.
Betty Ford *(1918-2011)*
American first lady

We all have ability. The difference is how we use it.
Charlotte Whitton *(1896-1975)*
Canadian politician

*I invented my life by taking for granted that everything I did
not like would have an opposite, which I would like.*
Coco Chanel *(1883-1971)*
French fashion designer

*Very few people possess true artistic ability. It is therefore both
unseemly and unproductive to irritate the situation by making
an effort. If you have a burning, restless urge to write or paint,
simply eat something sweet and the feeling will pass.*
Fran Lebowitz *(1950-)*
American writer

*Ah, mastery ... what a profoundly satisfying feeling when one finally
gets on top of a new set of skills ... and then sees the light under the
new door those skills can open, even as another door is closing.*
Gail Sheehy *(1937-)*
American writer, lecturer

Where I was born and where and how I have lived is unimportant. It is what I have done with where I have been that should be of interest.
Georgia O'Keeffe *(1887-1986)*
American artist

Ability hits the mark where presumption overshoots and diffidence falls short.
Golda Meir *(1898-1978)*
Ukrainian-born Israeli leader

My mother implanted in me as a young girl...you can either be an actor in your own life, or a reactor in somebody else's.
Hillary Rodham Clinton *(1947-)*
American, Secretary of State

It is our choices that show what we truly are, far more than our abilities.
J. K. Rowling *(1965-)*
English writer

A sobering thought: What if, at this very moment, I am living up to my full potential?
Jane Wagner *(1935-)*
American writer, director

They asked me, How did you learn to sing the blues like that? How did you learn to sing that heavy? I just opened my mouth and that's what I sounded like. You can't make up something that you don't feel. I didn't make it up. I just opened my mouth and it existed.
Janis Joplin *(1943-1970)*
American singer

A bird does not sing because it has an answer. It sings because it has a song.
Joan Walsh Anglund *(1926-)*
American author

I would always advise that you aim a lot higher because you've got that ability in you. If somebody says you can't do something, don't listen.
Kavita Oberoi *(1970-)*
British entrepreneur

If you only believe that you're an artist when you have a big advance in your pocket and a single coming out, I would say that's quite soulless. You have to have a sense of your own greatness and your own ability from a very deep place inside you. I am the one with the litmus test in my hands of what people need to hear next.
Lady Gaga *(1986-)*
American performance artist

I am not a has-been. I am a will be.
Lauren Bacall *(1924-)*
American actress

If you can't do what you want, do what you can.
Lois McMaster Bujold *(1949-)*
American author

Ability is of little account without opportunity.
Lucille Ball *(1911-1989)*
American comedian, actress

I think knowing what you cannot do is more important than knowing what you can do.
Lucille Ball *(1911-1989)*
American comedian, actress

Have enough sense to know ahead of time when your skills will not extend to wallpapering.
Marilyn vos Savant *(1946-)*
American writer

It was ability that mattered, not disability, which is a word I'm not crazy about using.
Marlee Matlin *(1965-)*
American actress

We don't know who we are until we see what we can do.
Martha Grimes *(1931-)*
American author detective fiction

I didn't have the same fitness or ability as the other girls so I had to beat them with my mind.
Martina Hingis *(1980-)*
Swiss tennis player

I believe every person has the ability to achieve something important and with that in mind I regard everyone as special.
Mary Kay Ash *(1918-2001)*
American entrepreneur

As simple as it sounds, we all must try to be the best person we can: by making the best choices, by making the most of the talents we've been given.
Mary Lou Retton *(1968-)*
American gymnast

I am a great realist in all aspects of life. Whatever I can do ... here it is.
Olga Korbut *(1955-)*
Soviet Olympic gymnast

To show your true ability is always, in a sense, to surpass the limits of your ability, to go a little beyond them: to dare, to seek, to invent; it is at such a moment that new talents are revealed, discovered, and realized.
Simone de Beauvoir *(1908-1986)*
French writer, philosopher

I can, therefore I am.
Simone Weil *(1909-1943)*
French philosopher

The ability of writers to imagine what is not the self, to familiarize the strange and mystify the familiar, is the test of their power.
Toni Morrison *(1931-)*
American novelist

The ability to think straight, some knowledge of the past, some vision of the future, some skill to do useful service, some urge to fit that service into the well-being of the community – these are the most vital things education must try to produce.
Virginia Crocheron Gildersleeve *(1877-1965)*
American educator

Acceptance

I learned that true forgiveness includes total self-acceptance. And out of acceptance wounds are healed and happiness is possible again.
Catharine Marshall *(1914-1983)*
American author

There are people who live lives little different than the beasts,
and I don't mean that badly. I mean they accept whatever
happens day to day without struggle or question or regret. To
them things just are, like the earth and sky and seasons.
Celestede Blasis *(1946-2001)*
American author

I am no longer what I was. I will remain what I have become.
Coco Chanel *(1883-1971)*
French fashion designer

I love my past. I love my present. I'm not ashamed of what
I've had, and I'm not sad because I have it no longer.
Colette *(1873-1954)*
French novelist

Whatever is – is best.
Ella Wheeler Wilcox *(1850-1919)*
American poet

Let's practice what we preach, and with the acceptance that we expect
from others, let's stop being so damn judgmental and crucifying everyone
who doesn't fit in to our boxed-in perception of what is right.
Gillian Anderson *(1968-)*
American actress

This is the precept by which I have lived: Prepare for the
worst; expect the best; and take what comes.
Hannah Arendt *(1906-1975)*
German philosopher

Understanding is the first step to acceptance, and
only with acceptance can there be recovery.
J. K. Rowling *(1965-)*
English writer

Acceptance and tolerance and forgiveness, those are life-altering lessons.
Jessica Lange *(1949-)*
American actress

The most beautiful thing is inevitability of events and the
most ugly thing is trying to resist inevitability.
Katharine Butler Hathaway *(1890-1942)*
American writer

Everything in life that we really accept undergoes a change.
Katherine Mansfield *(1888 - 1923)*
New Zealand-born writer

Conversion for me was not a Damascus Road experience. I slowly moved into an intellectual acceptance of what my intuition had always known.
Madeleine L'Engle *(1918-)*
American novelist

I accept the universe!
Margaret Fuller *(1810-1850)*
American journalist, author

*The minute you settle for less than you deserve,
you get even less than you settled for.*
Maureen Dowd *(1952-)*
American columnist

Gratitude unlocks the fullness of life. It turns what we have into enough and more. It turns denial into acceptance, chaos to order, confusion to clarity. It can turn a meal into a feast, a house into a home, a stranger into a friend. Gratitude makes sense of our past, brings peace for today and creates a vision for tomorrow.
Melody Beattie *(1948-)*
American author

I'm not wise, but the beginning of wisdom is there; it's like relaxing into – and an acceptance of – things.
Tina Turner *(1939-)*
American singer

Accomplishment

No matter what accomplishments you make, somebody helped you.
Althea Gibson *(1927-2003)*
American tennis player

Had I been a man I might have explored the Poles, or climbed Mount Everest, but as it was, my spirit found outlet in the air.
Amy Johnson *(1903-1941)*
English aviator

To follow without halt, one aim; there is the secret of success.
And success? What is it? I do not find it in the applause of the
theatre. It lies rather in the satisfaction of accomplishment.
Anna Pavlova *(1881-1931)*
Russian ballerina

Everyone has inside of them a piece of good news. The good
news is that you don't know how great you can be! What
you can accomplish! And what your potential is.
Anne Frank *(1929-1945)*
German writer, holocaust victim

I decided, very early on, just to accept life unconditionally; I
never expected it to do anything special for me, yet I seemed
to accomplish far more than I had ever hoped. Most of the
time it just happened to me without my ever seeking it.
Audrey Hepburn *(1929-1993)*
Belgian-born actress

They say an actor is only as good as his parts. Well,
my parts have done me pretty well, darling.
Barbara Windsor *(1937-)*
English actress

It's about connections. I want to connect with people; I want to make people
think Yeah, that's how I feel. And if I can do that, that's an accomplishment.
Carole King *(1942-)*
American musician

If you can react the same way to winning and losing, that's
a big accomplishment. That quality is important because it
stays with you the rest of your life, and there's going to be a
life after tennis that's a lot longer than your tennis life.
Chris Evert *(1954-)*
American tennis player

When you cease to make a contribution you begin to die.
Eleanor Roosevelt *(1884 - 1962)*
American First Lady

It had long since come to my attention that people of
accomplishment rarely sat back and let things happen
to them. They went out and happened to things.
Elinor Smith *(1911-2010)*
American aviatrix

For me, just being on the cover of a magazine wasn't enough. I began to think, what value is there in doing something in which you have no creative input?
Elle Macpherson *(1964-)*
Australian model

Most people, after accomplishing something, use it over and over again like a gramophone record till it cracks, forgetting that the past is just the stuff with which to make more future.
Freya Stark *(1893-1993)*
French-born travel writer, explorer

You get whatever accomplishment you are willing to declare.
Georgia O'Keeffe *(1887-1986)*
American artist

When I heard the BBC was putting on a retrospective season of my films I thought, 'Oh my God, I must have died.'
Glenda Jackson *(1936-)*
English actress

Everybody starts at the top, and then has the problem of staying there. Lasting accomplishment, however, is still achieved through a long, slow climb and self-discipline.
Helen Hayes *(1900-1993)*
American actress

Out of the strain of the Doing,/ Into the peace of the Done.
Julia Louisa M. Woodruff *(1833-1909)*
American writer

I longed to arrest all beauty that came before me, and at length the longing has been satisfied.
Julia Margaret Cameron *(1815-1879)*
English photographer

If you have everything, then you don't want to go on. It's the lacking that makes you search for something better.
Juliette Binoche *(1964-)*
French actress

Our being is subject to all the chances of life. There are so many things we are capable of that we could be or do. The potentialities are so great that we never any of us are more than one-fourth fulfilled.
Katherine Anne Porter *(1890-1980)*
American journalist

I yield to no one in my admiration for the office as a social center, but it's no place actually to get any work done.
Katherine Whitehorn *(1914-1956)*
British columnist

If I could learn to treat triumph and disaster the same, then I would find bliss.
Kathie Lee Gifford *(1953-)*
American entertainer

Look at a day when you are supremely satisfied at the end. It's not a day when you lounge around doing nothing; it's when you've had everything to do, and you've done it.
Margaret Thatcher *(1925-)*
English Prime Minister

You can eat an elephant one bite at a time.
Mary Kay Ash *(1918-2001)*
American entrepreneur

May it be a presidency where I the President can sing to you, citizens of Ireland, the joyous refrain of the 14th century poet as recalled by W.B. Yeats: 'I am of Ireland...come dance with me in Ireland.'
Mary Robinson *(1944-)*
Irish president

Many people say I'm the best women's soccer player in the world. I don't think so. And because of that, someday I just might be.
Mia Hamm *(1972-)*
American soccer player

But with the right kind of coaching and determination you can accomplish anything and the biggest accomplishment that I feel I got from the film was overcoming that fear.
Reese Witherspoon *(1976-)*
American actress

To be somebody you must last.
Ruth Gordon *(1896-1985)*
American actress, writer

My hope is that 10 years from now after I've been across the street at work for a while they'll all be glad they gave me that wonderful vote.
Sandra Day O'Connor *(1930-)*
American Supreme Court Justice

I value the momentum of making the list and the drive to tick. Sometimes I add stuff I've already accomplished so I can get going on my feelings of accomplishment.
Sara Genn *(1972-)*
Canadian-born artist

Being varied is something I do instinctively and naturally. I feel a tremendous sense of accomplishment.
Sarah Brightman *(1960-)*
English actress

I can now successfully drive a stick. That's a huge accomplishment.
Shannon Miller *(1977-)*
American gymnast

It doesn't matter what you're trying to accomplish. It's all a matter of discipline. I was determined to discover what life held for me beyond the inner-city streets.
Wilma Rudolph *(1940-1994)*
American Olympic runner

My mother taught me very early to believe I could achieve any accomplishment I wanted to. The first was to walk without braces.
Wilma Rudolph *(1940-1994)*
American Olympic runner

The love of these people and of my fans mean more than any award or special accomplishment.
Wynonna Judd *(1964-)*
American musician

Achievement

Achievement brings with it its own anticlimax.
Agatha Christie *(1890-1976)*
English detective novelist

I wish people could achieve what they think would bring them happiness in order for them to realize that that's not really what happiness is.
Alanis Morissette *(1974-)*
Canadian singer

Events that are predestined require but little management. They manage themselves. They slip into place while we sleep and suddenly we are aware that the thing we fear to attempt is already accomplished.
Amelia E. Barr *(1831-1919)*
British novelist

We know it matters not what we have been but this and always this: what we shall be.
Angelina Weld Grimké *(1805-1879)*
American abolitionist

A finished person is a boring person.
Anna Quindlen *(1952-)*
American journalist

Authority without wisdom is like a heavy axe without an edge, fitter to bruise than polish.
Anne Bradstreet *(1612-1672)*
American, first published poet

A creative person is motivated by the desire to achieve, not by the desire to beat others.
Ayn Rand *(1905-1982)*
Russian-American novelist

The Babe is here. Who's coming in second?
Babe Didrikson Zaharias *(1911-1956)*
American golfer

Yesterday I dared to struggle. Today I dare to win.
Bernadette Devlin *(1947-)*
Irish, member of Parliament

I'm always making a comeback but nobody ever tells me where I've been.
Billie Holiday *(1915-1959)*
American jazz singer

It doesn't matter what anybody thinks of what I do. The clock doesn't lie.
Bonnie Blair *(1964-)*
American Olympic speed skater

The most important thing to strive for in life is some kind of personal and professional achievement. Not as a man or a woman, but as a person.
Candace Bushnell *(1959-)*
American writer

How many cares one loses when one decides not to
be something, but (instead) someone.
Coco Chanel *(1883-1971)*
French fashion designer

In Italian there is an expression: We don't sleep on the fame.
Donatella Versace *(1955-)*
Italian designer

Greatness is not measured by what a man or woman accomplishes,
but by the opposition they have to overcome to reach their goals.
Dorothy Height *(1912-2010)*
American activist

All your youth you want to have your greatness taken for granted;
when you find it taken for granted, you are unnerved.
Elizabeth Bowen *(1899-1973)*
Irish novelist

Our achievements speak for themselves. What we have to keep track
of are our failures, discouragements and doubts. We tend to forget the
past difficulties, the many false starts, and the painful groping.
Ethel Barrymore *(1879-1959)*
American actress

Some people think they are worth a lot of money just because they have it.
Fannie Hurst *(1889-1968)*
American novelist

The controversial overachiever is someone whose grasp
exceeds his reach. This is possible but not attractive.
Fran Lebowitz *(1950-)*
American writer

You're never too young or too old to make your own kind of
mark in your own kind of time. You're never the wrong age to
release the power within you to create the life you deserve.
Georgette Mosbacher *(1947-)*
American, CEO of Borghese

The only way to enjoy anything in this life is to earn it first.
Ginger Rogers *(1911-1995)*
American actress, dancer

As an artist, you dream about accumulating enough successful music to someday do just one greatest-hits album, but to reach the point where you're releasing your second collection of hits is beyond belief.
Gloria Estefan *(1957-)*
American songwriter, musician

Trust yourself. Create the kind of self that you will be happy to live with all your life. Make the most of yourself by fanning the tiny, inner sparks of possibility into flames of achievement.
Golda Meir *(1898-1978)*
Ukrainian-born Israeli leader

Mere longevity is a good thing for those who watch life from the side lines. For those who play the game, an hour may be a year, a single day's work an achievement for eternity.
Helen Hayes *(1900-1993)*
American actress

I think my biggest achievement is that after going through a rather difficult time I consider myself comparatively sane. I'm proud of that.
Jacqueline Kennedy Onassis *(1929-1994)*
American First Lady

I don't care what they say to the press. I've never met an actor in my life who doesn't have an acceptance speech going through their head every day.
Jane Fonda *(1937-)*
American actress

It is hard to achieve what is great. Let's do what's hard. Let's achieve what is great.
Jennifer Lopez *(1970-)*
American musician

Show me a person who has never made a mistake and I'll show you somebody who has never achieved much.
Joan Collins *(1933-)*
British actress

I began to have an idea of my life not as the slow shaping of achievement to fit my preconceived purposes but as the gradual discovery and growth of a purpose which I did not know.
Joanna Field *(1900-1998)*
British psychoanalyst

The measure of achievement is not winning awards. It's doing something that you appreciate, something you believe is worthwhile. I think of my strawberry soufflé. I did that at least twenty-eight times before I finally conquered it.
Julia Child *(1912-2004)*
American cookbook author

If you want to achieve things in life, you've just got to do them, and if you're talented and smart, you'll succeed.
Juliana Hatfield *(1967-)*
American musician

In knowing how to overcome little things, a centimeter at a time, gradually when bigger things come, you're prepared.
Katherine Dunham *(1912-2006)*
American actress

I don't confuse greatness with perfection. To be great anyhow is the higher achievement.
Lois McMaster Bujold *(1949-)*
American author

The thing that makes you exceptional, if you are at all, is inevitably that which must also make you lonely.
Lorraine Hansberry *(1930-1965)*
American playwright

Innocence of heart and violence of feeling are necessary in any kind of superior achievement: The arts cannot exist without them.
Louise Bogan *(1897-1970)*
American critic, poet

I had rather die in the adventure of noble achievements, than live in obscure and sluggish security.
Margaret Lucas Cavendish *(1623-1674)*
English aristocrat, writer

People think that at the top there isn't much room. They tend to think of it as an Everest. My message is that there is tons of room at the top.
Margaret Thatcher *(1925-)*
English Prime Minister

*Generally speaking, we are all happier when we are still striving
for achievement than when the prize is in our hands.*
Margot Fonteyn *(1919-1991)*
English ballerina

I was taught that the way of progress is neither swift nor easy.
Marie Curie *(1897-1966)*
Polish-French physicist

My real achievement is my daughter and my three beautiful grandchildren.
Marilyn Horne *(1934-)*
American musician

*Dancing appears glamorous, easy, delightful. But the path to
paradise of the achievement is not easier than any other. There
is fatigue so great that the body cries, even in its sleep. There are
times of complete frustration, there are daily small deaths.*
Martha Graham *(1894-1991)*
American dancer, choreographer

I have not done what I wanted to, but I tried to make a good fight.
Mary Cassatt *(1844-1926)*
American impressionist artist

*For six years, I kept my five Olympic medals wrapped
in a plastic bread bag beneath my bed.*
Mary Lou Retton *(1968-)*
American gymnast

Achievement brings its own anticlimax.
Maya Angelou *(1928-)*
American poet, memoirist

To fly, we have to have resistance.
Maya Lin *(1959-)*
American artist

It is more difficult to stay on top than to get there.
Mia Hamm *(1972-)*
American soccer player

Although the circumstances of our lives may seem very disengaged, with me standing here as the First Lady of the United States of America and you just getting through school, I want you to know we have very much in common. For nothing in my life ever would have predicted that I would standing here as the first African-American First Lady.

Michelle Obama *(1964-)*
American First Lady

I am an example of what is possible when girls from the very beginning of their lives are loved and nurtured by people around them. I was surrounded by extraordinary women in my life who taught me about quiet strength and dignity.

Michelle Obama *(1964-)*
American First Lady

We ourselves feel that what we are doing is just a drop in the ocean. But if that drop was not in the ocean, I think the ocean would be less because of that missing drop. I do not agree with the big way of doing things.

Mother Teresa *(1910-1997)*
Albanian Roman Catholic nun

I don't care who you are. When you sit down to write the first page of your screenplay, in your head, you're also writing your Oscar acceptance speech.

Nora Ephron *(1941-)*
American director, screenwriter

When you're young, the silliest notions seem the greatest achievements.

Pearl Bailey *(1918-1990)*
American entertainer

The young do not know enough to be prudent, and therefore they attempt the impossible — and achieve it, generation after generation.

Pearl S. Buck *(1892-1973)*
American writer

If we have not achieved our early dreams, we must either find new ones or see what we can salvage from the old. If we have accomplished what we set out to do in our youth, we need not weep like Alexander the Great that we have no more worlds to conquer.

Rosalynn Carter *(1927-)*
American First Lady

There is clearly much left to be done, and whatever else
we are going to do, we had better get on with it.
Rosalynn Carter *(1927-)*
American First Lady

I would much rather be known as the mother of a great son than
the author of a great book or the painter of a great masterpiece.
Rose Kennedy *(1890-1995)*
American, Kennedy family matriarch

I couldn't stop looking at the award when I received it. It was
as if my whole career flashed in front of me, from beginning
to the moment I was handed the Golden Globe.
Sharon Stone *(1958-)*
American actress

I draw from my family and my friends and I feel like that small-
town person. The achievements, the materialistic possessions
have really come to mean less. They mean nothing.
Sheryl Crow *(1962-)*
American musician

I don't measure America by its achievement but by its potential.
Shirley Chisholm *(1924-2005)*
American politician

I've been rich and I've been poor; Believe me, honey, rich is better.
Sophie Tucker *(1884-1966)*
Russian/Ukranian born entertainer

I'm not an outsider at all. I'm on every bloody A-list there is in the art world.
Tracey Emin *(1963-)*
English artist

Where you see valid achievements or virtue being attacked,
it's by someone viewing them as a mirror of their own
inadequacy instead of an inspiring beacon for excellence.
Vanna Bonta *(1958-)*
American novelist, poet

What it comes down to is that anybody can win with the best horse. What
makes you good is if you can take the second or third best horse and win.
Vicky Aragon *(1965-)*
American jockey

Desire is creation, is the magical element in that process. If there were an
instrument by which to measure desire, one could foretell achievement.
Willa Cather *(1873-1947)*
American writer

Action

I begin to think that a calm is not desirable in any situation in life....
People were made for action and for bustle too, I believe.
Abigail Adams *(1744-1818)*
American First Lady

The most effective way to do it, is to do it.
Amelia Earhart *(1897-1937)*
American aviator

Our life is composed greatly from dreams, from the unconscious, and they
must be brought into connection with action. They must be woven together.
Anais Nin *(1902-1977)*
French author, diarist

There are really only three types of people; those who make things happen,
those who watch things happen, and those who say, 'What happened?'
Ann Landers *(1918-2002)*
American advice columnist

Hope doesn't come from calculating whether the good news is
winning out over the bad. It's simply a choice to take action.
Anna Lappe *(1973-   )*
American author

Every action we take, everything we do, is either a victory or
defeat in the struggle to become what we want to be.
Anne Bronte *(1820-1849)*
British novelist, poet

One sad thing about this world is that the acts that take the most out
of you are usually the ones that other people will never know about.
Anne Tyler *(1941-   )*
American novelist

Better remain silent, better not even think, if you are not prepared to act.
Annie Besant *(1847-1933)*
British writer, activist

People create their own questions because they are afraid to look straight. All you have to do is look straight and see the road, and when you see it, don't sit looking at it – walk.
Ayn Rand *(1905-1982)*
Russian-American novelist

It's not enough just to swing at the ball. You've got to loosen your girdle and let 'er fly.
Babe Didrikson Zaharias *(1911-1956)*
American golfer

Think first of the action that is right to take, think later about coping with one's fears.
Barbara Deming *(1917-1984)*
American author

You may be disappointed if you fail, but you are doomed if you don't try.
Beverly Sills *(1929-2007)*
American operatic soprano

Tennis is a perfect combination of violent action taking place in an atmosphere of total tranquility.
Billie Jean King *(1934-)*
American tennis player

Actions lie louder than words.
Carolyn Wells *(1862-1942)*
American author, poet

Instant gratification takes too long.
Carrie Fisher *(1956-)*
American actress

You can express a lot of things, a lot of action without speaking.
Catherine Deneuve *(1943-)*
French actress

It is in vain to say human beings ought to be satisfied with tranquility: they must have action; and they will make it if they cannot find it.
Charlotte Bronte *(1816-1855)*
English novelist

We do not need, and indeed never will have, all the answers before we act. It is often only through taking action that we can discover some of them.
Charlotte Bunch *(1944-)*
American author, activist

When it comes to getting things done, we need
fewer architects and more bricklayers.
Colleen C. Barrett *(1944-   )*
American, President Emerita Southwest Airlines

The world can only be grasped by action, not by contemplation.
The hand is the cutting edge of the mind.
Diane Arbus *(1923-1971)*
American photographer

Act as if it were impossible to fail.
Dorothea Brande *(1893-1948)*
American writer, editor

In a world where there is so much to be done, I felt strongly
impressed that there must be something for me to do.
Dorothea Dix *(1802-1887)*
American, Civil War activist

Young people say 'What is the sense of our small effort?' They cannot
see that we must lay one brick at a time, take one step at a time; we
can be responsible only for the one action of the present moment.
Dorothy Day *(1897-1980)*
American journalist, activist

They sicken of calm, who know the storm.
Dorothy Parker *(1893-1967)*
American writer, satirist

We're off and running. People are holding our feet to the fire.
Elaine Agather *(1956-   )*
American, CEO, JP Morgan Chase

To leap is not only to leap, it is to hit the ground somewhere.
Elizabeth Bowen *(1899-1973)*
Irish novelist

Energy is beauty – a Ferrari with an empty tank doesn't run.
Elsa Peretti *(1892-1973)*
American model, designer

You always feel when you look it straight in the eye that you could
have put more into it, could have let yourself go and dug harder.
Emily Carr *(1945-   )*
Canadian artist

Forever is composed of nows.
Emily Dickinson *(1830-1886)*
American poet

To live is so startling it leaves little time for anything else.
Emily Dickinson *(1830-1886)*
American poet

*I'd always thought, 'When I finish modeling, I'm going to pursue
this.' But then it really kind of hit me. I realized, 'Well, no, you
can't do it when it's convenient. If I'm going to do it, I've got to do
it right now.' (talking about pursuing her career as a singer)*
Erica Baxter *(1977-)*
Australian singer, model

*Remember, people will judge you by your actions, not your intentions.
You may have a heart of gold – but so does a hard-boiled egg.*
Erma Bombeck *(1927-1996)*
American writer, humorist

I think of who I am as what I've done.
Esther Dyson *(1951-)*
American commentator

*Go do something about it. Write a letter. Make a call.
There's no end of things that can be done!*
Esther Peterson *(1906-1997)*
American activist

*One's feelings waste themselves in words; they ought all
to be distilled into action ... which bring results.*
Florence Nightingale *(1820-1910)*
English nurse, writer

The biggest sin is sitting on your ass.
Florynce Kennedy *(1916-2000)*
American activist, lawyer

*If you are of the opinion that the contemplation of
suicide is sufficient evidence of a poetic nature, do not
forget that actions speak louder than words.*
Fran Lebowitz *(1950-)*
American writer

It is better to wear out than to rust out.
Frances E. Willard *(1839-1898)*
American educator, suffragist

*The most ominous of fallacies: the belief that
things can be kept static by inaction.*
Freya Stark *(1893-1993)*
French-born travel writer, explorer

*I don't waste time. I move. I finish things. I don't try and do things to
the nth degree. I know what's important and what's not. I've really
learned that. That's a judgment I've learned, what really matters.*
Gail Kelly *(1956-)*
American, CEO Westpac

*It will never rain roses: when we want / To have
more roses we must plant more trees.*
George Eliot *(1819-1880)*
English novelist

I don't waste time thinking, Am I doing it right? I say, Am I doing it?
Georgette Mosbacher *(1947-)*
American, CEO of Borghese

*We fought hard. We gave it our best. We did what
was right and we made a difference.*
Geraldine Ferraro *(1935-2011)*
American politician

Act quickly, think slowly.
Germaine Greer *(1939-)*
Australian-born writer

*It is funny that people who are supposed to be scientific cannot
get themselves to realize the basic principle of physics, that action
and reaction are equal and opposite, that when you persecute
people you always rouse them to be strong and stronger.*
Gertrude Stein *(1874-1946)*
American writer

*When you're frightened don't sit still, keep on doing something.
The act of doing will give you back your courage.*
Grace Ogot *(1934-)*
Kenyan author

Action without a name, a who attached to it, is meaningless.
Hannah Arendt *(1906-1975)*
German philosopher

If you rest, you rust.
Helen Hayes *(1900-1993)*
American actress

Science may have found a cure for most evils; but it has found no remedy for the worst of them all – the apathy of human beings.
Helen Keller *(1880-1968)*
American author, educator

*Multitasking? I can't even do two things at once.
I can't even do one thing at once.*
Helena Bonham Carter *(1966-)*
British actress

My view is that life unfolds at its own rhythm. I have never lived a life that I thought I could plan out. And I'm just trying to do the best I can every day. I find I have a lot to get done between the time I get up and the time I go to bed.
Hillary Rodham Clinton *(1947-)*
American, Secretary of State

You must learn to be still in the midst of activity, and to be vibrantly alive in repose.
Indira Gandhi *(1917-1984)*
Indian Prime Minister

The world is round and the place which may seem like the end may also be only the beginning.
Ivy Baker Priest *(1905-1975)*
American politician

I work hard, and I tend to play hard. I very seldom rest hard.
Jacqueline Bisset *(1944-)*
English actress

I want to live my life, not record it.
Jacqueline Kennedy Onassis *(1929-1994)*
American First Lady

Action indeed is the sole medium of expression for ethics.
Jane Addams *(1860-1935)*
American activist

Why not seize the pleasure at once? How often is happiness destroyed by preparation, foolish preparation!
Jane Austen *(1775-1817)*
English novelist

Action is the antidote to despair.
Joan Baez *(1941-)*
American folksinger, songwriter

I believe that words are easy. I believe the truth is told in the actions we take. And I believe that if enough ordinary people back up our desire for a better world with action, I believe we can, in fact, accomplish absolutely extraordinary things.
Jody Williams *(1901-1978)*
American Nobel Prize Recipient

What you do matters. All you need is to do it.
Judy Grahn *(1940-)*
American poet

To make big steps, you've got to take action yourself and not listen to other people.
Juliana Hatfield *(1967-)*
American musician

If you obey all the rules you miss all the fun.
Katharine Hepburn *(1907-2003)*
American actress

Once I decide to do something, I can't have people telling me I can't. If there's a roadblock, you jump over it, walk around it, crawl under it.
Kitty Kelley *(1942-)*
American journalist

Being told to sit still and enjoy myself is logically incompatible.
Lesley Glendower Peabody *(1870-?)*
American author, outdoorswoman

Our high resolves / Look down upon our slumbering acts.
Letitia Landon *(1802-1838)*
English poet, novelist

Nothing, of course, begins at the time you think it did.
Lillian Hellman *(1905-1984)*
American playwright

For fast-acting relief, try slowing down.
Lily Tomlin *(1939-)*
American actress, comedian

I always wondered why somebody doesn't do something about that. Then I realized I was somebody.
Lily Tomlin *(1939-)*
American actress, comedian

When you choose an action, you choose the consequences of that action... when you desire a consequence you had damned well better take the action that would create it.
Lois McMaster Bujold *(1949-)*
American author

If you want something done, ask a busy person to do it. The more things you do, the more you can do.
Lucille Ball *(1911-1989)*
American comedian, actress

It's more important to know where you are going than to get there quickly. Do not mistake activity for achievement.
Mabel Newcomer *(1873-1951)*
American economist

The greatest happiness is to transform one's feelings into action.
Madame de Stael *(1766-1817)*
French writer

I'm a woman of very few words, but lots of action.
Mae West *(1893-1980)*
American actress

Thinking is the place where intelligent actions begin. We pause long enough to look more carefully at a situation, to see more of its character, to think about why it's happening, to notice how it's affecting us and others.
Margaret J. Wheatley *(1934-)*
American organization expert

Tis the motive exalts the action. 'Tis the doing and not the deed.
Margaret Junkin Preston *(1820-1897)*
American poet, author

Whatever is not an energy source, is an energy sink.
Marge Piercy *(1936-)*
American novelist, poet

Study as if you were going to live forever; live as
if you were going to die tomorrow.
Maria Mitchell *(1818-1889)*
American scientist

Fear tells you what action to take to prove that your inner critic is wrong.
Maria Shriver *(1955-)*
American journalist, author

Talk without effort is nothing.
Maria W. Stewart *(1803-1879)*
American essayist

One never notices what has been done; one can
only see what remains to be done.
Marie Curie *(1897-1966)*
Polish-French physicist

There is only one proof of ability: action.
Marie von Ebner-Eschenbach *(1830-1916)*
Austrian writer

We've been taught to believe that actions speak louder
than words. But I think words speak pretty loud all of
our lives; we carry these words in our head.
Marlo Thomas *(1937-)*
American actress

There is a vitality, a life force, an energy, a quickening, that
is translated through you into action, and because there is
only one of you in all time, this expression is unique.
Martha Graham *(1894-1991)*
American dancer, choreographer

Live with intention. Walk to the edge. Listen hard. Practice wellness.
Play with abandon. Laugh. Choose with no regret. Appreciate
your friends. Continue to learn. Live as if this is all there is.
Mary Anne Radmacher *(1957-)*
American writer

Action without study is fatal. Study without action is futile.
Mary Beard *(1955-)*
British writer, literary critic

Let no one be deluded that a knowledge of the path can
substitute for putting one foot in front of the other.
Mary Caroline Richards *(1916-1999)*
American poet, potter

You guard against decay, in general, and stagnation,
by moving, by continuing to move.
Mary Daly *(1928-2010)*
American theologian

The time when you need to do something is when no one else is
willing to do it, when people are saying it can't be done.
Mary Frances Berry *(1938-)*
American educator

If our impulses were confined to hunger, thirst and desire, we might
be nearly free, but now we are moved by every wind that blows,
and a chance word or scene that that word may convey to us.
Mary Shelley *(1797-1851)*
British novelist

Life loves to be taken by the lapel and told, 'I'm with you, kid. Let's go.'
Maya Angelou *(1928-)*
American poet, memoirist

Ideas are powerful things, requiring not a studious contemplation
but an action, even if it is only an inner action.
Midge Dector *(1927-)*
American journalist

Never retract, never explain, never apologize –
get the thing done and let them howl.
Nellie McClung *(1873-1951)*
Canadian activist

For those of us who have a ground of knowledge which we cannot transmit
to outsiders, it is perhaps more profitable to act fearlessly than to argue.
Olive Schreiner *(1855-1920)*
South African author

I was a handful growing up.
Olivia Wilde *(1984-)*
American actress

People of action, whose minds are too busy with the day's work to see beyond it...are essential, we cannot do without them, and yet we must not allow all our vision to be bound by the limitations of people of action.
Pearl S. Buck *(1892-1973)*
American writer

To fight evil one must also recognize one's own responsibility. The values for which we stand must be expressed in the way we think of, and how we deal with, our fellow humans.
Queen Beatrix of the Netherlands *(1938-)*
Netherlands royalty

One must fight for a life of action, not reaction.
Rita Mae Brown *(1944-)*
American novelist

The most difficult thing is the decision to act, the rest is merely tenacity. The fears are paper tigers. You can do anything you decide to do. You can act to change and control your life; and the procedure, the process, is its own reward.
Robyn Davidson *(1950-)*
Australian writer

Life begets life. Energy creates energy. It is by spending oneself that one becomes rich.
Sarah Bernhardt *(1845-1923)*
French actress

Each decision we make, each action we take, is born out of an intention.
Sharon Salzberg *(1952-)*
American author

Don't even make a list. Do everything right now.
Sigourney Weaver *(1949-)*
American actress

Live with no time out.
Simone de Beauvoir *(1908-1986)*
French writer, philosopher

We should do only those righteous actions which we cannot stop ourselves from doing.
Simone Weil *(1909-1943)*
French philosopher

*The important thing is that when you come to understand
something you act on it, no matter how small that act is.
Eventually it will take you where you need to go.*
Sister Helen Prejean *(1944-)*
American Roman Catholic nun

*The word Action! frees me – the transformation is something
I cannot explain – too much analysis might destroy it.*
Sophia Loren *(1934-)*
Italian actress

The most effective way to do it, is to do it.
Toni Cade Bambara *(1939-1995)*
American author, filmmaker

*When action grows unprofitable gather information;
when information grows unprofitable sleep.*
Ursula K. LeGuin *(1929-)*
American novelist

*I am enjoying to a full that period of reflection which
is the happiest conclusion to a life of action.*
Willa Cather *(1873-1947)*
American writer

I don't know why I run so fast. I just run.
Wilma Rudolph *(1940-1994)*
American Olympic runner

Adventure

*Your travel life has the aspect of a dream. It is something outside the normal,
yet you are in it. It is peopled with characters you have never seen before and
in all probability will never see again. It brings occasional homesickness,
and loneliness, and pangs of longing... But you are like the Vikings who have
gone into a world of adventure, and home is not home until you return.*
Agatha Christie *(1890-1976)*
English detective novelist

Adventure is worthwhile in itself.
Amelia Earhart *(1897-1937)*
American aviator

Never forget that life can only be nobly inspired and rightly lived if you take it bravely and gallantly, as a splendid adventure in which you are setting out into an unknown country, to meet many a joy, to find many a comrade, to win and lose many a battle.
Annie Besant *(1847-1933)*
British writer, activist

Nobody is ever met at the airport when beginning a new adventure. It's just not done.
Elizabeth Warnock Fernea *(1927-2008)*
American anthropologist

Travel can also be the spirit of adventure somewhat tamed, for those who desire to do something they are a bit afraid of.
Ella Maillart *(1903-1997)*
Swiss writer

Acting, to me, is about the incredible adventure of examining the landscape of human heart and soul. That's basically what we do.
Glenn Close *(1947-)*
American actress

Life is either a daring adventure or nothing. To keep our faces toward change and behave like free spirits in the presence of fate is strength undefeatable.
Helen Keller *(1880-1968)*
American author, educator

I am a migratory bird. Ever since I was a little girl, I have looked for new things – I have longed for big adventures.
Ingrid Bergman *(1915-1982)*
Swedish-born, American actress

To the well-organized mind, death is but the next great adventure.
J. K. Rowling *(1965-)*
English writer

I have found adventure in flying, in world travel, in business, and even close at hand... adventure is a state of mind – and spirit.
Jacqueline Cochran *(1910-1980)*
American aviator

We owe something to extravagance, for thrift and adventure seldom go hand in hand.
Jennie Jerome Churchill *(1854-1921)*
American celebrity

What I love most about this crazy life is the adventure of it.
Juliette Binoche *(1964-)*
French actress

Adventure is something you see for pleasure, or even for profit, like a gold rush or invading a country...but experience is what really happens to you in the long run, the truth that finally overtakes you.
Katherine Anne Porter *(1890-1980)*
American journalist

We live at the edge of the world, so we live on the edge. Kiwis will always sacrifice money and security for adventure and challenge.
Lucy Lawless *(1968-)*
New Zealand actress

Sure, give me an adventure and I'll ride it.
Melissa Auf der Maur *(1972-)*
Canadian musician

Life is an opportunity, benefit from it. Life is a beauty, admire it. Life is a dream, realize it. Life is a challenge, meet it. Life is a duty, complete it. Life is a game, play it. Life is a promise, fulfill it. Life is sorrow, overcome it. Life is a song, sing it. Life is a struggle, accept it. Life is a tragedy, confront it. Life is an adventure, dare it. Life is luck, make it. Life is life, fight for it!
Mother Teresa *(1910-1997)*
Albanian Roman Catholic nun

Life is a marvelous, transitory adventure.
Nikki Giovanni *(1943-)*
American poet, author

An adventure may be worn as a muddy spot or it may be worn as a proud insignia. It is the woman wearing it who makes it the one thing or the other.
Norma Shearer *(1900-1983)*
American actress

But even if I'm left high and dry at the end of this wild journey, just taking it is a great feeling.
Olivia Wilde *(1984-)*
American actress

The biggest adventure you can ever take is to live the life of your dreams.
Oprah Winfrey *(1954-)*
American media mogul

Life ought to be a struggle of desire toward adventures
whose nobility will fertilize the soul.
Rebecca West *(1892-1983)*
Irish-born, British writer

We must continuously discipline ourselves to
remember how it felt the first moment.
Sarah Caldwell *(1924-2006)*
American opera conductor

Advice

Good advice is always certain to be ignored,
but that's no reason not to give it.
Agatha Christie *(1890-1976)*
English detective novelist

A lot of girls ask for advice on how to get into acting, and I'm
kind of the worst person to ask, because it just kind of fell in
my lap… I was just in the right place at the right time.
Alexis Bledel *(1981-)*
American actress

A lot of people think I'm cynical when I talk about acting. The
truth of the matter is, I just don't want someone to get some
lame advice that will send them in the wrong direction.
Amber Tamblyn *(1983-)*
American actress

Don't give advice unless you're asked.
Amy Alcott *(1956-)*
American golfer

If I were asked to give what I consider the single most useful bit
of advice, it would be this: Expect trouble as an inevitable part of
life, and when it comes, hold your head high. Look it squarely in the
eye, and say, I will be bigger than you. You cannot defeat me.
Ann Landers *(1918-2002)*
American advice columnist

It gets really tricky giving advice. The older I get, the less advice I give.
Anne Heche *(1969-)*
American actress

*The best advice on the art of being happy is about as easy
to follow as advice to be well when one is sick.*
Anne Sophie Swetchine *(1752-1857)*
Russian mystic

*It's queer how ready people always are with advice in any real or
imaginary emergency, and no matter how many times experience
has shown them to be wrong, they continue to set forth their
opinions, as if they had received them from the Almighty!*
Anne Sullivan Macy *(1866-1936)*
American teacher, companion Helen Keller

*It is very difficult to live among people you love and
hold back from offering them advice.*
Anne Tyler *(1941-)*
American novelist

*The wanting of advice is the sign that the spirit in you has not
yet spoken with the compelling voice that you ought to obey.*
Annie Besant *(1847-1933)*
British writer, activist

*It is not advisable to venture unsolicited opinions. You should spare
yourself the embarrassing discovery of their exact value to your listener.*
Ayn Rand *(1905-1982)*
Russian-American novelist

*Advice is a habit-forming drug. You give a dear friend a bit of advice
today, and next week you find yourself advising two or three friends,
and the week after, a dozen, and the week following, crowds!*
Carolyn Wells *(1862-1942)*
American author, poet

Advice is one of those things it is far more blessed to give than to receive.
Carolyn Wells *(1862-1942)*
American author, poet

*The best advice I got was to carry on. It would have been
difficult to set foot back inside a TV studio if I hadn't carried
on – I don't know if I would have ever gone back in.*
Cilla Black *(1943-)*
British musician

34

Nobody had ever told me how to do these things, ... I didn't want anyone giving me advice until I had it all figured out on my own.
Diana Gabaldon *(1952-)*
American author

We only make a dupe of the friend whose advice we ask, for we never tell them all; and it is usually what we have left unsaid that decides our conduct.
Diane de Poitiers *(1499-1566)*
French noblewoman

I am glad that I paid so little attention to good advice; had I abided by it I might have been saved from some of my most valuable mistakes.
Edna Saint Vincent Millay *(1892-1950)*
American poet, playwright

Please give me some good advice in your next letter. I promise not to follow it.
Edna Saint Vincent Millay *(1892-1950)*
American poet, playwright

The strongest possible piece of advice I would give any young woman is: Don't screw around, and don't smoke.
Edwina Currie *(1946-)*
British politician

I agree with every word you write, and I can prove this in no better way than by taking your advice from beginning to end.
Ellen Glasgow *(1873-1945)*
American novelist

Advice is what we ask for when we already know the answer but wish we didn't.
Erica Jong *(1942-)*
American writer

When your mother asks, 'Do you want a piece of advice?' it is a mere formality. It doesn't matter if you answer yes or no. You're going to get it anyway.
Erma Bombeck *(1927-1996)*
American writer, humorist

As far as advice, that will be in my next book, my next collection. I certainly never like to instruct anyone, but just say as I feel. That's the same as advice, isn't it?
Fay Wray *(1907-2004)*
American actress

*I don't want to give any advice to a 19-year-old, because I want a
19-year-old to make mistakes and learn from them. Make mistakes,
make mistakes, make mistakes. Just make sure they're your mistakes.*
Fiona Apple *(1977-)*
American musician

*I am very handy with my advice and then when anybody
appears to be following it, I get frantic.*
Flannery O'Connor *(1925-1964)*
American writer

*The true secret of giving advice is, after you have honestly
given it, to be perfectly indifferent whether it is taken or
not, and never persist in trying to set people right.*
Hannah Whitall Smith *(1832-1911)*
American author, suffragist

Many receive advice, only the wise profit from it.
Harper Lee *(1926-)*
American author

*It was, perhaps, one of those cases in which advice
is good or bad only as the event decides.*
Jane Austen *(1775-1817)*
English novelist

*Listen to advice. You don't know how many writer's conferences I've taught
at where at least half the audience fights all the conventions of the field.*
Jane Haddam *(1951-)*
American writer

Advice is such a tricky thing when you're young.
Jena Malone *(1984-)*
American actress

*I would never offer advice without the person asking for it. I, in general,
don't believe in giving advice, actually, as a human being I don't.*
Joan Chen *(1961-)*
Chinese actress

*I don't give advice. I can't tell anybody what to do. Instead
I say this is what we know about this problem at this time.
And here are the consequences of these actions.*
Joyce Brothers *(1927-)*
American psychologist

I don't think anybody can be told how to act. I think you can give advice. But you have to find your own way through it.
Judi Dench *(1934-)*
English actress

My only advice is to stay aware, listen carefully, and yell for help if you need it.
Judy Blume *(1938-)*
American author of children's books

I'm not a very good advice-giver.
Juliana Hatfield *(1967-)*
American musician

I'm not in the business of becoming famous. That's the advice I give to younger aspiring actors. Work onstage and do the little roles. It's not important to be seen. It's important to do. There's a lot of disappointment in this business, but my family keeps me grounded.
Kristen Bell *(1980-)*
American actress

Nobody ever seems to want my advice about serious stuff. People will be like: 'Who made that sweater?' Or 'How did you get your hair so straight?' They don't come to me for the relationship advice or deep stuff. In fact, my little sister actually hides from me.
Lauren Graham *(1967-)*
American actress

Adversity does teach who your real friends are.
Lois McMaster Bujold *(1949-)*
American author

Don't ever take advice from anyone who starts a sentence with, 'You may not like me for this, but it's for your own good.' It never is.
Lois Wyse *(1926-2007)*
American advertising executive

As time passes we all get better at blazing a trail through the thicket of advice.
Margot Bennett *(1912-1980)*
Scottish mystery writer

No vice is so bad as advice.
Marie Dressler *(1868-1934)*
Canadian actress

I give myself, sometimes, admirable advice, but I am incapable of taking it.
Mary Wortley Montagu *(1689-1762)*
British author, poet

Interestingly, young people don't come to you for advice.
Especially the ones who are related to you.
Meryl Streep *(1949-)*
American actress

Pull yourself together is seldom said to anyone who can.
Mignon McLaughlin *(1913-1983)*
American journalist

Among the most disheartening and dangerous of advisors, you will often
find those closest to you, your dearest friends, members of your own
family, perhaps, loving, anxious, and knowing nothing whatever.
Minnie Maddern Fiske *(1865-1932)*
American actress

A good scare is worth more to a person than good advice.
Nadine Gordimer *(1923-)*
South African novelist, activist

This is the gist of what I know: Give advice and buy a foe.
Phyllis Mcginley *(1905-1978)*
American writer

Strange, when you ask anyone's advice you see yourself what is right.
Selma Lagerlof *(1858-1940)*
Swedish author

My advice, Be healthy, reach your own goals and
don't be afraid to impersonate an SNL star.
Teri Hatcher *(1964-)*
American actress

Ambition

Far be it from me to disclaim the influence of ambition and fame.
No living soul ever was more imbued with it than myself.
Ada Lovelace *(1815-1852)*
English mathematician

*I may have aimed too high sometimes, asked too much of
myself and demanded too little from those around me.*
Agnetha Faltskog *(1950-)*
Swedish musician

I have the desire to work as an actress, but I have no ambition to be a star.
Ally Sheedy *(1962-)*
American actress

*I always wanted to be somebody. If I made it, it's half because I was
game enough to take a lot of punishment along the way and half
because there were a lot of people who cared enough to help me.*
Althea Gibson *(1927-2003)*
American tennis player

*Women like myself, CEOs, can pave the way
for more women to get to the top.*
Andrea Jung *(1959-)*
Canadian-American, CEO Avon

*I don't believe you are simply born with the ambition of becoming
chancellor. But if you want to make a difference, if you enjoy
putting ideas into practice, then the post of chancellor has to
be the one presenting the biggest opportunity of all.*
Angela Merkel *(1954-)*
German Chancellor

*My biggest ambition is never to be bored. I'm not aggressive
enough to strongly run after being an actress.*
Anjelica Huston *(1951-)*
American actress

I do not care for the money, just for the glory.
Anna Held *(1872-1918)*
Polish-born stage performer

*How wonderful it is that nobody need wait a single
moment before starting to improve the world.*
Anne Frank *(1929-1945)*
German writer, holocaust victim

All of my life I've always had the urge to do things better than anybody else.
Babe Didrikson Zaharias *(1911-1956)*
American golfer

I have had no expectations, and the desire for posthumous glory seems to me an inordinate aspiration. My ambition is limited to trying to record something fleeting, anything, the least of things. Yet even this ambition is excessive.
Berthe Morisot *(1841-1895)*
French impressionist painter

My passions were all gathered together like fingers that made a fist. Drive is considered aggression today; I knew it then as purpose.
Bette Davis *(1908-1989)*
American actress

My desire to get here was like miners' coal dust, it was under my fingers and I couldn't scrub it out.
Betty Boothroyd *(1929-)*
British politician

To survive there, you need the ambition of a Latin-American revolutionary, the ego of a grand opera tenor, and the physical stamina of a cow pony.
Billie Burke *(1884-1970)*
American actress

When you have a dream you've got to grab it and never let go.
Carol Burnett *(1933-)*
American actress, comedian

Odd, the years it took to learn one simple fact: that the prize just ahead, the next job, publication, love affair, marriage always seemed to hold the key to satisfaction but never, in the longer run, sufficed.
Carolyn Heilbrun *(1926-2003)*
American academic, author

There is no point at which you can say, Well, I'm successful now. I might as well take a nap.
Carrie Fisher *(1956-)*
American actress

I had a burning ambition. Otherwise, I wouldn't have accomplished it.
Claire Bloom *(1931-)*
British actress

I hope I shall have ambition until the day I die.
Clare Boothe Luce *(1903 - 1987)*
American playwright, diplomat

You have to learn the rules of the game. And then
you have to play better than anyone else.
Dianne Feinstein *(1933-)*
American politician

I'm not going to limit myself just because people won't
accept the fact that I can do something else.
Dolly Parton *(1946-)*
American singer-songwriter

I didn't have high goals and high ambitions, and that I was going
to become the world's greatest jewel thief. It got out of hand.
Doris Payne *(1930-)*
American, notorious jewel thief

Set your sights high, the higher the better. Realize that nothing is too
good. Allow absolutely nothing to hamper you or hold you up in any way.
Eileen Caddy *(1917-2006)*
British educator

Ambition is pitiless. Any merit that it cannot use it finds despicable.
Eleanor Roosevelt *(1884 - 1962)*
American First Lady

On what strange stuff Ambition feeds!
Eliza Cook *(1818-1889)*
English author, poet

I did not want to be depressed by the gap existing
between my weakness and my ambition.
Ella Maillart *(1903-1997)*
Swiss writer

Bite off more than you can chew, then chew it.
Ella Williams *(1919-)*
American operatic soprano

I have been ambitious to be a somebody from the time I was 5 years old.
Ethel Merman *(1908-1984)*
American singer

A youthful mind is seldom totally free from ambition; to curb that is the first
step to contentment, since to diminish expectation is to increase enjoyment.
Frances Burney *(1752-1840)*
English author

You are never too old to be what you might have been.
George Eliot *(1819-1880)*
English novelist

I have decided that when I am a star, I will be
every inch and every moment a star.
Gloria Swanson *(1899-1983)*
American actress

We're not all nice, and there are a lot of levels of ambition and niceness.
Heather Donahue *(1974-)*
American actress

One can never consent to creep when one feels the impulse to soar.
Helen Keller *(1880-1968)*
American author, educator

I always believed that I could make it or I would never
have spent so many years trying to get here.
Helen Reddy *(1941-)*
Australian actress

My motto – sans limites.
Isadora Duncan *(1878-1927)*
American dancer

I never expected to be in the papers. I personally never expected to be in
the papers. The height of my ambition for these books was, well frankly,
to get reviewed. A lot of children's books don't even get reviewed...
forget good review, bad review. Personally, no, I never expected to be
in the papers so it's an odd experience when it happens to you.
J. K. Rowling *(1965-)*
English writer

It's better to look ahead and prepare than to look back and regret.
Jackie Joyner-Kersee *(1962-)*
American Olympic athlete

I just knew that was what I wanted to do. I was going to perform as a singer;
I was going to perform as a dancer, and I was, you know, going to do movies
and be an actress. I was going to do it or die trying. That's what my life was.
Jennifer Lopez *(1970-)*
American musician

Ambition is destruction; only competence matters.
Jill Robinson *(1955-)*
English activist

I think I look good out there. I'm strong, powerful, and artistic. But I have my doubts as much as anyone. And there are so many more things to life than skating – I hope.
Jill Trenary *(1968-)*
American figure skater

I felt a comedy ego beginning to grow, which gave me the courage to begin tentatively looking into myself for material.
Joan Rivers *(1933-)*
American comedian

If your energy is as boundless as your ambition, total commitment may be a way of life you should seriously consider.
Joyce Brothers *(1927-)*
American psychologist

Drama is very important in life: You have to come on with a bang. You never want to go out with a whimper.
Julia Child *(1912-2004)*
American cookbook author

My ambition is to have beautiful encounters, not to make money.
Juliette Binoche *(1964-)*
French actress

I wanted to develop the idea of torch and twang, that's what's inside me and it pretty much sums up the kind of music that interests me.
K. D. Lang *(1962-)*
American singer

If ambition doesn't hurt you, you haven't got it.
Kathleen Norris *(1880-1966)*
American poet, novelist

When I'm dead, I want people to say: That woman made a difference. I don't want that to seem like a conceited remark .... But I think we all have an obligation to make life a little better – and a little pleasanter – for others.
Lillian Vernon *(1929-)*
German entrepreneur

I don't know many ambition-ridden people who really enjoy themselves.
Even success doesn't seem to still the insatiable, gnawing hunger
of their ambition. Ambition is a good gift, but it cannot be all.
Loretta Young *(1913-2000)*
American actress

I ... resolved to take Fate by the throat and shake a living out of her.
Louisa May Alcott *(1832-1888)*
American author

Some people go through life trying to find out what the
world holds for them only to find out too late that it's
what they bring to the world that really counts.
Lucy Maud Montgomery *(1874-1942)*
Canadian writer

Being effective is more important to me than being recognized.
Margaret Beckett *(1943-)*
British Labour politician

One only gets to the top rung of the ladder by steadily climbing up
one at a time, and suddenly all sorts of powers, all sorts of abilities
which you thought never belonged to you suddenly become within
your own possibility and you think, 'Well, I'll have a go, too.'
Margaret Thatcher *(1925-)*
English Prime Minister

What's the need of working if it doesn't get you anywhere?
What's the use of boring around in the same hold like
a worm? Making the hole bigger to stay in?
Marita Bonner *(1899-1971)*
American writer

You are unique, and if that is not fulfilled, then something has been lost.
Martha Graham *(1894-1991)*
American dancer, choreographer

I'm very determined and stubborn. There's a desire in me that makes me
want to do more and more, and to do it right. Each one of us has a fire in
our heart for something. It's our goal in life to find it and to keep it lit.
Mary Lou Retton *(1968-)*
American gymnast

The past cannot be changed. The future is yet in your power.
Mary Pickford *(1893-1979)*
Canadian-American actress

What great changes have not been ambitious?
Melinda Gates *(1964-)*
American philanthropist

Writing is my ultimate ambition. I respect it above all. I didn't strive to be a performer. It's come so easily for me. In some ways I feel guilty about that. On the other hand, I enjoy it precisely because I'm not consumed by it.
Mia Sara *(1967-)*
American actress

Make your own music. It can be done.
Michelle Shocked *(1962-)*
American musician

If you have a great ambition, take as big a step as possible in the direction of fulfilling it. The step may only be a tiny one, but trust that it may be the largest one possible for now.
Mildred McAfee *(1900-1994)*
American, first director WAVES U.S. Navy

A person without ambition is dead. A person with ambition but no love is dead. A person with ambition and love for their blessings here on earth is ever so alive. Having been alive, it won't be so hard in the end to lie down and rest.
Pearl Bailey *(1918-1990)*
American entertainer

My ambition is to be happy.
Penelope Cruz *(1974-)*
Spanish actress

As far back as I can remember, I've had only one real ambition: to be an actress.
Piper Laurie *(1932-)*
American actress

I used to think I had ambition... but now I'm not so sure. It may have been only discontent. They're easily confused.
Rachel Field *(1894-1942)*
American novelist

Ambition can be a disease, and it feeds on itself.
Rebecca Miller *(1962-)*
American director

I really have no ulterior motive in taking on certain roles.
I have no larger issue that I really want to show people.
I'm an actor, that's all. I just do what I do.
Sally Field *(1946-)*
American actress

I proved to myself that if I believe in something and set
my mind to it I could actually accomplish it.
Salma Hayek *(1966-)*
Mexican actress

I want everything – all of it.
Sophia Loren *(1934-)*
Italian actress

Ambition if it feeds at all, does so on the ambition of others.
Susan Sontag *(1933-2004)*
American activist, writer

I have been absolutely hag-ridden with ambition. If I could wish to
have anything in the world it would be to be free of ambition.
Tallulah Bankhead *(1902-1968)*
American actress

Obscurity can be a fire of ambition in those who have stalwart souls.
Taylor Caldwell *(1900-1985)*
American author

I never said Well, I don't have this and I don't have that. I
said, I don't have this yet, but I'm going to get it.
Tina Turner *(1939-)*
American singer

Make a difference about something other than yourselves.
Toni Morrison *(1931-)*
American novelist

Ambition, old as mankind, the immemorial weakness of the strong.
Vita Sackville-West *(1892-1962)*
English author

Mama exhorted her children at every opportunity to jump at de sun. We might not land on the sun, but at least we would get off the ground.
Zora Neale Hurston *(1891-1960)*
American dramatist

Attitude

Crime is terribly revealing. Try and vary your methods as you will, your tastes, your habits, your attitude of mind, and your soul is revealed by your actions.
Agatha Christie *(1890-1976)*
English detective novelist

I think a lot of times we don't pay enough attention to people with a positive attitude because we assume they are naive or stupid or unschooled.
Amy Adams *(1974-)*
American actress

If you can't change your fate, change your attitude.
Amy Tan *(1952-)*
American writer (Chinese descent)

The truth is, laughter always sounds more perfect than weeping. Laughter flows in a violent riff and is effortlessly melodic. Weeping is often fought, choked, half strangled, or surrendered to with humiliation.
Anne Rice *(1941-)*
American author

Why does a person even get up in the morning? You have breakfast, you floss your teeth so you'll have healthy gums in your old age, and then you get in your car and drive down I-10 and die. Life is so stupid I can't stand it.
Barbara Kingsolver *(1946-1989)*
American writer

Egotism – usually just a case of mistaken nonentity.
Barbara Stanwyck *(1907-1990)*
American actress

I am a believer in 'Breed.' I am descended from generations of yeomen and weavers; obstinate, hard-headed, matter-of-fact folk.
Beatrix Potter *(1866-1943)*
English author, illustrator

Champions take responsibility. When the ball is coming over the net you can be sure I want the ball.
Billie Jean King *(1934-)*
American tennis player

When are you going to realize that if it doesn't apply to me it doesn't matter?
Candace Bergen *(1946-)*
American actress

I don't have a star-type attitude. I tend to laugh at my success. I don't take myself all that seriously. If you take yourself too seriously in this business, you'll get hurt badly.
Christine McVie *(1943-)*
American rock singer

Everybody's business is nobody's business, and nobody's business is my business.
Clara Barton *(1821-1912)*
American nurse

The surest test of discipline is its absence.
Clara Barton *(1821-1912)*
American nurse

Just because I have my standards they think I'm a bitch.
Diana Ross *(1944-)*
American singer, actress

Attitude is everything.
Diane Von Furstenberg *(1946-)*
Belgian-born fashion designer

We cannot direct the wind, but we can adjust the sails.
Dolly Parton *(1946-)*
American singer-songwriter

Life isn't one damn thing after another. It's the same damn thing again and again.
Edna Saint Vincent Millay *(1892-1950)*
American poet, playwright

Attitude is more important than reality.
Elaine Agather *(1956-)*
American, CEO, JP Morgan Chase

Go big or go home. Because it's true. What do you have to lose?
Eliza Dushku *(1980-)*
American actress

It has begun to occur to me that life is a stage I'm going through.
Ellen Goodman *(1950-)*
American journalist

Is it worse to be scared than to be bored?
Gertrude Stein *(1874-1946)*
American writer

If I am one of Blair's babes, well I've been called a damn sight worse.
Glenda Jackson *(1936-)*
English actress

I don't mean this in a stuck-up way, but I needed an attitude song.
Gwen Stefani *(1969-)*
American musician

I say what I think, and I stand behind what I say.
Gwyneth Paltrow *(1972-)*
American actress

I can excuse everything but boredom. Boring
people don't have to stay that way.
Hedy Lamarr *(1914-2000)*
Austrian actress

A happy childhood can't be cured. Mine'll hang around my
neck like a rainbow, that's all, instead of a noose.
Hortense Calisher *(1911-2009)*
American writer

Having a child makes you strong and gives you chutzpah. It relaxed my
attitude to the job; my center of focus shifted, which I think is very helpful,
because even if you're not a very indulgent actor you spend a lot of time
thinking about yourself. I don't think that is particularly healthy.
Imelda Staunton *(1956-)*
English actress

Civilization is a method of living, an attitude of equal respect for all.
Jane Addams *(1860-1935)*
American activist

Nobody minds having what is too good for them.
Jane Austen *(1775-1817)*
English novelist

*I think it has something to do with being British. We don't take ourselves
as seriously as some other countries do. I think a lot of people take
themselves far too seriously; I find that a very tedious attitude.*
Joan Collins *(1933-)*
British actress

*My painted smile is always genuine but sometimes
I think it gives off no warmth.*
Joanna Lumley *(1946-)*
British actress

*Fame can be just so annoying because people are so critical
of you. You can't just say, 'hi.' You say hi and people whisper
'man did you see the way she said hi? What an attitude.'*
Juliette Lewis *(1973-)*
American actress

*Could we change our attitude, we should not only see life differently,
but life itself would come to be different. Life would undergo a change of
appearance because we ourselves had undergone a change in attitude.*
Katherine Mansfield *(1888-1923)*
New Zealand-born writer

The name we give to something shapes our attitude to it.
Katherine Paterson *(1932-)*
China-born author of children's books

*You can't start worrying about what's going to happen. You get
spastic enough worrying about what's happening now.*
Lauren Bacall *(1924-)*
American actress

The ball went in and out. That's the way the game bounces.
Lisa Leslie *(1972-)*
American basketball player

Life's under no obligation to give us what we expect.
Margaret Mitchell *(1900-1949)*
American novelist

I always cheer up immensely if an attack is particularly wounding because I think, well, if they attack me personally, it means they have not a single political argument left.
Margaret Thatcher *(1925-)*
English Prime Minister

The greatest revolution in our generation is that of human beings, who by changing the inner attitudes of their minds, can change the outer aspects of their lives.
Marilyn Ferguson *(1938-2008)*
American author

All we need, really, is a change from a near frigid to a tropical attitude of mind.
Marjory Stoneman Douglas *(1890-1998)*
American journalist

Great dancers are not great because of their technique, they are great because of their passion.
Martha Graham *(1894-1991)*
American dancer, choreographer

I've learned from experience that the greater part of our happiness or misery depends on our dispositions and not on our circumstances.
Martha Washington *(1731-1802)*
American First Lady

The mark of great athletes is not how good they are at their best, but how good they are at their worst.
Martina Navratilova *(1956-)*
Czech American tennis player

Every Body has so good an Opinion of their own Understanding as to think their own way the best.
Mary Astell *(1666-1731)*
English writer

Every failure, obstacle or hardship is an opportunity in disguise. Success in many cases is failure turned inside out. The greatest pollution problem we face today is negativity. Eliminate the negative attitude and believe you can do anything. Replace 'if I can, I hope, maybe' with 'I can, I will, I must.'
Mary Kay Ash *(1918-2001)*
American entrepreneur

I think what's fun about the '60s was the exhilaration of this, 'We're going to change the world,' attitude. That huge group of young people with all this energy and idealism saying, Let's make it better. I miss that movement.
Mary Travers *(1936-2009)*
American singer

In aid, the proper attitude is one omitting gratitude.
Marya Mannes *(1904-199*
American author, critic

If you don't like something, change it. If you can't change it, change your attitude.
Maya Angelou *(1928-)*
American poet, memoirist

I will not get very far with this attitude.
Nancy Cartwright *(1957-)*
American actress

If the President has a bully pulpit, then the First Lady has a white glove pulpit...more refined, restricted, ceremonial, but it's a pulpit all the same.
Nancy Reagan *(1923-)*
American First Lady

A strong positive mental attitude will create more miracles than any wonder drug.
Patricia Neal *(1926-2010)*
American actress

We are not amused!
Queen Victoria *(1819-1901)*
English royalty

I'm doing pretty well considering. In the past, when anyone left the Royal family they had you beheaded.
Sarah, Duchess of York *(1959-)*
English, former royalty

Take a step back, evaluate what is important, and enjoy life.
Teri Garr *(1944-)*
American actress

I think people want very much to simplify their lives enough so that they can control the things that make it possible to sleep at night.
Twyla Tharp *(1941-)*
American dancer

Hot air expands, and seriously pompous attitude is the inflation of choice by those lacking substance.
Vanna Bonta *(1958-)*
American novelist, poet

I grew up thinking that whatever I wanted to do, I could do.
Victoria Principal *(1946-)*
American actress

Sometimes, I feel discriminated against, but it does not make me angry. It merely astonishes me. How can any deny themselves the pleasure of my company? It's beyond me.
Zora Neale Hurston *(1891-1960)*
American dramatist

Boss

Well, what I tried to do is to just listen to my voice, because my voice is my boss.
Cecilia Bartoli *(1966-)*
Italian musician

I don't think you can ever question the decision that your boss makes. If he would have said 'race' or 'don't race,' that's what I would have done. I race for him. . . .
Danica Patrick *(1982-)*
American race car driver

The person who knows how will always have a job. The person who knows why will always be their boss.
Diane Ravitch *(1945-)*
American educator

To make a long story short, there's nothing like having a boss walk in.
Doris Lilly *(1926-1991)*
American journalist

For years it never occurred to me to question the judgment of those in charge at the studio.
Gene Tierney *(1920-1991)*
American actress

*To me, success was not having to have a boss and not having a
day job. I've been living my own version of success since the early
'90s when I first got signed. I haven't had a job since then.*
Juliana Hatfield *(1967-)*
American musician

*I am convinced that any feeling of exaltation because we
have people under us should be conquered, for I am sure that
if we enjoy being over people, there will be something in our
manner which will make them dislike being under us.*
Mary Parker Follett *(1868-1933)*
American management consultant

*Boards and bosses may say they want change, but in fact they
don't want too much disruption, controversy or agitation.*
Rosabeth Moss Kanter *(1943-)*
American academic, author

*If the boss is a jerk, get over it. ...just keep your head down and do the
work. Usually, if you put in maximum effort and produce excellent
results, someone in the company is going to take notice. Either you
will get promoted or your jerky boss will get the heave-ho.*
Suze Orman *(1951-)*
American, personal finance author

*The type of contract between players and producers is, I feel, antiquated
in form and abstract in concept. We have no privacies which producers
cannot invade, they trade us like cattle, boss us like children.*
Teresa Wright *(1918-2005)*
American actress

Career

*I happen to be lucky in that I knew what I wanted to
do as far as a career since I was nine years old.*
Alanis Morisette *(1974-)*
Canadian singer

*Some people just wait for someone to take them under their wings
but they should just find someone's wings to grab onto.*
Andrea Jung *(1959-)*
Canadian-American, CEO Avon

*My mother was against me being an actress – until
I introduced her to Frank Sinatra.*
Angie Dickinson *(1931-)*
American actress

*Whether we call it a job or a career work is more than
just something we do. It is a part of who we are.*
Anita Hill *(1956-)*
American, professor of law

*Clearly society has a tremendous stake in insisting on a woman's natural
fitness for the career of mother: the alternatives are all too expensive.*
Ann Oakley *(1944-)*
British sociologist, writer

I do not like vaudeville, but what can I do? It likes me.
Anna Held *(1872-1918)*
Polish-born stage performer

*I probably hold the distinction of being one movie star
who, by all laws of logic, should never have made it. At
each stage of my career, I lacked the experience.*
Audrey Hepburn *(1929-1993)*
Belgian-born actress

*Where I am today has everything to do with the years I
spent hanging on to a career by my fingernails.*
Barbara Aronstein Black *(1933-)*
American legal scholar

*Career is too pompous a word. It was a job, and I have
always felt privileged to be paid for what I love doing.*
Barbara Stanwyck *(1907-1990)*
American actress

*A job is not a career. I think I started out with a job.
It turned into a career and changed my life.*
Barbara Walters *(1929-)*
American broadcast journalist, author

*Acting should be bigger than life. Scripts should be
bigger than life. It should all be bigger than life.*
Bette Davis *(1908-1989)*
American actress

My voice had a long, nonstop career. It deserves to be put to bed with quiet and dignity, not yanked out every once in a while to see if it can still do what it used to do. It can't.
Beverly Sills *(1929-2007)*
American operatic soprano

I am just at that stage of wondering where I go from here. I came into this business almost by accident, but now it has become serious. What started as a bit of fun, something to do other than be a model, has taken on a different career curve. I have been forced to ask where that curve is going to end up.
Cameron Diaz *(1972-)*
American actress

Other people's perspective, just seeing the sexy image, might be that I take my sexuality very seriously. But I really don't. I like being sexy. It's fun, and I have had a nice little career off it.
Carmen Electra *(1972-)*
American model, actress

If I lose, I'm going to retire from politics, practice law and wear bright leather pants.
Carol Moseley Braun *(1947-)*
American politician, author

I shall be an autocrat: that's my trade. And the good lord will forgive me: that's his.
Catherine the Great *(1729-1796)*
Russian royalty

Food, love, career, and mothers, the four major guilt groups.
Cathy Guisewhite *(1950-)*
American cartoonist

I think, first of all, you need to love what you're doing.
Cecilia Bartoli *(1966-)*
Italian musician

Nothing is a career move. Everything I've done this year has so not been a career move.
Cilla Black *(1943-)*
British musician

56

No letters after your name are ever going to be a total guarantee
of competence any more than they are a guarantee against fraud.
Improving competence involves continuing professional development
... That is the really crucial thing, not just passing an examination.
Colette Bowe *(1946-)*
English, CEO of Ofcom

Don't let someone else define who you are...My advice
is, do what you love and forget the rest of it.
Condoleezza Rice *(1954-)*
American, Secretary of State

I wanted to use what I was, to be what I was born to be – not to have a
career, but to be that straightforward obvious unmistakable animal, a writer.
Cynthia Ozick *(1929-)*
American novelist

I don't believe in careers. I believe in work. I'm not interested
in some 'big picture that would be really good for me.'
Debra Winger *(1955-)*
American actress

A human being must have occupation, if he or she
is not to become a nuisance to the world.
Dorothy L. Sayers *(1893-1957)*
English crime writer

The question was not how to get a job, but how
to live by such jobs as I could get.
Dorothy M. Richardson *(1873-1957)*
British journalist

I must have something to engross my thoughts, some object in life which
will fill this vacuum, and prevent this sad wearing away of the heart.
Elizabeth Blackwell *(1821-1910)*
British, first U.S. woman doctor

My career at Warner Brothers consisted of one musical short
subject. I was running around in a bear skin. Very chic.
Ethel Merman *(1908-1984)*
American singer

I know what my job is: I write the songs, I sing them, I play them on the piano.
Fiona Apple *(1977-)*
American musician

Follow what you love!...Don't deign to ask what they are looking for out there. Ask what you have inside. Follow not your interests, which change, but what you are and what you love, which will and should not change.
Georgie Anne Geyer *(1935-)*
American journalist

You'll be old and you never lived, and you kind of feel silly to lie down and die and to never have lived, to have been a job chaser and never have lived.
Gertrude Stein *(1874-1946)*
American writer

The key is to figure out what you want out of life, not what you want out of your career.
Goldie Hawn *(1945-)*
American actress

Analyzing what you haven't got as well as what you have is a necessary ingredient of a career.
Grace Moore *(1898-1947)*
American operatic soprano

The word career is a divisive word. It's a word that divides the normal life from business or professional life.
Grace Paley *(1922-2007)*
American writer

Starting out to make money is the greatest mistake in life. Do what you feel you have a flair for doing, and if you are good enough at it, the money will come.
Greer Garson *(1904-1996)*
British-born actress

I've had a very interesting career. I get to do amazing things and work with amazing people and travel and learn languages – things most people don't get the opportunity to do.
Gwyneth Paltrow *(1972-)*
American actress

*Nearly every glamorous, wealthy, successful career woman
you might envy now started out as some kind of schlep.*
Helen Gurley Brown *(1922-)*
American author, publisher

Don't confuse having a career with having a life.
Hillary Rodham Clinton *(1947-)*
American, Secretary of State

*I have tried to be as eclectic as I possibly can with my
professional life, and so far it's been pretty fun.*
Holly Hunter *(1958-)*
American actress

*Stay out of the politics, stay out of running for office, focus on the job at
hand – and if you do those three, it does not matter if you are international,
locally born, man, woman, I think you'll find yourself moving ahead.*
Indra Nooyi *(1955-)*
Indian, CEO of Pepsico

*When I left the Yale campus back in 1980, I did not have my
sights set on being CEO of PepsiCo or any other company.*
Indra Nooyi *(1955-)*
Indian, CEO of Pepsico

*I was told to avoid the business all together because of the rejection. People
would say to me, 'Don't you want to have a normal job and a normal family?'
I guess that would be good advice for some people, but I wanted to act.*
Jennifer Aniston *(1969-)*
American actress

*My parents wanted me to be a lawyer. But I don't think I would
have been very happy. I'd be in front of the jury singing.*
Jennifer Lopez *(1970-)*
American musician

*This is the man my mother lived for. My career means
something now because I've worked with Robert Redford.*
Jennifer Lopez *(1970-)*
American musician

*Dynasty was the opportunity to take charge of my career rather
than waiting around like a library book waiting to be loaned out.*
Joan Collins *(1933-)*
British actress

Probably any successful career has 'X' number of breaks in it and maybe the difference between successful people and those who aren't superachievers is taking advantage of those breaks.
Joan Ganz Cooney *(1929-)*
American television producer

Seriously, though, I think I never ceased to be grateful of the fact that I am able to do a job that I really love – I never got over that.
Judi Dench *(1934-)*
English actress

I suppose that if I could have quit, I would have, because in those days I never wanted to be an actress, the acting was something to do while I waited for a chance to study writing and directing. But I guess I was just meant to be an actress. Because, here I am.
Judy Holliday *(1921-1965)*
American actress

I'm just an ordinary person who has an extraordinary job.
Julia Roberts *(1967-)*
American actress

It's been certainly more than a job, it's been giving me a charmed life ... If I could've dreamt what the outcome of my career would've been when I'd auditioned 20 years ago, you know, I would have never believed it. It's just given me the greatest blessings and gifts and rewards and challenges. It's really been quite a trip.
Julie Kent *(1969-)*
American ballerina

I'm on top, I'm 35 years old, and there are other things I want to do. Physically, there is a lot of pain. I don't want to be hurt again. I have nothing left to prove.
Julie Krone *(1963-)*
American jockey

To love what you do and feel that it matters – how could anything be more fun?
Katharine Graham *(1917-2001)*
American publisher

Acting is the most minor of gifts and not a very high-class way to earn a living. After all, Shirley Temple could do it at the age of four.
Katharine Hepburn *(1907-2003)*
American actress

*I wasn't concerned about the hardships, because I always felt I was doing
what I had to do, what I wanted to do and what I was destined to do.*
Katherine Dunham *(1912-2006)*
American actress

*The best career advice given to the young is, Find out what you
like doing best and get someone to pay you for doing it.*
Katherine Whitehorn *(1914-1956)*
British columnist

*I am focused on the work. I am constantly creating. I am a busy girl.
I live and breathe my work. I love what I do. I believe in the message.
There's no stopping. I didn't create the fame, the fame created me.*
Lady Gaga *(1986-)*
American performance artist

Always be smarter than the people who hire you.
Lena Horne *(1917-2010)*
American singer, actress

I was just born to swing, that's all.
Lil Hardin Armstrong *(1898-1971)*
American bandleader, 1930s

*I have always wanted to be somebody, but I see
now I should have been more specific.*
Lily Tomlin *(1939-)*
American actress, comedian

*Being on stage is the best part of my career. I just say whatever comes
into my head. It's the only time I feel grown-up and in control of things.*
Loretta Lynn *(1935-)*
American musician

*From the first day in school until the day I graduated, everyone
gave me one hundred plus in art. Well, where do you go in life?
You go to the place where you got one hundred plus.*
Louise Nevelson *(1899-1988)*
American sculptor, painter

*I just feel that I'm in tune with the right vibrations in
the universe when I'm in the process of working.*
Louise Nevelson *(1899-1988)*
American sculptor, painter

I regret the passing of the studio system. I was very appreciative of it because I had no talent.
Lucille Ball *(1911-1989)*
American comedian, actress

I had to make my own living and my own opportunity! But I made it! Don't sit down and wait for the opportunities to come. Get up and make them!
Madame C. J. Walker *(1867-1919)*
American entrepreneur

My career is chequered. Then I think I got pigeon-holed in humour; Shakespeare is not my thing.
Maggie Smith *(1934-)*
British actress

The great thing to learn about life is first not to do what you don't want to do and second to do what you do want to do.
Margaret Anderson *(1886-1973)*
American publisher

Never work just for money or for power. They won't save your soul or help you sleep at night.
Marian Wright Edelman *(1939-)*
American, founder Children's Defense Fund

You have to know exactly what you want out of your career. If you want to be a star, you don't bother with other things.
Marilyn Horne *(1934-)*
American musician

A career is wonderful, but you can't curl up with it on a cold night.
Marilyn Monroe *(1926-1962)*
American actress

Glamour is what I sell. It's my stock in trade.
Marlene Dietrich *(1901-1992)*
German-born actress

I feel like it's important to use this gift God gave me, my life and my career to do something to make the world a better place. It's an easy thing for me to do.
Martina McBride *(1966-)*
American singer

I've been in the twilight of my career longer than
most people have had their career.
Martina Navratilova *(1956-)*
Czech American tennis player

Our career is a dream. I mean, we get to act, travel around
the world, and meet cool people. What's not to love!
Mary-Kate Olsen *(1986-)*
American actress, entrepreneur

Through it all, I have remained consistently and nauseatingly
adorable. In fact, I have been known to cause diabetes.
Meg Ryan *(1961-)*
American actress

Having been let out of the barn once, I know I wouldn't
be happy if I were home all the time.
Meryl Streep *(1949-)*
American actress

I want a big career... and a big life. You have to
think big. That's the only way to get it.
Mia Farrow *(1945-)*
American actress

If you don't love what you do, you won't do it
with much conviction or passion.
Mia Hamm *(1972-)*
American soccer player

I try to look at this music career thing as the means to an end. And really,
at the end of it, I see myself on a sailboat, sailing off the edge of the world.
Michelle Shocked *(1962-)*
American musician

I'm out of a job. London wants flappers and I can't flap.
Mrs. Patrick Campbell *(1865-1940)*
English actress

Being the first woman speaker and breaking the marble
ceiling is pretty important. Now it's time to move on.
Nancy Pelosi *(1940-)*
American politician

I'm going to college. I don't care if it ruins my career.
I'd rather be smart than a movie star.
Natalie Portman *(1981-)*
American actress

Competitive skaters must be prepared for lots of work,
challenges, self-discipline, and motivation. The desire must
be there, but more importantly, your love for the sport.
Oksana Baiul *(1977-)*
Ukrainian Olympic skater

Sometimes I say, Enough ... all my life I've done gymnastics. Let's do
something else. But I was born in gymnastics, and it is in my heart.
Olga Korbut *(1955-)*
Soviet Olympic gymnast

From a very early age, I made my decisions based on careers
that I admire. The one thing that all the actresses I love have
in common is that they have diversity in their careers.
Olivia Wilde *(1984-)*
American actress

Adults are always asking kids what they want to be when
they grow up because they are looking for ideas.
Paula Poundstone *(1959-)*
American comedian

I don't choose to take a role to prove to someone what I can do. It's an August
Wilson play. I met with the playwright, I read for the playwright. In my
career, that's like meeting Bill Cosby – meeting him is enough for me.
Phylicia Rashad *(1948-)*
American actress

Women want men, careers, money, children, friends,
luxury, comfort, independence, freedom, respect, love,
and a three-dollar pantyhose that won't run.
Phyllis Diller *(1917-)*
American comedian

Many people worry so much about managing their careers, but rarely
spend half that much energy managing their LIVES. I want to make my
life, not just my job, the best it can be. The rest will work itself out.
Reese Witherspoon *(1976-)*
American actress

The boomers' biggest impact will be on eliminating the term 'retirement' and inventing a new stage of life ... the new career arc.
Rosabeth Moss Kanter *(1943-)*
American academic, author

I haven't strength of mind not to need a career.
Ruth Benedict *(1887-1948)*
American scientist

I never got a job I didn't create for myself.
Ruth Gordon *(1896-1985)*
American actress, writer

[C]celebrity .... is a sort of octopus with innumerable tentacles. It throws out to right and left, in front and behind, its clammy arms, and gathers in, through its thousand little suckers, all the gossip and slander and praise afloat, to spit out again at the public.
Sarah Bernhardt *(1845-1923)*
French actress

My gift is that I'm not beautiful. My career was never about looks. It's about health and being in good shape.
Shirley MacLaine *(1934-)*
American actress

No other job in the world could possibly dispossess one so completely as this job of teaching. You could stand all day in a laundry, for instance, still in possession of your mind. But this teaching utterly obliterates you. It cuts right into your being essentially, it takes over your spirit. It drags it out from where it would hide.
Sylvia Ashton-Warner *(1908-1984)*
New Zealand writer, poet

My career always took me away from home, I was always away from home and I just wanted to be at home.
Tina Turner *(1939-)*
American singer

And I don't believe that I have to stay on one side of the fence or the other. I don't believe that there is any good career move or bad career move. I believe there are only the things that make me happy.
Whoopi Goldberg *(1955-)*
American actress, comedian

A lot of young girls have looked to their career paths and have said they'd like to be chief. There's been a change in the limits people see.
Wilma Pearl Mankiller *(1945-2010)*
American Cherokee leader

People ask me what I do and I say I don't really know. I get paid to be a fool.
Zoe Ball *(1970-)*
British television presenter

Challenges

Never interrupt someone doing what you said couldn't be done.
Amelia Earhart *(1897-1937)*
American aviator

When you find a burden in belief or apparel, cast it off.
Amelia Jenks Bloomer *(1818 - 1894)*
American reformist

Life's challenges are not supposed to paralyze you, they are supposed to help you discover who you are.
Bernice Johnson Reagon *(1942-)*
American historian

Live with intention. Walk to the edge. Listen hard. Practice wellness. Play with abandon. Laugh. Choose with no regret. Continue to learn. Appreciate your friends. Do what you love. Live as if this is all there is.
Bertha Adams Backus *(1900-1940)*
American poet

Magic lies in challenging what seems impossible.
Carol Moseley Braun *(1947-)*
American politician, author

It is not easy to be a pioneer – but oh, it is fascinating! I would not trade one moment, even the worst moment, for all the riches in the world.
Elizabeth Blackwell *(1821-1910)*
British, first U.S. woman doctor

For me it's the challenge – the challenge to try to beat myself or do better than I did in the past. I try to keep in mind not what I have accomplished but what I have to try to accomplish in the future.
Jackie Joyner-Kersee *(1962-)*
American Olympic athlete

You don't get to choose how you're going to die. Or when.
You can decide how you're going to live now.
Joan Baez *(1941-)*
American folksinger, songwriter

The first rule of holes: when you're in one, stop digging.
Molly Ivens *(1944-2007)*
American political commentator

I have reached a point in my life where I understand
the pain and the challenges; and my attitude is one of
standing up with open arms to meet them all.
Myrlie Evers *(1933-)*
American activist

Challenges are gifts that force us to search for a new center of
gravity. Don't fight them. Just find a different way to stand.
Oprah Winfrey *(1954-)*
American media mogul

I hate to complain...No one is without difficulties, whether in high or
low life, and every person knows best where their own shoe pinches.
Abigail Adams *(1744-1818)*
American First Lady

It's astonishing in this world how things don't turn
out at all the way you expect them to.
Agatha Christie *(1890-1976)*
English detective novelist

It's just such a freeing thing to set these great challenges for
yourself, to travel, to learn more about the world, to just go
out there and get crazy and get free and get strong.
Angelina Jolie *(1975-)*
American actress

Providence has hidden a charm in difficult undertakings which
is appreciated only by those who dare to grapple with them.
Anne Sophie Swetchine *(1752-1857)*
Russian mystic

Nothing is impossible – the word itself says 'I'm possible!'
Audrey Hepburn *(1929-1993)*
Belgian-born actress

*Real obstacles don't take you in circles. They can be
overcome. Invented ones are like a maze.*
Barbara Sher *(1869-1942)*
American writer

*For me life is a challenge. And it will be a challenge if I
live to be a hundred or if I get to be a trillionaire.*
Beah Richards *(1920-2000)*
American actress

*The key to life is accepting challenges. Once
someone stops doing this, they're dead.*
Bette Davis *(1908-1989)*
American actress

*What is genius, anyway, if it isn't the ability to give
an adequate response to a great challenge.*
Bette Green *(1934-)*
American author children's books

*You can be up to your boobies in white satin, with gardenias in your hair
and no sugar cane for miles, but you can still be working on a plantation.*
Billie Holiday *(1915-1959)*
American jazz singer

We're so overburdened with all the bullshit in the system.
Carol Bartz *(1948-)*
American, former Yahoo CEO

*The hardest times for me were not when people challenged
what I said, but when I felt my voice was not heard.*
Carol Gilligan *(1936-)*
American ethnicist

*Those who wait to take action until they find themselves in a
desperate situation face more difficulties than they need to.*
Catherine Pulsifer *(1957-)*
American glass artist, author

*To swallow and follow, whether old doctrine or new propaganda,
is a weakness still dominating the human mind.*
Charlotte Perkins Gilman *(1860-1935)*
American sociologist, novelist

To succeed in life in today's world, you must have
the will and tenacity to finish the job.
Chin-Ning Chu *(1947-2009)*
Chinese business author

Challenges make you discover things about yourself you never knew. They're
what make the instrument stretch, what make you go beyond the norm.
Cicely Tyson *(1933-)*
American actress

I wanted to be scared again... I wanted to feel unsure again.
That's the only way I learn, the only way I feel challenged.
Connie Chung *(1946-)*
Chinese-American journalist

Struggle is a never ending process. Freedom is never really
won—you earn it and win it in every generation.
Coretta Scott King *(1927-2006)*
American civil rights activist

I have learned to live each day as it comes, and not
borrow trouble by dreading tomorrow. It is the dark
menace of the future that makes cowards of us.
Dorothy Dix *(1861-1951)*
American journalist

The game of life is a game of boomerangs. Our thoughts, deeds and
words return to us sooner or later with astounding accuracy.
Florence Scovel Shinn *(1871-1940)*
American artist, book illustrator

To be tested is good. The challenged life may be the best therapist.
Gail Sheehy *(1937-)*
American writer, lecturer

Trying to make order out of my life was like trying to pick up a jellyfish.
Gene Tierney *(1920-1991)*
American actress

If you can do it then why do it?
Gertrude Stein *(1874-1946)*
American writer

I wanted a perfect ending. Now I've learned, the hard way, that some poems don't rhyme, and some stories don't have a clear beginning, middle, and end. Life is about not knowing, having to change, taking the moment and making the best of it without knowing what's going to happen next.
Gilda Radner *(1946-1989)*
American comedian

It was very difficult. We don't advertise this much, but those years that we went through were hell.
Gina Rinehart *(1954-)*
Australian business woman

Whether you are making leadership changes, integrating an acquisition or executing a major transformation, move quickly because in hindsight you will always wish you moved faster.
Irene Rosenfeld *(1953-)*
American, CEO Kraft Foods

The cure for anything is salt water – sweat, tears, or the sea.
Isak Dineson *(1885-1962)*
Danish writer

You can do one of two things; just shut up, which is something I don't find easy, or learn an awful lot very fast, which is what I tried to do.
Jane Fonda *(1937-)*
American actress

Get up tomorrow early in the morning, and earlier than you did today, and do the best that you can. Always stay near me, for tomorrow I will have much to do and more than I ever had, and tomorrow blood will leave my body above the breast.
Joan of Arc *(1412-1431)*
French heroine

Part of me longs to do a job where there's not a gray area.
Jodie Foster *(1962-)*
American actress

It frustrates me about myself when I see I'm not taking the road that demands more of me.
Judith Light *(1949-)*
American actress

There are no laurels in life ... just new challenges.
Katharine Hepburn *(1907-2003)*
American actress

*To fear is one thing. To let fear grab you by the
tail and swing you around is another.*
Katherine Paterson *(1932-)*
China-born author of children's books

*Life is easier than you'd think; all that is necessary is to accept the
impossible, do without the indispensable, and bear the intolerable.*
Kathleen Norris *(1880-1966)*
American poet, novelist

*I look for a role that hopefully I feel empathy with and that I can understand
and love, but also that has that challenge for me to play – a different
kind of role, a different type of character, a different time period.*
Kathy Bates *(1948-)*
American actress

*My family gave me values that have sustained me through
situations that would challenge any person.*
Kathy Ireland *(1963-)*
American entrepreneur

*This business is very challenging – you must get used to rejection
no matter what level you are at. Not everyone is going to like what
you do or what you have to offer; however, if you can't see yourself
doing anything else, and you have the drive and ambition, get the
training and go for it. Because there is nothing more rewarding.*
Kristin Chenoweth *(1968-)*
American singer, actress

*The sentimentalist ages far more quickly than the person
who loves his work and enjoys new challenges.*
Lillie Langtry *(1853-1929)*
British actress

The road to success is always under construction.
Lily Tomlin *(1939-)*
American actress, comedian

*A tactical retreat is not a bad response to a surprise assault, you know. First
you survive. Then you choose your own ground. Then you counterattack.*
Lois McMaster Bujold *(1949-)*
American author

The mystery of existence is the connection between
our faults and our misfortunes.
Madame de Stael *(1766-1817)*
French writer

Never be limited by other people's limited imaginations...If you
adopt their attitudes, then the possibility won't exist because
you'll have already shut it out ... You can hear other people's
wisdom, but you've got to re-evaluate the world for yourself.
Mae Jemison *(1956-   )*
American astronaut

When people keep telling you that you can't do
a thing, you kind of like to try it.
Margaret Chase Smith *(1897-1995)*
American politician

I was never one to patiently pick up broken fragments and glue them
together again and tell myself that the mended whole was as good as
new. What is broken is broken and I'd rather remember it as it was at
its best than mend it and see the broken places as long as I lived.
Margaret Mitchell *(1900-1949)*
American novelist

If my critics saw me walking over the Thames they
would say it was because I couldn't swim.
Margaret Thatcher *(1925-   )*
English Prime Minister

I was a queen, and you took away my crown; a wife, and you killed
my husband; a mother, and you deprived me of my children. My
blood alone remains: take it, but do not make me suffer long.
Marie Antoinette *(1755-1793)*
Austrian-born, Queen of France

I have frequently been questioned, especially by women, of how I could
reconcile family life with a scientific career. Well, it has not been easy.
Marie Curie *(1867-1934)*
Polish-French physicist

You have to stand up for some things in this world.
Marjory Stoneman Douglas *(1890-1998)*
American journalist

I think loss of loved ones is the hardest blow in life.
Marlo Thomas *(1937-)*
American actress

Consider calling it a challenge rather than calling it a crisis
Mary Anne Radmacher *(1957-)*
American writer

*For every failure, there's an alternative course of action. You just
have to find it. When you come to a roadblock, take a detour.*
Mary Kay Ash *(1918-2001)*
American entrepreneur

*Having a dream is what keeps you alive ... Overcoming
the challenges make life worth living.*
Mary Tyler Moore *(1936-)*
American actress

*There are always new, grander challenges to confront,
and a true winner will embrace each one.*
Mia Hamm *(1972-)*
American soccer player

*People might say I'm difficult, but did you ever hear anyone describe
a label as 'difficult'? By nature, artists should challenge. When they
call you difficult, it is a reflection of the imbalance of power.*
Michelle Shocked *(1962-)*
American musician

*I don't run away from a challenge because I am afraid. Instead, I run toward
it because the only way to escape fear is to trample it beneath your feet.*
Nadia Comaneci *(1961-)*
Romanian Olympic gymnast

*We have so much room for improvement. Every aspect of our lives must
be subjected to an inventory... of how we are taking responsibility.*
Nancy Pelosi *(1940-)*
American politician

*Life is one long struggle to disinter oneself, to keep one's head above the
accumulations of the ever deepening layers of objects ... which attempt
to cover one over steadily, almost irresistibly, like falling snow.*
Rose Macaulay *(1881-1958)*
British writer

Perhaps the greatest challenge has been trying to keep my time to myself and my private life private in order to do my job. Everything that is most mine belongs to everyone now.
Sandra Cisneros *(1954-)*
American author

Everyone has obstacles, and you're not going to have the right answer or do the right thing every single time.
Shannon Miller *(1977-)*
American gymnast

One should never be sorry one has attempted something new – never, never, never.
Sybil Thorndike *(1882-1976)*
English actress

I have the wherewithal to challenge myself for my entire life. That's a great gift.
Twyla Tharp *(1941-)*
American dancer

The worst walls are never the ones you find in your way. The worst walls are the ones you put there – you build yourself. Those are the high ones, the thick ones, the ones with no doors in.
Ursula K. LeGuin *(1929-)*
American novelist

Change

I'm doing it because I choose it. And if it's not working, I can make a change.
Alanis Morisette *(1974-)*
Canadian singer

Every small, positive change we make in ourselves repays us in confidence in the future.
Alice Walker *(1944-)*
American writer

The problem is, of course, that these interest groups are all asking for changes, but their enthusiasm for change rapidly disappears when it affects the core of their own interests.
Angela Merkel *(1954-)*
German Chancellor

*The question is not whether we are able to change
but whether we are changing fast enough.*
Angela Merkel *(1954-)*
German Chancellor

I feel very strongly that change is good because it stirs up the system.
Ann Richards *(1933-2006)*
American politician

*There is no sin punished more implacably by nature
than the sin of resistance to change.*
Anne Morrow Lindbergh *(1906-2001)*
American aviator, author

In this world, nothing which comes stays, and nothing which goes is lost.
Anne Sophie Swetchine *(1752-1857)*
Russian mystic

*Our task, of course, is to transmute the anger that is affliction into
the anger that is determination to bring about change. I think,
in fact, that one could give that as a definition of revolution.*
Barbara Deming *(1917-1984)*
American author

*It's important to be active in the causes that are important
to you... That's how we make changes in this world.*
Cameron Diaz *(1972-)*
American actress

*My parents were always philosophizing about how to bring about change.
To me, people who didn't try to make the world a better place were strange.*
Carol Moseley Braun *(1947-)*
American politician, author

*A great wind is blowing, and that gives you
either imagination or a headache.*
Catherine the Great *(1729-1796)*
Russian royalty

*The softest, freest, most pliable and changeful living substance
is the brain – the hardest and most iron-bound as well.*
Charlotte Perkins Gilman *(1860-1935)*
American sociologist, novelist

I have an almost complete disregard of precedent, and a faith in the possibility of something better. It irritates me to be told how things have always been done. I defy the tyranny of precedent. I go for anything new that might improve the past.
Clara Barton *(1821-1912)*
American nurse

It doesn't matter how strong your opinions are. If you don't use your power for positive change, you are, indeed, part of the problem.
Coretta Scott King *(1927 - 2006)*
American author, activist

Change, when it comes, cracks everything open.
Dorothy Allison *(1949-)*
American writer, speaker

Come, come, my conservative friend, wipe the dew off your spectacles, and see that the world is moving.
Elizabeth Cady Stanton *(1815-1902)*
American reformist, writer

Yesterday people were permitted to change things. They will be permitted to advocate changing them tomorrow. It is only dangerous to think of changing anything today.
Elizabeth Hawes *(1903-1971)*
American fashion designer

If one is going to change things, one has to make a fuss and catch the eye of the world.
Elizabeth Janeway *(1913-2005)*
American author, critic

Change is the watchword of progression. When we tire of well-worn ways, we seek for new. This restless craving in the souls of everyone spurs them to climb, and to seek the mountain view.
Ella Wheeler Wilcox *(1850-1919)*
American poet

All change is not growth, as all movement is not forward.
Ellen Glasgow *(1873-1945)*
American novelist

*I have never been especially impressed by the heroics of people who
are convinced they are about to change the world. I am more awed by
those who struggle to make one small difference after another.*
Ellen Goodman *(1950-)*
American journalist

*A change of heart is the essence of all other change, and it
has brought about me a reeducation of the mind.*
Emmeline Pethick-Lawrence *(1867-1954)*
British women's rights activist

*I have accepted fear as part of my life—specifically the fear of change...I
have gone ahead despite the pounding in the heart that says: turn back . . .*
Erica Jong *(1942-)*
American writer

*Things good in themselves...perfectly valid in the integrity
of their origins, become fetters if they cannot alter.*
Freya Stark *(1893-1993)*
French-born travel writer, explorer

If we don't change, we don't grow. If we don't grow, we aren't really living.
Gail Sheehy *(1937-)*
American writer, lecturer

When you get there, there isn't any there there.
Gertrude Stein *(1874-1946)*
American writer

*Life is about not knowing, having to change, taking the moment and
making the best of it, without knowing what's going to happen next.*
Gilda Radner *(1946-1989)*
American comedian

*Humans are allergic to change. They love to say, We've
always done it this way. I try to fight that. That's why I
have a clock on my wall that runs counter-clockwise.*
Grace Murray Hopper *(1906-1992)*
American Rear Admiral, U.S. Navy

*Always remember you have within you the strength, the patience,
and the passion to reach for the stars to change the world.*
Harriet Tubman *(1913-)*
American abolitionist

*In trying to make something new, half the undertaking
lies in discovering whether it can be done. Once it has been
established that it can, duplication is inevitable.*
Helen Gahagan Douglas *(1900-1980)*
American politician, singer

*The challenges of change are always hard. It is important that
we begin to unpack those challenges that confront this nation
and realize that we each have a role that requires us to change
and become more responsible for shaping our own future.*
Hillary Rodham Clinton *(1947-)*
American, Secretary of State

For me, words are a form of action, capable of influencing change.
Ingrid Benqis *(1944-)*
American essayist

*We have been straightforward with employees and because
of that they trust us. Transformation is a serious word. There
is an expectation that the changes made will last.*
Irene Rosenfeld *(1953-)*
American, CEO Kraft Foods

To change, that is the most difficult thing to accomplish.
Isabelle Adjani *(1955-)*
French actress

*I am full of the sorrow that goes with changes in surroundings, those
successive stages of annihilation that slowly lead to the great and final void.*
Isabelle Eberhardt *(1877-1904)*
Swiss explorer

*It is only in romances that people undergo a sudden
metamorphosis. In real life, even after the most terrible
experiences, the main character remains exactly the same.*
Isadora Duncan *(1878-1927)*
American dancer

*At my time of life opinions are tolerably fixed. It is not likely
that I should now see or hear anything to change them.*
Jane Austen *(1775-1817)*
English novelist

Change happens by listening and then starting a dialogue with the people who are doing something you don't believe is right.
Jane Goodall *(1934-)*
English, chimpanzee researcher

So often I heard people paying blind obeisance to change – as though it had some virtue of its own. Change or we will die. Change or we will stagnate. Evergreens don't stagnate.
Judith Rossner *(1935-2005)*
American novelist

There is no good reason why we should not develop and change until the last day we live.
Karen Horney *(1885-1952)*
American psychologist

A person needs at intervals to separate themself from family and companions and go to new places. They must go without their familiars in order to be open to influence, to change.
Katharine Butler Hathaway *(1890-1942)*
American writer

Disconnecting from change does not recapture the past. It loses the future.
Kathleen Norris *(1880-1966)*
American poet, novelist

None of us knows what the next change is going to be, what unexpected opportunity is around the corner waiting to change the tenor of our lives.
Kathleen Norris *(1880-1966)*
American poet, novelist

It never occurred to me that I couldn't change things that needed changing or couldn't have what I wanted if I worked hard enough and was good enough.
Kathleen Turner *(1954-)*
American actress

I've learned that you'll never be disappointed if you always keep an eye on uncharted territory, where you'll be challenged and growing and having fun.
Kirstie Alley *(1951-)*
American actress

And now, I'm just trying to change the world, one sequin at a time.
Lady Gaga *(1986-)*
American performance artist

People change and forget to tell each other.
Lillian Hellman *(1905-1984)*
American playwright

*I knew here could never be as sweet as there; going
was a question, staying was an answer.*
Linda Ellerbee *(1944-)*
American journalist

*That's the risk you take if you change, that people you've been involved
with won't like the new you. But other people who do will come along.*
Lisa Alther *(1944-)*
American author

*The only people in the whole world who can change
things are those who can sell ideas.*
Lois Wyse *(1926-2007)*
American advertising executive

*Not everything that is faced can be changed, but
nothing can be changed until it is faced.*
Lucille Ball *(1911-1989)*
American comedian, actress

*The great secret that all old people share is that you really haven't
changed in seventy or eighty years. Your body changes, but you
don't change at all. And that, of course, causes great confusion.*
Maggie Kuhn *(1905-1995)*
American activist

Better never means better for everyone. It always means worse, for some.
Margaret Atwood *(1939-)*
Canadian poet, novelist

*The mind of the most logical thinker goes so easily from one point
to another that it is not hard to mistake motion for progress.*
Margaret Collier Graham *(1850-1910)*
American writer

*There is no power for change greater than a
community discovering what it cares about.*
Margaret J. Wheatley *(1934-)*
American organization expert

*Never doubt that a small number of dedicated people can
change the world; indeed it is the only thing that ever has.*
Margaret Mead *(1901-1978)*
American cultural anthropologist

Never doubt that you can change history. You already have.
Marge Piercy *(1936-)*
American novelist, poet

*People don't alter. They may with enormous difficulty
modify themselves, but they never really change.*
Margery Allingham *(1904-1966)*
English crime writer

*If you don't like the way the world is, change it. You have an
obligation to change it. You do it one step at a time.*
Marian Wright Edelman *(1939-)*
American, founder Children's Defense Fund

*Cultural transformation announces itself in sputtering fits and starts,
sparked here and there by minor incidents, warmed by new ideas
that may smolder for decades. In many different places at different
times the kindling is laid for the real conflagration – the one that
will consume the old landmarks and alter the landscape forever.*
Marilyn Ferguson *(1938-2008)*
American author

*No one can persuade another to change. Each of us guards a gate
of change that can only be opened from the inside. We cannot open
the gate of another, either by argument or emotional appeal.*
Marilyn Ferguson *(1938-2008)*
American author

*I am invariably late for appointments – sometimes as much
as two hours. I've tried to change my ways but the things
that make me late are too strong, and too pleasing.*
Marilyn Monroe *(1926-1962)*
American actress

Fluidity and discontinuity are central to the reality in which we live.
Mary Catherine Bateson *(1939-)*
American anthropologist

If you don't like something change it; if you can't
change it, change the way you think about it.
Mary Engelbreit *(1952-)*
American children's book illustrator

The need for change bulldozed a road down the center of my mind.
Maya Angelou *(1928-)*
American poet, memoirist

People are always telling me that change is good. But all that means
is that something you didn't want to happen has happened.
Meg Ryan *(1961-)*
American actress

We need big change … not just the shifting of power among insiders.
We need to change the game, because the game is broken.
Michelle Obama *(1964-)*
American First Lady

When you're really trying to make serious change, you don't want people
to get caught up in emotion because change isn't emotion. It's real work
and organization and strategy.. that's just the truth of it. I mean, you
pull people in with inspiration, but then you have to roll up your sleeves
and you've got to make sacrifices and you have got to have structure.
Michelle Obama *(1964-)*
American First Lady

It's the most unhappy people who most fear change.
Mignon McLaughlin *(1913-1983)*
American journalist

It is not the conscious changes made in their lives by men and women – a
new job, a new town, a divorce – which really shape them, like the chapter
headings in a biography, but a long, slow mutation of emotion, hidden,
all-penetrative; something by which they may be so taken up that the
practical outward changes of their lives in the world, noted with surprise,
scandal, or envy by others, pass almost unnoticed by themselves.
Nadine Gordimer *(1923-)*
South African novelist, activist

The main dangers in this life are the people who
want to change everything… or nothing.
Nancy Astor *(1879-1964)*
American born, British politician

Everything will change. The only question is growing up or decaying.
Nikki Giovanni *(1943-)*
American poet, author

*If you want your life to be more rewarding, you
have to change the way you think.*
Oprah Winfrey *(1954-)*
American media mogul

*Every change is a form of liberation. My mother used to say
a change is always good even if it's for the worse.*
Paula Rego *(1935-)*
Portuguese painter

We must change in order to survive.
Pearl Bailey *(1918-1990)*
American entertainer

All birth is unwilling.
Pearl S. Buck *(1892-1973)*
American writer

*Neither situations nor people can be altered by the interference of an
outsider. If they are to be altered, that alteration must come from within.*
Phyllis Bottome *(1884-1963)*
British novelist

*When people made up their minds that they wanted to
be free and took action, then there was a change.*
Rosa Parks *(1949-)*
American Civil Rights Activist

*Change masters are – literally – the right people
in the right place at the right time.*
Rosabeth Moss Kanter *(1943-)*
American academic, author

*Change can be exhilarating, refreshing – a chance to meet challenges, a
chance to clean house. It means excitement when it is considered normal,
when people expect it routinely, like a daily visit from the mail carrier
– known – bringing a set of new messages – unknown. Change brings
opportunities when people have been planning for it, are ready for it, and
have just the thing in mind to do when the new state comes into being.*
Rosabeth Moss Kanter *(1943-)*
American academic, author

The key to change... is to let go of fear.
Roseanne Cash *(1955-)*
American singer, songwriter

Am I going to change the world, or am I going to change me? Or maybe change the world a little bit, just by changing me?
Sadie Delaney *(1877-1965)*
American educator

Life is like an ever-shifting kaleidoscope – a slight change, and all patterns alter.
Sharon Salzberg *(1952-)*
American author

It's unbelievable the primitive feelings that are aroused by rapid change.
Sheila Ballantyne *(1933-2007)*
American novelist

I am, was, and always will be a catalyst for change.
Shirley Chisholm *(1924-2005)*
American politician

I realized that if what we call human nature can be changed then absolutely anything is possible. And from that moment my life changed.
Shirley MacLaine *(1934-)*
American actress

Someday change will be accepted as life itself.
Shirley MacLaine *(1934-)*
American actress

Change your life today. Don't gamble on the future, act now, without delay.
Simone de Beauvoir *(1908-1986)*
French writer, philosopher

When you change the way you look at things, the things you look at change.
Susan Jenkins *(1958-)*
English actress

The past itself, as historical change continues to accelerate, has become the most surreal of subjects – making it possible to see a new beauty in what is vanishing.
Susan Sontag *(1933-2004)*
American activist, writer

In every crisis there is a message. Crises are nature's way of forcing change – breaking down old structures, shaking loose negative habits so that something new and better can take their place.
Susan Taylor *(1946-)*
American journalist

I wanted change and excitement and to shoot off in all directions myself, like the colored arrows from a Fourth of July rocket.
Sylvia Plath *(1932-1963)*
American writer

Our generation has an incredible amount of realism, yet at the same time it loves to complain and not really change because if it does change then it won't have anything to complain about.
Tori Amos *(1963-)*
American singer, songwriter

The only thing I fear more than change is no change. The business of being static makes me nuts.
Twyla Tharp *(1941-)*
American dancer

You must not change one thing, one pebble, one grain of sand, until you know what good and evil will follow on that act.
Ursula K. LeGuin *(1929-)*
American novelist

Character

It is not in the still calm of life, or the repose of a pacific station, that great characters are formed...the habits of a vigorous mind are formed in contending with difficulties.
Abigail Adams *(1744-1818)*
American First Lady

The best index to a person's character is how they treat people who can't do them any good, and how they treat people who can't fight back.
Abigail Van Buren *(1918-2002)*
American advice columnist

If one sticks too rigidly to one's principles one would hardly see anybody.
Agatha Christie *(1890-1976)*
English detective novelist

People who cannot recognize a palpable absurdity
are very much in the way of civilization.
Agnes Repplier *(1855-1950)*
American essayist

My theory is that everyone, at one time or another, has been at the fringe
of society in some way: an outcast in high school, a stranger in a foreign
country, the best at something, the worst at something, the one who's
different. Being an outsider is the one thing we all have in common.
Alice Hoffman *(1887-1964)*
American writer

Activism is my rent for living on this planet.
Alice Walker *(1944-)*
American writer

The shell is America's most active contribution to the
formation of character. A tough hide. Grow it early.
Anais Nin *(1902-1977)*
French author, diarist

Each person has a literature inside them. But when people lose language,
when they have to experiment with putting their thoughts together
on the spot – that's what I love most. That's where character lives.
Anna Deavere Smith *(1950-)*
American actress, playwright

Parents can only give good advice or put them on the right paths, but
the final forming of a person's character lies in their own hands.
Anne Frank *(1929-1945)*
German writer, holocaust victim

The most exhausting thing in life is being insincere.
Anne Morrow Lindbergh *(1906-2001)*
American aviator, author

It's most important to play to your strengths and not to
conform to someone else's image of leadership. It allows you
to have integrity of style and consistency of character.
Anne Mulcahy *(1952-)*
American, former CEO Xerox

Playing our parts. Yes, we all have to do that and from childhood on, I have found that my own character has been much harder to play worthily and far harder at times to comprehend than any of the roles I have portrayed.
Bette Davis *(1908-1989)*
American actress

Mirrors in a room, water in a landscape, eyes in a face – those are what give character.
Brooke Astor *(1902-2007)*
American philanthropist

Even when it wasn't easy or convenient, both my mother and father were ultimately true to themselves... Their definition of greatness was about greatness of character.
Carly Fiorina *(1954-)*
American, Former HP CEO

Good enough never is.
Debbi Fields *(1956-)*
American entrepreneur

I have long since come to believe that people never mean half of what they say, and that it is best to disregard their talk and judge only their actions.
Dorothy Day *(1897-1980)*
American journalist, activist

People grow through experience if they meet life honestly and courageously. This is how character is built.
Eleanor Roosevelt *(1884 - 1962)*
American First Lady

Happiness must be cultivated. It is like character. It is not a thing to be safely let alone for a moment or it will run to weeds.
Elizabeth Stuart Phelps *(1844-1911)*
American author

The world may take your reputation from you, but it cannot take your character.
Emma Dunham Kelley-Hawkins *(1863-1938)*
American writer

I never like anyone till I've seen them at their worst.
Ethel M. Dell *(1881-1939)*
English writer

Character builds slowly but it can be torn down with incredible swiftness.
Faith Baldwin *(1893-1978)*
American author

Sow and act and you reap a habit; sow a habit and you reap a character; sow a character and you reap destiny.
Frances E. Willard *(1839-1898)*
American educator, suffragist

There can be no happiness if the things we believe in are different from the things we do.
Freya Stark *(1893-1993)*
French-born travel writer, explorer

I don't choose to stay in the state of sadness any more than I would choose to stay in a room with a smoke alarm going off.
Gloria Jones *(1946-)*
African-American singer

Don't be so humble. You're not that great.
Golda Meir *(1898-1978)*
Ukrainian-born Israeli leader

Character isn't inherited. One builds it daily by the way one thinks and acts, thought by thought, action by action.
Helen Gahagan Douglas *(1900-1980)*
American politician, singer

Character cannot be developed in ease and quiet. Only through experience of trial and suffering can the soul be strengthened, ambition inspired, and success achieved.
Helen Keller *(1880-1968)*
American author, educator

Our whole life is an attempt to discover when our spontaneity is whimsical sentimental irresponsibility and when it is a valid expression of our deepest desires and values.
Helen Merrell Lynd *(1896-1982)*
American sociologist, philosopher

The farther behind I leave the past, the closer I am to forging my own character.
Isabelle Eberhardt *(1877-1904)*
Swiss-Algerian explorer and writer

Virtuous people are simply those who have not been tempted sufficiently, because they live in a vegetative state, or because their purposes are so concentrated in one direction that they have not had the leisure to glance around them.
Isadora Duncan *(1878-1927)*
American dancer

Character contributes to beauty. It fortifies a woman as her youth fades. A mode of conduct, a standard of courage, discipline, fortitude and integrity can do a great deal to make a woman beautiful.
Jacqueline Bisset *(1944-)*
English actress

Watch your thoughts, for they become words. Watch your words, for they become actions. Watch your actions, for they become habits. Watch your habits, for they become character. Watch your character, for it becomes your destiny.
Jane Austen *(1775-1817)*
English novelist

Beauty is a radiance that originates from within and comes from inner security and strong character.
Jane Seymour *(1508-1537)*
English, Queen consort

Cultural constraints condition and limit our choices, shaping our characters with their imperatives.
Jeane Kirkpatrick *(1926-2006)*
American ambassador

Character – the willingness to accept responsibility for one's own life – is the source from which self respect springs.
Joan Didion *(1934-)*
American writer

You can be true to the character all you want but you've got to go home with yourself.
Julia Roberts *(1967-)*
American actress

To keep your character intact you cannot stoop to filthy acts. It makes it easier to stoop the next time.
Katharine Hepburn *(1907-2003)*
American actress

You have to be unique, and different, and shine in your own way.
Lady Gaga *(1986-)*
American performance artist

Don't worry so much about your self-esteem. Worry more about your character. Integrity is its own reward.
Laura Schlessinger *(1947-)*
American talk radio host

They were so strong in their beliefs that there came a time when it hardly mattered what exactly those beliefs were; they all fused into a single stubbornness.
Louise Erdrich *(1954-)*
American author

The voice of conscience is so delicate that it is easy to stifle it; but it is also so clear that it is impossible to mistake it.
Madame de Stael *(1766-1817)*
French writer

Because you're not what I would have you be, I blind myself to who, in truth, you are.
Madeleine L'Engle *(1918-)*
American novelist

Success does not implant bad characteristics in people. It merely steps up the growth rate of the bad characteristics they already had.
Margaret Halsey *(1910-1997)*
American writer

Conscience is a treacherous thing, and mine behaves badly whenever there is a serious danger of being found out.
Margaret Lane *(1850-1910)*
American writer

To succeed is nothing – it's an accident. But to feel no doubts about oneself is something very different: it is character.
Marie Leneru *(1875-1918)*
French diarist, playwright

Character is what you know you are, not what others think you have.
Marva Collins *(1936-)*
American educator

To have character is to be big enough to take life on.
Mary Caroline Richards *(1916-1999)*
American poet, potter

*It is a farce to call any being virtuous whose virtues do
not result from the exercise of its own reason.*
Mary Shelley *(1797-1851)*
British novelist

*Sometimes you have to get to know someone really
well to realize you're really strangers.*
Mary Tyler Moore *(1936-)*
American actress

*And Barack and I were raised with so many of the same values, like you
work hard for what you want in life. That your word is your bond; that you
do what you say you're going to do. That you treat people with dignity and
respect, even if you don't know them and even if you don't agree with them.*
Michelle Obama *(1964-)*
American First Lady

It's never too late – in fiction or in life – to revise.
Nancy Thayer *(1923-1971)*
American writer

*I reject the term guru because it is associated with pandering
to the masses, providing inspiration without substance.
There is a little bit of the shaman in a guru.*
Rosabeth Moss Kanter *(1943-)*
American academic, author

*I was raised to sense what someone else wanted me to
be and to be that kind of person. It took me a long time
not to judge myself through someone else's eyes.*
Sally Field *(1946-)*
American actress

It's better to be a lion for a day than a sheep all your life.
Sister Elizabeth Kenny *(1910-1997)*
Australian nurse

*It never pays to deal with the flyweights of the world. They take
far too much pleasure in thwarting you at every turn.*
Sue Grafton *(1940-)*
American author detective novels

Fortune does not change people, it unmasks them.
Suzanne Necker *(1739-1794)*
French patroness

Character, I am sure, lies in the genes.
Taylor Caldwell *(1900-1985)*
American author

*If you do not tell the truth about yourself you
cannot tell it about other people.*
Virginia Woolf *(1882-1941)*
English author

It is easier to influence strong than weak characters in life.
Margot Asquith *(1864-1945)*
Anglo-Scottish socialite

Communication

*It is not what we learn in conversation that enriches us. It is the elation
that comes of swift contact with tingling currents of thought.*
Agnes Repplier *(1855-1950)*
American essayist

*The inventions and the great discoveries have opened up whole continents
to reciprocal communication and interchange, provided we are willing.*
Alva Myrdal *(1902-1986)*
Swedish diplomat

A good message will always find a messenger.
Amelia E. Barr *(1831-1919)*
British novelist

There can be too much communication between people.
Ann Beattie *(1947-)*
American short story writer

*Good communication is as stimulating as black
coffee, and just as hard to sleep after.*
Anne Morrow Lindbergh *(1906-2001)*
American aviator, author

If one talks to more than four people, it is an audience; and one cannot really think or exchange thoughts with an audience.
Anne Morrow Lindbergh *(1906-2001)*
American aviator, author

There must be a reason why photographers are not very good at verbal communication. I think we get lazy.
Annie Leibovitz *(1949-)*
American photographer

If I waited to be right before I spoke, I would be sending little cryptic messages on the Ouija board, complaints from the other side.
Audre Lorde *(1934-1992)*
Caribbean-American writer

Art is the indispensable medium for the communication of a moral idea.
Ayn Rand *(1905-1982)*
Russian-American novelist

I've found that if I say what I'm really thinking and feeling, people are more likely to say what they really think and feel. The conversation becomes a real conversation.
Carol Gilligan *(1936-)*
American ethnicist

Just because people can express themselves through their art doesn't mean they are great communicators in person.
Christie Brinkley *(1954-)*
American model

Communication is a continual balancing act, juggling the conflicting needs for intimacy and independence. To survive in the world, we have to act in concert with others, but to survive as ourselves, rather than simply as cogs in a wheel, we have to act alone.
Deborah Tannen *(1945-)*
American academic, linguist

Talk uses up ideas...Once I have spoken them aloud, they are lost to me, dissipated into the noisy air like smoke. Only if I bury them, like bulbs, in the rich soil of silence do they grow.
Doris Grumbach *(1918-)*
American novelist, biographer

A passage is not plain English – still less is it good English – if
we are obliged to read it twice to find out what it means.
Dorothy L. Sayers *(1893-1957)*
English crime writer

The real art of conversation is not only to say the right thing in the right
place but to leave unsaid the wrong thing at the tempting moment.
Dorothy Nevill *(1826-1913)*
English writer, horticulturist

This wasn't conversation. This was oral death.
Edna Ferber *(1885-1968)*
American novelist

Each of us keeps, battened down inside themself, a sort of lunatic giant
– impossible socially, but full-scale. It's the knockings and batterings we
sometimes hear in each other that keep our intercourse from utter banality.
Elizabeth Bowen *(1899-1973)*
Irish novelist

It seemed rather incongruous that in a society of super sophisticated
communication, we often suffer from a shortage of listeners.
Erma Bombeck *(1927-1996)*
American writer, humorist

No mechanical device can ever take the place of that mysterious
communication between players and the public, that sense of an experience
directly shared which gives to the living theatre its unique appeal.
Eva Le Gallienne *(1899-1991)*
English-American actress, director

Sometimes there is a greater lack of communication
in facile talking than in silence.
Faith Baldwin *(1893-1978)*
American author

It is not the correct thing to invite many people who like to monopolize
conversation; one of this kind will be found amply sufficient.
Florence Howe Hall *(1845-1922)*
American etiquette author

Polite conversation is rarely either.
Fran Lebowitz *(1950-)*
American writer

*I'll paint it big and they will be surprised into taking the time to look at it – I
will make even busy New Yorkers take time to see what I see of flowers.*
Georgia O'Keeffe *(1887-1986)*
American artist

It is always a mistake to be plain-spoken.
Gertrude Stein *(1874-1946)*
American writer

*I cannot expect even my own art to provide all of the answers
– only to hope it keeps asking the right questions.*
Grace Hartigan *(1922-2008)*
American abstract expressionist painter

*Never fail to know that if you are doing all the
talking, you are boring somebody.*
Helen Gurley Brown *(1922-)*
American author, publisher

*I think in many cases the challenge of communicating your ideas in a way
that can get everybody to buy into them and to get managers to give up on
the short term win for the longer term benefit was a big piece of my learning.*
Irene Rosenfeld *(1953-)*
American, CEO Kraft Foods

*As you share the stories of an organization you're able to
bring to life concepts and strategies in a way that's real
and understandable and makes people proud.*
Irene Rosenfeld *(1953-)*
American, CEO Kraft Foods

*We put a premium on communication from day one. Communication is the
job of every senior leader. We celebrate success often because people want
to know they are noticed for making a difference and are appreciated.*
Irene Rosenfeld *(1953-)*
American, CEO Kraft Foods

I cannot speak well enough to be unintelligible.
Jane Austen *(1775-1817)*
English novelist

*One of the large consolations for experiencing anything
unpleasant is the knowledge that one can communicate it.*
Joyce Carol Oates *(1938-)*
American writer

I have seen faces age and sag under the onslaught of amiable extroversion.
Kate O'Brien *(1897-1974)*
Irish playwright

Their civil discussions weren't interesting, and their interesting discussions weren't civil.
Lisa Alther *(1944-)*
American author

A gossip is someone who talks to you about others, a bore is someone who talks to you about himself, and a brilliant conversationalist is one who talks to you about yourself.
Lisa Kirk *(1925-1990)*
American actress

We all need somebody to talk to. It would be good if we talked ... not just pitter-patter but real talk. We shouldn't be so afraid because most people really like this contact; that you show you are vulnerable makes them free to be vulnerable.
Liv Ullmann *(1938-)*
Norwegian actress, director

If you can't add to the discussion, don't subtract by talking.
Lois Wyse *(1926-2007)*
American advertising executive

Say what you will in two words and get through. Long, frilly Palaver is silly.
Madame de Boufflers *(1711-1787)*
French noblewoman

Where no interest is taken in science, literature and liberal pursuits, mere facts and insignificant criticisms necessarily become the themes of discourse; and minds, strangers alike to activity and meditation, become so limited as to render all intercourse with them at once tasteless and oppressive.
Madame de Stael *(1766-1817)*
French writer

The whole art of life is knowing the right time to say things.
Maeve Binchy *(1940-)*
Irish novelist

Most conversations are simply monologues delivered in the presence of a witness.
Margaret Millar *(1915-1994)*
Canadian mystery writer

Too much brilliance has its disadvantages, and misplaced wit may raise a laugh, but often beheads a topic of profound interest.
Margot Asquith *(1864-1945)*
Anglo-Scottish socialite

I explained it when I danced it.
Margot Fonteyn *(1919-1991)*
English ballet dancer

We are suffering from too much sarcasm.
Marianne Moore *(1887-1972)*
American poet, writer

Email, instant messaging, and cell phones give us fabulous communication ability, but because we live and work in our own little worlds, that communication is totally disorganized.
Marilyn vos Savant *(1946-)*
American writer

Sometimes, I tell them more than they wanted to know.
Marjory Stoneman Douglas *(1890-1998)*
American journalist

Everyone knows, that the mind will not be kept from contemplating what it loves in the midst of crowds and business. Hence come those frequent absences, so observable in conversation; for whilst the body is confined to present company, the mind is flown to that which it delights in.
Mary Astell *(1666-1731)*
English writer

There is a world of communication which is not dependent on words. ... The communication is in the work and words are no substitute for this.
Mary Martin *(1913-1990)*
American actress

The more people are reached by mass communications, the less they communicate with each other.
Marya Mannes *(1904-1990)*
American author, critic

To talk easily with people, you must firmly believe that either you or they are interesting. And even then it's not easy.
Mignon McLaughlin *(1913-1983)*
American journalist

A speech does not need to be eternal to be immortal.
Muriel Humphrey Brown *(1912-1998)*
American politician

It is impossible to persuade a person who does not disagree, but smiles.
Muriel Spark *(1906-1992)*
Scottish author

It makes a great difference to a speaker whether they
have something to say, or have to say something.
Nellie McClung *(1873-1951)*
Canadian activist

Self-expression must pass into communication for its fulfillment.
Pearl S. Buck *(1892-1973)*
American writer

Remember the waterfront shack with the sign FRESH FISH
SOLD HERE. Of course it's fresh, we're on the ocean. Of course
it's for sale, we're not giving it away. Of course it's here, otherwise
the sign would be someplace else. The final sign: FISH.
Peggy Noonan *(1950-   )*
American author, columnist

Up here in the hills you hardly ever get down to business right off.
First you say your howdys and then you talk about anything else but
what you come for, and finally, when the mosquitos start to bite, you
say what's on your mind. But you always edge into it, not to offend.
Phyllis Reynolds Naylor *(1933-   )*
American author

There is no such thing as conversation. It is an illusion.
There are intersecting monologues, that is all.
Rebecca West *(1892-1983)*
Irish-born, British writer

I know that after all is said and done, more is said than done.
Rita Mae Brown *(1944-   )*
American novelist

Leaders must pick causes they won't abandon easily, remain
committed despite setbacks, and communicate their big
ideas over and over again in every encounter.
Rosabeth Moss Kanter *(1943-   )*
American academic, author

The best impromptu speeches are the ones written well in advance.
Ruth Gordon *(1896-1985)*
American actress, writer

I see dance being used as communication between body and soul, to express what is too deep to find for words.
Ruth St. Denis *(1878-1968)*
American dancer

The key to any good relationship, on-screen and off, is communication, respect, and I guess you have to like the way the other person smells – and he smelled real nice.
Sandra Bullock *(1964-   )*
American actress

If you have anything to tell me of importance for God's sake begin at the end.
Sara Jeannette Duncan *(1861-1922)*
Canadian journalist

They talked with more claret than clarity.
Susan Ertz *(1894-1985)*
British writer

To feel as well as hear what someone says requires whole attention.
Sylvia Ashton-Warner *(1908-1984)*
New Zealand writer, poet

God, the illogic! The impossibility of communication in this house. The sheer operation alone of getting something through to somebody.
Sylvia Ashton-Warner *(1908-1984)*
New Zealand writer, poet

Once a human being has arrived on this earth, communication is the largest single factor determining what kinds of relationships they make with others and what happens to them in the world about them.
Virginia Satir *(1916-1988)*
American author, psychotherapist

It is not hard to converse for a short space of time on a subject about which one knows little, and it is indeed often amusing to see how cunningly one can steer the conversational barque, hoisting and lowering her sails, tacking this way and that to avoid reefs, and finally racing feverishly for home with the outboard engine making a loud and cheerful noise.
Virginia Graham *(1912-1998)*
American talk show host

*If one cannot state a matter clearly enough so that even an
intelligent twelve-year-old can understand it, one should remain
within the cloistered walls of the university and laboratory
until one gets a better grasp of one's subject matter.*
Margaret Mead *(1901-1978)*
American cultural anthropologist

Compassion

*No kind action ever stops with itself. One kind action leads to another.
Good example is followed. A single act of kindness throws out roots in all
directions, and the roots spring up and make new trees. The greatest work
that kindness does to others is that it makes them kind themselves.*
Amelia Earhart *(1898-1937)*
American aviator

*But my experience is that people who have been through
painful, difficult times are filled with compassion.*
Amy Grant *(1960-)*
American singer, songwriter

Make no judgments where you have no compassion.
Anne McCaffrey *(1926-)*
American author

*It's that wonderful old-fashioned idea that others come first and you
come second. This was the whole ethic by which I was brought up.
Others matter more than you do, so 'don't fuss, dear; get on with it.'*
Audrey Hepburn *(1929-1993)*
Belgian-born actress

*I took it to heart that in order to be a good person, you
never said anything mean about anybody.*
Carly Simon *(1945-)*
American singer, songwriter

*So once I shut down my privilege of disliking anyone I
choose and holding myself aloof if I could manage it, greater
understanding, growing compassion came to me.*
Catharine Marshall *(1914-1983)*
American author

It's compassion that makes gods of us.
Dorothy Gilman *(1923-)*
American mystery writer

*I feel beautiful when I'm at peace with myself. When I'm serene,
when I'm a good person, when I've been considerate of others.*
Elle Macpherson *(1964-)*
Australian model

*Guard within yourself that treasure kindness. Know how to give without
hesitation, how to lose without regret, how to acquire without meanness.*
George Sand *(1804-)*
French novelist, memoirist

*In its sentimental mode, compassion is an exercise in moral
indignation, in feeling good rather than doing good...In its
unsentimental mode, compassion seeks above all to do good.*
Gertrude Himmelfarb *(1922-)*
American historian

*Forgiveness is the economy of the heart... forgiveness saves the
expense of anger, the cost of hatred, the waste of spirits.*
Hannah More *(1745-1833)*
English writer, philanthropist

*I guess we'd be living in a boring, perfect world if
everybody wished everybody else well.*
Jennifer Aniston *(1969-)*
American actress

Compassion is not a popular virtue.
Karen Armstrong *(1944-)*
English writer

As we grow in wisdom, we pardon more freely.
Madame de Stael *(1766-1817)*
French writer

Nobody who is somebody looks down on anybody.
Margaret Deland *(1857-1945)*
American short story writer

It helps I think to consider ourselves on a very long journey:
the main thing is to keep to the faith, to endure, to help each
other when we stumble or tire, to weep and press on.
Mary Caroline Richards *(1916-1999)*
American poet, potter

Some people are filled by compassion and a desire to do good, and
some simply don't think anything's going to make a difference.
Meryl Streep *(1949-)*
American actress

For me music is a vehicle to bring our pain to the surface,
getting it back to that humble and tender spot where, with
luck, it can lose its anger and become compassion again.
Paula Cole *(1968-)*
American musician

Compassionate action starts with seeing yourself when you start to make
yourself right and when you start to make yourself wrong. At that point
you could just contemplate the fact that there is a larger alternative to
either of those, a more tender, shaky kind of place where you could live.
Pema Chodron *(1936-)*
Tibetan Buddhist teacher

Everyone needs to be valued. Everyone has the
potential to give something back.
Princess Diana *(1961-1997)*
British princess

If you only try to please others, you're going to resent those
people you're trying to please; the ones who are often closest to
you. If you choose a path that you yourself want to take, then
you're going to be much kinder to the people in your life.
Sarah McLachlan *(1968-)*
Canadian singer, songwriter

Any ordinary favor we do for someone or any compassionate reaching
out may seem to be going nowhere at first, but may be planting a
seed we can't see right now. Sometimes we need to just do the best
we can and then trust in an unfolding we can't design or ordain.
Sharon Salzberg *(1952-)*
American author

*I think it's really important that the people who are going
to make decisions for other people have fair, truthful and
compassionate regard for all people, not just some people.*
Sharon Stone *(1958-)*
American actress

*One's life has value so long as one attributes value to the life of
others, by means of love, friendship, indignation and compassion*
Simone de Beauvoir *(1908-1986)*
French writer, philosopher

*Difficult as it is really to listen to someone in affliction, it is just as
difficult for them to know that compassion is listening to them.*
Simone Weil *(1909-1943)*
French philosopher

*It is above all by the imagination that we achieve
perception and compassion and hope.*
Ursula K. LeGuin *(1929-)*
American novelist

*When I listen to these women, it makes what I thought
were my hard knocks feel like little nudges.*
Whoopi Goldberg *(1955-)*
American actress, comedian

Competition

I am out to beat everybody in sight, and that is just what I'm going to do.
Babe Didrikson Zaharias *(1911-1956)*
American golfer

*If you're able to be yourself, then you have no competition. All
you have to do is get closer and closer to that essence.*
Barbara Cook *(1927-)*
American singer, actress

If you're going to play the game properly you'd better know every rule.
Barbara Jordan *(1936-1996)*
American politician

A champion is someone who does not settle for that day's practice, that day's competition, that day's performance. They are always striving to be better. They don't live in the past.
Briana Scurry *(1971-)*
American soccer player

When they play against us, they bring it. How you've done previously doesn't matter when we play each other.
Briana Scurry *(1971-)*
American soccer player

Competition, you know, is a lot like chastity. It is widely praised, but alas, too little practiced.
Carol Tucker *(1925-)*
American agricultural official

If you're a champion, you have to have it in your heart.
Chris Evert *(1954-)*
American tennis player

Never compete. Never. Watching the other person is what kills all forms of energy.
Diana Vreeland *(1903-1989)*
French journalist

Competition is easier to accept if you realize it is not an act of oppression or abrasion. ... I've worked with my best friends in direct competition.
Diane Sawyer *(1945-)*
American broadcast journalist

I don't have to be enemies with someone to be in competition with them.
Jackie Joyner-Kersee *(1962-)*
American Olympic athlete

The great disadvantage of being in a rat race is that it is humiliating. The competitors in a rat race are, by definition, rodents.
Margaret Halsey *(1910-1997)*
American writer

Whoever said, It's not whether you win or lose that counts, probably lost.
Martina Navratilova *(1956-)*
Czech American tennis player

*When the going got tough, I really had to draw on many of the
same competitive instincts I did when I was skating. I really
had to put my head down and stay positive. I had to fight.*
Peggy Fleming *(1948-)*
American Olympic skater

*I'm a competitor. I really enjoyed the race more
than just going out and running to run.*
Shannon Miller *(1977-)*
American gymnast

*When I go in to compete, whether it's gymnastics or anything
else, I do my own thing. I compete with myself.*
Shannon Miller *(1977-)*
American gymnast

*I'm generally competing with the ideal I have set for
myself, and I've found that served me very well.*
Victoria Principal *(1946-)*
American actress

*I loved the feeling of freedom in running, the fresh air, the
feeling that the only person I'm competing with is me.*
Wilma Rudolph *(1940-1994)*
American Olympic runner

Composure

*It is to me a most affecting thing to hear myself prayed for, in particular
as I do every day in the week, and disposes me to bear with more
composure, some disagreeable circumstances that attend my situation.*
Abigail Adams *(1744-1818)*
American First Lady

*Dogs are wise. They crawl away into a quiet corner and lick their
wounds and do not rejoin the world until they are whole once more.*
Agatha Christie *(1890-1976)*
English detective novelist

Nothing is a matter of life and death except life and death.
Angela Carter *(1940-1992)*
English novelist, journalist

I have to have a little bit of time to myself right before whatever it is that I have to do because most of the time I'm sitting in my head convincing myself to calm down, all right, slow down.
Christina Milian *(1981-)*
American musician

I'm going to try to be good but I can't help it. I have to be me.
Clare Short *(1946-)*
British Labour politician

Since everything is in our heads, we better not lose them.
Coco Chanel *(1883-1971)*
French fashion designer

But when I lose my temper, I find it difficult to forgive myself. I feel I've failed. I can be calm in a crisis, in the face of death or things that hurt badly. I don't get hysterical, which may be masochistic of me.
Emma Thompson *(1959-)*
British actress

Anger is a signal, and one worth listening to.
Harriet Lerner *(1944-)*
American psychologist

This morning I threw up at a board meeting. I was sure the cat was out of the bag, but no one seemed to think anything about it; apparently it's quite common for people to throw up at board meetings.
Jane Wagner *(1935-)*
American writer, director

If you can keep your head when all about are losing theirs, it's just possible you haven't grasped the situation.
Jean Kerr *(1923-2003)*
American author

Screaming at people may not be the most efficient way. I'm going to stay back a little from now on. I'm learning how to listen to people instead of preaching at them so much.
Joan Baez *(1941-)*
American folksinger, songwriter

People in a temper often say a lot of silly, terrible things they mean.
Katherine Whitehorn *(1914-1956)*
British columnist

I am angry nearly every day of my life, but I have learned
not to show it; and I still try to hope not to feel it, though
it may take me another forty years to do it.
Louisa May Alcott *(1832-1888)*
American author

Nothing contributes so much to tranquilize the mind as a steady
purpose – a point on which the soul may fix its intellectual eye.
Mary Shelley *(1797-1851)*
British novelist

I am a danger to myself if I get angry.
Oriana Fallaci *(1929-2006)*
Italian journalist, writer

A further sign of health is that we don't become undone by fear
and trembling, but we take it as a message that it's time to stop
struggling and look directly at what's threatening us.
Pema Chodron *(1936-)*
Tibetan Buddhist teacher

Compromise

I've a theory that one can get anything one wants if one will pay the price.
And do you know what the price is, nine times out of ten? Compromise.
Agatha Christie *(1890-1976)*
English detective novelist

I am a journalist in the field of etiquette. I try to find out what
the most genteel people regularly do, what traditions they
have discarded, what compromises they have made.
Amy Vanderbilt *(1908-1974)*
American author, journalist

If you look at life one way, there is always cause for alarm.
Elizabeth Bowen *(1899-1973)*
Irish novelist

To be or not to be is not a question of compromise.
Either you be or you don't be.
Golda Meir *(1898-1978)*
Ukrainian-born Israeli leader

Compromise and tolerance are magic words. It took
me 40 years to become philosophical.
Hedy Lamarr *(1914-2000)*
Austrian actress

Lasting change is a series of compromises. And compromise
is all right, as long your values don't change.
Jane Goodall *(1934-)*
English, chimpanzee researcher

Learn the wisdom of compromise, for it is better
to bend a little than to break.
Jane Wells *(1961-)*
American news reporter

Don't compromise yourself. You are all you've got.
Janis Joplin *(1943-1970)*
American singer

I saw people willing to compromise themselves, or change themselves, to
acquire what they thought was important. I don't judge what other people
do, many choices that may be right for others are definitely not right for me.
Kathy Ireland *(1963-)*
American entrepreneur

I never liked the middle ground—the most boring place in the world.
Louise Nevelson *(1899-1988)*
American sculptor, painter

What we call reality is an agreement that people
have arrived at to make life more livable.
Louise Nevelson *(1899-1988)*
American sculptor, painter

If you just set out to be liked, you would be prepared to compromise
on anything at any time, and you would achieve nothing.
Margaret Thatcher *(1925-)*
English Prime Minister

Whilst our Hearts are violently set upon any thing, there is
no convincing us that we shall ever be of another Mind.
Mary Astell *(1666-1731)*
English writer

I think people have to choose between living with contradictions or painting themselves into a corner. I have a lot of contradictions.
Michelle Shocked *(1962-)*
American musician

Compromise, if not the spice of life, is its solidity. It is what makes nations great and marriages happy.
Phyllis Mcginley *(1905-1978)*
American writer

They say it is better to be poor and happy than rich and miserable, but how about a compromise like moderately rich and just moody?
Princess Diana *(1961-1997)*
British princess

It is a measure of the framers' fear that a passing majority might find it expedient to compromise 4th Amendment values that these values were embodied in the Constitution itself.
Sandra Day O'Connor *(1930-)*
American Supreme Court Justice

Confidence

Class is an aura of confidence that is being sure without being cocky. Class has nothing to do with money. Class never runs scared. It is self-discipline and self-knowledge. It's the sure footedness that comes with having proved you can meet life.
Ann Landers *(1918-2002)*
American advice columnist

I was always looking outside myself for strength and confidence but it comes from within. It is there all the time.
Anna Freud *(1895-1982)*
Austrian psychoanalyst

Confidence is a plant of slow growth.
Anna Leonowens *(1831-1915)*
English travel writer

The more we refuse to buy into our inner critics – and our external ones too – the easier it will get to have confidence in our choices, and to feel comfortable with who we are.
Arianna Huffington *(1950-)*
American journalist

I was thought to be stuck up. I wasn't. I was just sure of myself. This is and always has been an unforgivable quality to the unsure.
Bette Davis *(1908-1989)*
American actress

You've got to take the initiative and play your game. In a decisive set, confidence is the difference.
Chris Evert *(1954-)*
American tennis player

Regardless of how you feel inside, always try to look like a winner. Even if you are behind, a sustained look of control and confidence can give you a mental edge that results in victory.
Diane Arbus *(1923-1971)*
American photographer

You gain strength, courage and confidence by every experience in which you really stop to look fear in the face. You are able to say to yourself, 'I have lived through this horror. I can take the next thing that comes along.' You must do the thing you think you cannot do.
Eleanor Roosevelt *(1884 - 1962)*
American First Lady

The usual channels of university studies or secretarial work did not appeal to me. I cherished difficult dreams through confidence in myself.
Ella Maillart *(1903-1997)*
Swiss writer

If one burdens the future with one's worries, it cannot grow organically. I am filled with confidence, not that I shall succeed in worldly things, but that even when things go badly for me I shall still find life good and worth living.
Esther Etty Hillesum *(1914-1943)*
Netherlands, Jewish prisoner at Auschwitz

Analysis gave me great freedom of emotions and fantastic confidence. I felt I had served my time as a puppet.
Hedy Lamarr *(1914-2000)*
Austrian actress

Optimism is the faith that leads to achievement. Nothing can be done without hope and confidence.
Helen Keller *(1880-1968)*
American author, educator

Play, then as now, is certainly about physical activity. But it's also about encouraging teamwork and stimulating creativity and confidence. Through collaborative play, I developed strength and coordination, interpersonal skills, a stronger self identity and an appreciation for tolerance and cultural diversity. Frankly, the lessons I learned from those early days on the playground have been essential to my success, as a student, as a young business person and today, as the chairman and CEO of a global corporation.
Irene Rosenfeld *(1953-)*
American, CEO Kraft Foods

[A difficult childhood gave me] a kind of cocky confidence. ... I could never have so little that I hadn't had less. It took away my fear.
Jacqueline Cochran *(1910-1980)*
American aviator

Confidence and superiority: It's the usual fundamentalist stuff: I've got the truth, and you haven't.
Jeanette Winterson *(1959-)*
British novelist

Upon reflection, I decided I had three main weaknesses: I was confused (evidenced by a lack of facts, an inability to coordinate my thoughts, and an inability to verbalize my ideas); I had a lack of confidence, which caused me to back down from forcefully stated positions; and I was overly emotional at the expense of careful, 'scientific' thought. I was thirty-seven years old and still discovering who I was.
Julia Child *(1912-2004)*
American cookbook author

The big gap between the ability of actors is confidence.
Kathleen Turner *(1954-)*
American actress

It is best to act with confidence, no matter how little right you have to it.
Lillian Hellman *(1905-1984)*
American playwright

I couldn't bear it if anyone knew I had hardly any self-confidence at all.
Loretta Young *(1913-2000)*
American actress

The self-confidence one builds from achieving difficult things and accomplishing goals is the most beautiful thing of all.
Madonna Ciccone *(1958-)*
American recording artist

*Life is not easy for any of us. But what of that? We must have
perseverance and above all confidence in ourselves. We must believe that
we are gifted for something and that this thing must be attained.*
Marie Curie *(1897-1966)*
Polish-French physicist

*Honesty is the cornerstone of all success, without which
confidence and ability to perform shall cease to exist.*
Mary Kay Ash *(1918-2001)*
American entrepreneur

*It is confidence in our bodies, minds and spirits that allows us
to keep looking for new adventures, new directions to grow in,
and new lessons to learn – which is what life is all about.*
Oprah Winfrey *(1954-)*
American media mogul

All anything takes, really, is confidence.
Rachel Ward *(1957-)*
British actress

Confidence is everything in this business.
Reese Witherspoon *(1976-)*
American actress

Humor comes from self-confidence. There's an aggressive element to wit.
Rita Mae Brown *(1944-)*
American novelist

*My parents...always told me I could do anything
but never told me how long it would take.*
Rita Rudner *(1953-)*
American comedian

*Hollywood is a suction for your confidence or your faith or your
togetherness. Just walking on the street you can feel it.*
Robin Wright Penn *(1966-)*
American actress

*Leaders deliver confidence, that's what they do. They make decisions,
they set strategy, they do all the technical stuff, but they also have
to make people feel confident that their efforts will pay off.*
Rosabeth Moss Kanter *(1943-)*
American academic, writer

You have to have confidence in your ability, and
then be tough enough to follow through.
Rosalynn Carter *(1927-)*
American First Lady

I was a pretty insecure kid, didn't have a lot of friends, and
was picked on a lot, and music gave me confidence.
Sarah McLachlan *(1968-)*
Canadian singer, songwriter

When I was as you are now, towering in the confidence of twenty-one,
little did I suspect that I should be at forty-nine, what I now am.
Sarah Orne Jewett *(1849-1909)*
American novelist

Self-confidence is the most important thing, and this comes from identifying
your goals, knowing your limits and roping in all the help you can get.
Shirley Conran *(1932-)*
American writer

Confidence is key. Sometimes, you need to look like
you're confident even when you're not.
Vanessa Hudgens *(1988-)*
American actress

Conflict

People who fight fire with fire usually end up with ashes.
Abigail Van Buren *(1918-2002)*
American advice columnist

Strength alone knows conflict, weakness is born vanquished.
Anne Sophie Swetchine *(1752-1857)*
Russian mystic

The moral absolute should be: if and when, in any dispute, one
side initiates the use of physical force, that side is wrong – and no
consideration or discussion of the issues is necessary or appropriate.
Ayn Rand *(1905-1982)*
Russian-American novelist

*One person who wants something is a hundred times
stronger than a hundred who want to be left alone.*
Barbara Ward *(1914-1981)*
British economist, writer

Sometimes it's worse to win a fight than to lose.
Billie Holiday *(1915-1959)*
American jazz singer

*My dad always used to tell me that if they challenge you to an after-
school fight, tell them you won't wait – you can kick their ass right now.*
Cameron Diaz *(1972-)*
American actress

*Even when you think people are wrong, it is easy to tell when they are right.
When they are right about something you are trying very hard to hide from
others and yourself, you know they are right because you want to kill them.*
Candace Bergen *(1946-)*
American actress

*Well, if you pick a fight with somebody that's smaller than
you and you beat them, where's the honor in that?*
Carol Moseley Braun *(1947-)*
American politician, author

*Unlike lions and dogs, we are a dissenting animal. We need to
dissent in the same way that we need to travel, to make money,
to keep a record of our time on earth and in dream, and to leave
a permanent mark. Dissension is a drive, like those drives.*
Carol Bly *(1930-2007)*
American author

Resentment is like drinking poison and waiting for the other person to die.
Carrie Fisher *(1956-)*
American actress

*I do not like strife, because I have always found that
in the end each remains of the same opinion.*
Catherine the Great *(1729-1796)*
Russian royalty

*This conflict is one thing I've been waiting for. I'm well and strong and young
– young enough to go to the front. If I can't be a soldier, I'll help soldiers.*
Clara Barton *(1821-1912)*
American nurse

I don't have a warm personal enemy left. They've all died off.
I miss them terribly because they helped define me.
Clare Boothe Luce *(1903-1987)*
American playwright, diplomat

Openly questioning the way the world works and challenging the
power of the powerful is not an activity customarily rewarded.
Dale Spender *(1943-)*
Australian writer

Creativity comes from a conflict of ideas.
Donatella Versace *(1955-)*
Italian designer

Peace is not the absence of conflict but the presence of creative
alternatives for responding to conflict – alternatives to passive
or aggressive responses, alternatives to violence.
Dorothy Thompson *(1893-1961)*
American journalist

Great art is the expression of a solution of the conflict between
the demands of the world without and that within.
Edith Hamilton *(1867-1963)*
American educator

I have spent many years of my life in opposition, and I rather like the role.
Eleanor Roosevelt *(1884 - 1962)*
American First Lady

To make laws that people cannot and will not obey
serves to bring all law into contempt.
Elizabeth Cady Stanton *(1815-1902)*
American reformist, writer

Even if I do not see the fruits, the struggle has been worthwhile.
If my life has taught me anything, it is that one must fight.
Ella Winter *(1898-1980)*
Australian-British journalist

I see those picketers, and I think you know, if I weren't a loving,
non-violent, spiritual person, I would really go over there and
grab those signs and smash them over their heads and shove
them up their asses. But...I'm a loving, spiritual person.
Ellen DeGeneres *(1958-)*
American comedian, television host

I make enemies deliberately. They are the sauce piquante to my dish of life.
Elsa Maxwell *(1883-1963)*
American gossip columnist

No real social change has ever been brought about without a revolution... revolution is but thought carried into action.
Emma Goldman *(1869-1940)*
Russian-born, American activist

The world is wide, and I will not waste my life in friction when it could be turned into momentum.
Frances E. Willard *(1839-1898)*
American educator, suffragist

Any coward can fight a battle when they're sure of winning, but give me the people who have pluck to fight when they're sure of losing. That's my way, sir; and there are many victories worse than a defeat.
George Eliot *(1819-1880)*
English novelist

Argument is to me the air I breathe. Given any proposition, I cannot help believing the other side and defending it.
Gertrude Stein *(1874-1946)*
American writer

When I hear that somebody's difficult, I think, Oh, I can't wait to work with them.
Glenn Close *(1947-)*
American actress

I had to kick their law into their teeth in order to save them.
Gwendolyn Brooks *(1917-2000)*
American poet

The most radical revolutionary will become a conservative the day after the revolution.
Hannah Arendt *(1906-1975)*
German philosopher

There's no use throwing down the gauntlet in front of me and daring me to pick it up. Pick it up yourself, I'd say.
Helen Lawrenson *(1908-1982)*
American writer

People tend to forget their duties but remember their rights.
Indira Gandhi *(1917-1984)*
Indian Prime Minister

The Department of Justice is committed to asking one central question of everything we do: What is the right thing to do? Now that can produce debate and I want it to be spirited debate. I want the lawyers of America to be able to call me and tell me: Janet have you lost your mind?
Janet Reno *(1938-)*
American Attorney General

We have war when at least one of the parties to a conflict wants something more than it wants peace.
Jeane Kirkpatrick *(1926-2006)*
American ambassador

I like to look at how people work together when they are put into stressful situations, when life stops being cozy.
Jeanette Winterson *(1959-)*
British novelist

You can no more win a war than you can win an earthquake.
Jeannette Rankin *(1880-1973)*
American, first Congresswoman

For good and evil, men and women are free creative spirits. This produces the very queer world we live in...A world in everlasting conflict between the new idea and the old allegiances, new arts and new inventions against the old establishment.
Joyce Cary *(1888-1957)*
Anglo-Irish novelist

Fortunately [psychoanalysis] is not the only way to resolve inner conflicts. Life itself still remains a very effective therapist.
Karen Horney *(1885-1952)*
American psychologist

In any free society, the conflict between social conformity and individual liberty is permanent, unresolvable, and necessary.
Kathleen Norris *(1880-1966)*
American poet, novelist

Well, that's your opinion, isn't it? And I'm not about
to waste my time trying to change it.
Lady Gaga *(1986-)*
American performance artist

I got what I have now through knowing the right time
to tell terrible people when to go to hell.
Leslie Caron *(1931-)*
French actress

The older one gets in this profession, the more people
there are with whom one would never work again.
Liv Ullmann *(1938-)*
Norwegian actress, director

Aggression only moves in one direction – it creates more aggression.
Margaret J. Wheatley *(1934-)*
American organization expert

Our first and most pressing problem is how to do away with warfare
as a method of solving conflicts between national groups within a
society who have different views about how the society is to run.
Margaret Mead *(1901-1978)*
American cultural anthropologist

Fighting is like champagne. It goes to the heads of
cowards as quickly as of heroes. Any fool can be brave on
a battlefield when it's be brave or else be killed.
Margaret Mitchell *(1900-1949)*
American novelist

I am in politics because of the conflict between good and
evil, and I believe that in the end good will triumph.
Margaret Thatcher *(1925-)*
English Prime Minister

As long as you keep a person down, some part of you has to be down there to
hold the person down, so it means you cannot soar as you otherwise might.
Marian Anderson *(1897-1993)*
American singer

It is human nature to stand in the middle of a thing.
Marianne Moore *(1887-1972)*
American poet, writer

I believed that all one did about a war was go to it, as a gesture of solidarity, and get killed, or survive if lucky until the war was over...I had no idea you could be what I became, an unscathed tourist of wars.
Martha Gellhorn *(1908-1998)*
American journalist

I can ruin my reputation in five minutes; I don't need help.
Martha Graham *(1894-1991)*
American dancer, choreographer

There can be no reconciliation where there is no open warfare. There must be a battle, a brave, boisterous battle, with pennants waving and cannon roaring, before there can be peaceful treaties and enthusiastic shaking of hands.
Mary Elizabeth Braddon *(1835-1915)*
British novelist

[when asked, at age 90, who had issued the permit to speak on the streets] Patrick Henry, Thomas Jefferson, and John Adams.
Mother Jones *(1830-1930)*
American activist

Disturbers are never popular – nobody ever really loved an alarm clock in action, no matter how grateful they may have been afterwards for its kind services.
Nellie McClung *(1873-1951)*
Canadian activist

We habitually erect a barrier called blame that keeps us from communicating genuinely with others, and we fortify it with our concepts of who's right and who's wrong. We do that with the people who are closest to us and we do it with political systems, with all kinds of things that we don't like about our associates or our society. It is a very common, ancient, well-perfected device for trying to feel better. Blame others. Blaming is a way to protect your heart, trying to protect what is soft and open and tender in yourself. Rather than own that pain, we scramble to find some comfortable ground.
Pema Chodron *(1936-)*
Tibetan Buddhist teacher

Any time three New Yorkers get into a cab without an argument, a bank has just been robbed.
Phyllis Diller *(1917-)*
American comedian

We might as well give up the fiction that we can argue any view.
For what in me is pure conviction is simple prejudice in you.
Phyllis Mcginley *(1905-1978)*
American writer

Any authentic work of art must start an argument
between the artist and their audience.
Rebecca West *(1892-1983)*
Irish-born, British writer

I believe in a lively disrespect for most forms of authority.
Rita Mae Brown *(1944-)*
American novelist

To argue over who is the more noble is nothing more than to dispute
whether dirt is better for making bricks or for making mortar.
Teresa of Avila *(1515-1582)*
Spanish Roman Catholic nun, saint

Mental fight means thinking against the current, not with it. It is
our business to puncture gas bags and discover the seeds of truth.
Virginia Woolf *(1882-1941)*
English author

I don't have pet peeves, I have whole kennels of irritation.
Whoopi Goldberg *(1955-)*
American actress, comedian

I tell you there is no such thing as creative hate!
Willa Cather *(1873-1947)*
American writer

It's our tendency to approach every problem as if it were a fight
between two sides. We see it in headlines that are always using
metaphors for war. It's a general atmosphere of animosity and
contention that has taken over our public discourse.
Deborah Tannen *(1945-)*
American academic, linguist

Courage

I'm not brave. When a thing is certain, there's nothing to be brave about. All you can do is find your consolation.
Agatha Christie *(1890-1976)*
English detective novelist

Courage is the price that life exacts for granting peace. The soul that knows it not, knows no release from little things.
Amelia Earhart *(1897-1937)*
American aviator

Life shrinks or expands in proportion to one's courage.
Anais Nin *(1902-1977)*
French author, diarist

Courage is saying, Maybe what I'm doing isn't working, maybe I should try something else.
Anna Lappe *(1973-)*
American author

The executioner is, I hear, very expert, and my neck is very slender.
Anne Boleyn *(1501-1536)*
English, Queen of England

Where there's hope, there's life. It fills us with fresh courage and makes us strong again. We'll need to be brave to endure the many fears and hardships and the suffering yet to come.
Anne Frank *(1929-1945)*
German writer, holocaust victim

Don't wish me happiness – I don't expect to be happy, it's gotten beyond that, somehow. Wish me courage and strength and a sense of humor – I will need them all.
Anne Morrow Lindbergh *(1906-2001)*
American aviator, author

It isn't for the moment you are stuck that you need courage, but for the long uphill climb back to sanity and faith and security.
Anne Morrow Lindbergh *(1906-2001)*
American aviator, author

You don't get a chance to live through a lot of crises. You've got to do it,
you've got to do it once, [and] you've got to have light at the end of the tunnel
or else you will lose people, you will lose talent, you will lose customers.
Anne Mulcahy *(1952-)*
American, former CEO Xerox

You can't test courage cautiously.
Annie Dillard *(1945-)*
American author

But you have to do what you dream of doing even while you're afraid.
Arianna Huffington *(1950-)*
American journalist

I became more courageous by doing the very things I needed to be
courageous for – first, a little, and badly. Then, bit by bit, more and better.
Audre Lorde *(1934-1992)*
Caribbean-American writer

Why do they always teach us that it's easy and evil to do what we
want and that we need discipline to restrain ourselves? It's the
hardest thing in the world – to do what we want. And it takes
the greatest kind of courage. I mean, what we really want.
Ayn Rand *(1905-1982)*
Russian-American novelist

In politics, guts is all.
Barbara Castle *(1910-2002)*
British politician

They call me Battling Bella, Mother Courage, and a Jewish mother with
more complaints than Portnoy...But whatever I am – and this ought
to be made very clear at the outset – I am a very serious woman.
Bella Abzug *(1920-1998)*
American politician

Anything I've ever done that ultimately was
worthwhile ... initially scared me to death.
Bette Midler *(1945-)*
American actress

In true courage there is always an element of choice, of an ethical choice, and of anguish, and also of action and deed. There is always a flame of spirit in it, a vision of some necessity higher than oneself.
Brenda Ueland *(1891-1985)*
American journalist

I can pretty much take care of myself; I don't walk around with much fear.
Carla Gugino *(1971-)*
American actress

I beg you take courage; the brave soul can mend even disaster.
Catherine the Great *(1729-1796)*
Russian royalty

In spite of your fear, do what you have to do.
Chin-Ning Chu *(1947-2009)*
Chinese business author

I may be compelled to face danger, but never fear it.
Clara Barton *(1821-1912)*
American nurse

Courage is the ladder on which all other virtues mount.
Clare Boothe Luce *(1903-1987)*
American playwright, diplomat

I would rather die a meaningful death than to live a meaningless life.
Corazon Aquino *(1933-2009)*
Philippine president

The bravest thing you can do when you are not brave is to profess courage and act accordingly.
Corra Harris *(1941-)*
American writer

Courage is as often the outcome of despair as hope; in the one case we have nothing to lose, in the other all to gain.
Diane de Poitiers *(1499-1566)*
French noblewoman

Think wrongly if you please but in all cases think for yourself.
Doris Lessing *(1919-)*
Persian-born British writer

Courage is fear that has said its prayers.
Dorothy Bernard *(1890-1955)*
American silent film actress

Courage, it would seem, is nothing less than the power to overcome danger, misfortune, fear, injustice, while continuing to affirm inwardly that life with all its sorrows is good; that everything is meaningful even if in a sense beyond our understanding; and that there is always tomorrow.
Dorothy Thompson *(1893-1961)*
American journalist

When you have decided what you believe, what you feel must be done, have the courage to stand alone and be counted.
Eleanor Roosevelt *(1884 - 1962)*
American First Lady

The moment we begin to fear the opinions of others and hesitate to tell the truth that is in us, and from motives of policy are silent when we should speak, the divine floods of light and life no longer flow into our souls.
Elizabeth Cady Stanton *(1815-1902)*
American reformist, writer

To know how to say what other people only think, is what makes people poets and sages; and to dare to say what others only dare to think, makes people martyrs or reformers.
Elizabeth Rundle Charles *(1828-1896)*
English writer

I've been through it all, baby, I'm mother courage.
Elizabeth Taylor *(1932-2011)*
British-born actress

To sin by silence when we should protest makes cowards out of people.
Ella Wheeler Wilcox *(1850-1919)*
American poet

As for keeping the attack dogs from nibbling away your courage? My theory, after decades in this business, is that you only give a few people the right to make you feel rotten. You have a handful of chits to give out, penuriously, to those you trust and respect. You don't give them to just anyone with an e-mail address and an epithet.
Ellen Goodman *(1950-)*
American journalist

Yes, as my swift days near their goal, 'tis all that I implore: In life and death a chainless soul, with courage to endure.
Emily Brontë *(1818-1848)*
English author

Always do the things you fear the most. Courage is an acquired taste, like caviar.
Erica Jong *(1942-)*
American writer

It takes courage to lead a life. Any life.
Erica Jong *(1942-)*
American writer

Great dreams... never even get out of the box. It takes an uncommon amount of guts to put your dreams on the line, to hold them up and say, How good or how bad am I? That's where courage comes in.
Erma Bombeck *(1927-1966)*
American writer, humorist

I can never remember being afraid of an audience. If the audience could do better, they'd be up here on stage and I'd be out there watching them.
Ethel Merman *(1908-1984)*
American singer

A person of courage never needs weapons, but they may need bail.
Ethel Watts Mumford *(1876-1940)*
American author

All serious daring starts from within.
Eudora Welty *(1909-2001)*
American writer

When they asked for those to raise their hands who'd go down to the courthouse the next day, I raised mine. Had it high up as I could get it. I guess if I'd had any sense I'd've been a little scared, but what was the point of being scared? The only thing they could do to me was kill me and it seemed like they'd been trying to do that a little bit at a time ever since I could remember.
Fannie Lou Hamer *(1917-1977)*
American activist

How cool, how quiet is true courage.
Fanny Burney *(1752-1840)*
English novelist, diarist

How very little can be done under the spirit of fear.
Florence Nightingale *(1820-1910)*
English nurse, writer

If one is willing to do a thing they are afraid to do, they do not have to ... face a situation fearlessly, and [if] there is no situation to face; it falls away of its own weight.
Florence Scovel Shinn *(1871-1940)*
American artist, book illustrator

Limit to courage? There is no limit to courage.
Gabriele D'Annunzio *(1863-1938)*
Italian poet

To create one's own world in any of the arts takes courage.
Georgia O'Keeffe *(1887-1986)*
American artist

A ship in port is safe, but that's not what ships are built for.
Grace Murray Hopper *(1906-1992)*
American Rear Admiral, U.S. Navy

Let us go forth with fear and courage and rage to save the world.
Grace Paley *(1922-2007)*
American writer

It is brave to be involved.
Gwendolyn Brooks *(1917-2000)*
American poet

I wanted you to see what real courage is, instead of getting the idea that courage is a man with a gun in his hand. It's when you know you're licked before you begin but you begin anyway and you see it through no matter what.
Harper Lee *(1926-)*
American author

Every human being on this earth is born with a tragedy... They are born with the tragedy that they have to grow up. That they have to leave the nest, the security, and go out to do battle. They have to lose everything that is lovely and fight for a new loveliness of their own making, and it's a tragedy. A lot of people don't have the courage to do it.
Helen Hayes *(1900-1993)*
American actress

There is plenty of courage among us for the abstract but not for the concrete.
Helen Keller *(1880-1968)*
American author, educator

It takes a great deal of courage to stand up to your enemies,
but even more to stand up to your friends.
J. K. Rowling *(1965-)*
English writer

You have to pick the places you don't walk away from.
Joan Didion *(1934-)*
American writer

I am not afraid...I was born to do this.
Joan of Arc *(1412-1431)*
French heroine

It takes far less courage to kill yourself than it takes to make
yourself wake up one more time. It's harder to stay where
you are than to get out. For everyone but you, that is.
Judith Rossner *(1935-2005)*
American novelist

Each of us has an inner dream that we can unfold if we will
just have the courage to admit what it is. And the faith to trust
our own admission. The admitting is often very difficult.
Julia Cameron *(1948-)*
American teacher, author

Kill the snake of doubt in your soul, crush the worms of fear
in your heart and mountains will move out of your way.
Kate Seredy *(1896-1975)*
Hungarian-born writer

Everyone thought I was bold and fearless and even
arrogant, but inside I was always quaking.
Katharine Hepburn *(1907-2003)*
American actress

A fear of the unknown keeps a lot of people from leaving bad situations.
Kathie Lee Gifford *(1953-)*
American entertainer

All that is necessary is to accept the impossible, do without the indispensable, and bear the intolerable.
Kathleen Norris *(1880-1966)*
American poet, novelist

If you are willing to take the punishment, you're halfway through the battle. That the issues may be trivial, the battle ugly, is another point.
Lillian Hellman *(1905-1984)*
American playwright

Courage is a word for others to use about us, not something we can seek for ourselves.
Lillian Smith *(1729-1796)*
American author

I think laughter may be a form of courage...As humans we sometimes stand tall and look into the sun and laugh, and I think we are never more brave than when we do that.
Linda Ellerbee *(1944-)*
American journalist

Fear is the single strongest motivating force in our lives ... The more frightened you become, the better your chances of achieving success.
Lois Korey *(1934-1990)*
American advertising executive

I'm not funny. What I am is brave.
Lucille Ball *(1911-1989)*
American comedian, actress

Courage of soul is necessary for the triumphs of genius.
Madame de Stael *(1766-1817)*
French writer

Stand before the people you fear and speak your mind – even if your voice shakes.
Maggie Kuhn *(1905-1995)*
American activist

Speak your mind, even if your voice shakes.
Maggie Smith *(1934-)*
British actress

The truly fearless think of themselves as normal.
Margaret Atwood *(1939-)*
Canadian poet, novelist

The right way is not always the popular and easy way. Standing for right when it is unpopular is a true test of moral character.
Margaret Chase Smith *(1897-1995)*
American politician

I have learned to love that which is meant to harm me, so that I can stand in the way of those who are less strong. I can take the bullets for those who aren't able to.
Margaret Cho *(1968-   )*
American comedian, actress

With enough courage, you can do without a reputation.
Margaret Mitchell *(1900-1949)*
American novelist

Courage is rarely reckless or foolish ... courage usually involves a highly realistic estimate of the odds that must be faced.
Margaret Truman *(1924-2008)*
American writer

Some people are capable of making great sacrifices, but few are capable of concealing how much the effort cost them.
Marguerite Blessington *(1789-1849)*
Irish-born English writer

Courage! I have shown it for years; think you I shall lose it at the moment when my sufferings are to end?
Marie Antoinette *(1755-1793)*
Austrian-born, Queen of France

No artist is ahead of their time. They are their time. It is just that others are behind the time. Nothing in life is to be feared. It is only to be understood.
Marie Curie *(1867-1934)*
Polish-French physicist

Ultimately we know deeply that the other side of every fear is freedom.
Marilyn Ferguson *(1938-2008)*
American author

Courage and grace are a formidable mixture. The only place to see it is in the bullring.
Marlene Dietrich *(1901-1992)*
German-born actress

I'm definitely a person who likes to control my own destiny. That's hard to do in this business because there are many creative people with great ideas and years of experience giving you advice, but what is right for one artist isn't always best for another. Knowing what's best for you and being willing to stand up and assert that is really a strong trait in this business.
Martina McBride *(1966-)*
American singer

Courage doesn't always roar. Sometimes courage is the quiet voice at the end of the day saying, 'I will try again tomorrow.'
Mary Anne Radmacher *(1957-)*
American writer

But screw up your courage to the sticking place, And we'll not fail.
Mary Bertone *(1869-1935)*
American writer

Courage is like – it's a habitus, a habit, a virtue: you get it by courageous acts. It's like you learn to swim by swimming. You learn courage by couraging.
Mary Daly *(1928-2010)*
American theologian

You can't be brave if you've only had wonderful things happen to you.
Mary Tyler Moore *(1936-)*
American actress

Courage is the most important of all virtues, because without it we can't practice any other virtue with consistency.
Maya Angelou *(1928-)*
American poet, memoirist

Courage is not the absence of fear but rather the judgment that something is more important than fear. The brave may not live forever but the cautious do not live at all.
Meg Cabot *(1967-)*
American author

You may not always have a comfortable life and you will not always be able to solve all of the world's problems at once but don't ever underestimate the importance you can have because history has shown us that courage can be contagious and hope can take on a life of its own.
Michelle Obama *(1964-)*
American First Lady

If you are brave too often, people will come to expect it of you.
Mignon McLaughlin *(1913-1983)*
American journalist

The only courage that matters is the kind that
gets you from one moment to the next.
Mignon McLaughlin *(1913-1983)*
American journalist

However confused the scene of our life appears, however torn we may be
who now do face that scene, it can be faced, and we can go on to be whole.
Muriel Rukeyser *(1913-1980)*
American poet, activist

Don't be afraid if things seem difficult in the beginning.
That's only the initial impression. The important thing
is not to retreat; you have to master yourself.
Olga Korbut *(1955-)*
Soviet Olympic gymnast

I have reached the conclusion that those who have physical courage
also have moral courage. Physical courage is a great test.
Oriana Fallaci *(1929-2006)*
Italian journalist, writer

I am old enough to know that victory is often a thing deferred,
and rarely at the summit of courage... What is at the summit
of courage, I think, is freedom. The freedom that comes with
the knowledge that no earthly think can break you.
Paula Giddings *(1947-)*
American historian, author

Part of courage is simple consistency.
Peggy Noonan *(1950-)*
American author, columnist

Being brave means doing or facing something frightening.
... Being fearless means being without fear.
Penelope Leach *(1937-)*
British psychologist

Cowards falter, but danger is often overcome by those who nobly dare.
Queen Elizabeth I *(1553-1603)*
English royalty

Fear is forward. No one is afraid of yesterday.
Renata Adler *(1938-)*
American journalist, critic

I have learned over the years that when one's mind is made up, this diminishes fear; knowing what must be done does away with fear.
Rosa Parks *(1949-)*
American Civil Rights Activist

The bravest thing you can do when you are not brave is to profess courage and act accordingly.
Rosalind Sussman Yalow *(1921-)*
American physicist

God, make me so uncomfortable that I will do the very thing I fear.
Ruby Dee *(1924-)*
American actress

Courage is very important. Like a muscle, it is strengthened by use.
Ruth Gordon *(1896-1985)*
American actress, writer

All adventures, especially into new territory, are scary.
Sally Ride *(1951-)*
American astronaut

I was silent as a child, and silenced as a young woman; I am taking my lumps and bumps for being a big mouth, now, but usually from those whose opinion I don't respect.
Sandra Cisneros *(1954-)*
American author

Anything can happen to anyone at any time and you shouldn't just live through the days, or you lose them. You should do what you can to enjoy every moment.
Sarah Brightman *(1960-)*
English actress

My greatest political asset, which professional politicians fear, is my mouth, out of which come all kinds of things one shouldn't always discuss for reasons of political expediency.
Shirley Chisholm *(1924-2005)*
American politician

To be a hero or a heroine, one must give an order to oneself.
Simone Weil *(1909-1943)*
French philosopher

It's only when we have nothing else to hold onto that we're willing to try something very audacious and scary.
Sonia Johnson *(1936-)*
American activist, writer

Cautious, careful people, always casting about to preserve their reputation and social standing, never can bring about a reform. Those who are really in earnest must be willing to be anything or nothing in the world's estimation, and publicly and privately, in season and out, avow their sympathy with despised and persecuted ideas and their advocates, and bear the consequences.
Susan B. Anthony *(1820-1906)*
American activist

In all realms of life it takes courage to stretch your limits, express your power, and fulfill your potential.
Suze Orman *(1951-)*
American, personal finance author

To have courage for whatever comes in life – everything lies in that.
Teresa of Avila *(1515-1582)*
Spanish Roman Catholic nun, saint

I am not afraid of a fight; I have to do my duty come what may.
Therese of Lisieux *(1873-1897)*
French carmelite nun

If you surrender to the wind, you can ride it.
Toni Morrison *(1931-)*
American novelist

Healing takes courage, and we all have courage, even if we have to dig a little to find it.
Tori Amos *(1963-)*
American singer, songwriter

What we look squarely in the eye rarely bites us in the butt.
Vanna Bonta *(1958-)*
American novelist, poet

Courage comes and goes. Hold on for the next supply.
Vicki Baum *(1888-1960)*
Austrian writer

This is the art of courage: to see things as they are and still believe that the victory lies not with those who avoid the bad, but those who taste, in living awareness, every drop of the good.
Victoria Lincoln *(1905-1981)*
American writer

This soul, or life within us, by no means agrees with the life outside us. If one has the courage to ask her what she thinks, she is always saying the very opposite to what other people say.
Virginia Woolf *(1882-1941)*
English writer

I have always had the courage for the new things that life sometimes offers.
Wallis Simpson *(1895-1986)*
American royalty

Creativity

It takes great passion and great energy to do anything creative, especially in the theater. You have to care so much that you can't sleep, you can't eat, you can't talk to people. It's just got to be right. You can't do it without that passion.
Agnes De Mille *(1905-1993)*
American dancer

The creative mind is not a mind full of stuff.
Alice Walker *(1944-)*
American writer

If you don't know what makes green, you're going to try every color combination.
Alison Krauss *(1971-)*
American musician

I believe in businesses where you engage in creative thinking, and where you form some of your deepest relationships. If it isn't about the production of the human spirit, we are in big trouble.
Anita Roddick *(1942-2007)*
English entrepreneur

Creative minds always have been known to survive any kind of bad training.
Anna Freud *(1895-1982)*
Austrian psychoanalyst

*I believe that true identity is found in creative activity
springing from within. It is found when one loses oneself.*
Anne Morrow Lindbergh *(1906-2001)*
American aviator, author

*Thank goodness I have walked in circles long enough to wear the soles of my
shoes so thin that the diamonds on which I stand can now get my attention.*
Anne Wilson Schaef *(1947-)*
American psychotherapist

*Our current obsession with creativity is the result of our continued striving
for immortality in an era when most people no longer believe in an after-life.*
Arianna Huffington *(1950-)*
American journalist

My left hand is my thinking hand. The right is only a motor hand.
Barbara Hepworth *(1903-1975)*
English sculptor

*Thank goodness I was never sent to school: it would
have rubbed off some of the originality.*
Beatrix Potter *(1866-1943)*
English author, illustrator

*Creativeness often consists of merely turning up what is
already there. Did you know that right and left shoes were
thought up only a little more than a century ago?*
Bernice Fitz-Gibbon *(1894-1982)*
American, advertising pioneer

Creativity varies inversely with the number of cooks involved with the broth.
Bernice Fitz-Gibbon *(1894-1982)*
American, advertising pioneer

*There is something about the creative process... which is that you can't talk
about it. You try to think of anecdotes about it, and you try to explain, but
you're never really saying what happened... it's a sort of happy accident.*
Betty Comden *(1917-2006)*
American lyricist

I learned...that inspiration does not come like a bolt, nor is it kinetic, energetic striving, but it comes into us slowly and quietly and all the time, though we must regularly and every day give it a little chance to start flowing, prime it with a little solitude and idleness.
Brenda Ueland *(1891-1985)*
American journalist

I've been relying very heavily on my instincts as of late, and my songwriting has come to depend on my ability to surrender to the inspiration whenever it strikes. When I clear my mind and let the music take over, my hands seem to move on their own... This is pure instinct. It's like riding a wave. You just take a deep breath, hop on, and hang on as long as you can.
Christine Anderson *(1983-)*
American musician

When I can no longer create anything I'll be done for.
Coco Chanel *(1883-1971)*
French fashion designer

Creativity belongs to the artist in each of us. To create means to relate. The root meaning of the word art is to fit together and we all do this every day. Each time we fit things together we are creating – whether it is to make a loaf of bread, a child, a day.
Corita Kent *(1918-1986)*
American, Roman Catholic nun, artist

Out of limitations comes creativity.
Debbie Allen *(1950-)*
American actress, dancer

What moves me about...what's called technique...is that it comes from some mysterious deep place... it comes mostly from some very deep choices somebody has made that take a long time and keep haunting them.
Diane Arbus *(1923-1971)*
American photographer

Just don't give up trying to do what you really want to do. Where there is love and inspiration, I don't think you can go wrong.
Ella Fitzgerald *(1917-1996)*
American jazz singer

I paint my own reality. The only thing I know is that I paint because I need to, and I paint whatever passes through my head without any other consideration.
Frida Kahlo *(1907 - 1954)*
Mexican artist

Creativity can be described as letting go of certainties.
Gail Sheehy *(1937-)*
American writer, lecturer

It takes a lot of time to be a genius. You have to sit around so much doing nothing, really doing nothing.
Gertrude Stein *(1874-1946)*
American writer

While we have the gift of life, it seems to me the only tragedy is to allow part of us to die – whether it is our spirit, our creativity, or our glorious uniqueness.
Gilda Radner *(1946-1989)*
American comedian

There's a time when what you're creating and the environment you're creating it in come together.
Grace Hartigan *(1922-2008)*
American abstract expressionist painter

I don't advise any one to take it [painting] up as a business proposition, unless they really have talent... But I will say that I have did remarkable for one of my years, and experience.
Grandma Moses *(1860-1961)*
American folk artist

To me, being creative is a very fragile thing, and somehow I've always felt the need to be very protective of that.
Holly Hunter *(1958-)*
American actress

What I am interested in doing is finding and expressing a new form of life.
Isadora Duncan *(1878-1927)*
American dancer

Creative endeavor requires physical and mental space; without privacy, solitude, and time it suffocates...it is impossible to pursue original thought in the scattered remnants of a day or of a lifetime.
Judith Groch *(1952-)*
American writer

Most artwork comes out of someplace you can just tap into, and make that so obvious. And then other people can look at it and say, I know that place too, that craving.
Judy Pfaff *(1946-)*
English artist

When we are angry or depressed in our creativity, we have misplaced our power. We have allowed someone else to determine our worth, and then we are angry at being undervalued.
Julia Cameron *(1948-)*
American teacher, author

Invention is the pleasure you give yourself when other people's stuff isn't good enough.
Julie Newmar *(1933-)*
American actress

I have never done any work cold...I have always worked with my blood, so to speak.
Kathe Kollwitz *(1867-1945)*
German sculptor

Human life itself may be almost pure chaos, but the work of the artist is to take these handfuls of confusion and disparate things and put them together in a frame to give them some kind of shape and meaning.
Katherine Anne Porter *(1890-1980)*
American journalist

As a rule, I am very careful to be shallow and conventional where depth and originality are wasted.
Lucy Maud Montgomery *(1874-1942)*
Canadian writer

On a lazy Saturday morning when you're lying in bed, drifting in and out of sleep, there is a space where fantasy and reality become one. Your mind and your body exist, but on separate planes. Time stands still. For me, this is the feeling I have when ideas come.
Lynn Johnston *(1947-)*
Canadian cartoonist

Genius is essentially creative; it bears the stamp
of the individual who possesses it.
Madame de Stael *(1766-1817)*
French writer

I like the fact that in ancient Chinese art the great painters always
included a deliberate flaw in their work: human creation is never perfect.
Madeleine L'Engle *(1918-)*
American novelist

Don't let anyone rob you of your imagination, your creativity, or
your curiosity. It's your place in the world; it's your life. Go on and
do all you can with it, and make it the life you want to live.
Mae Jemison *(1956-)*
American astronaut

The things we fear most in organizations – fluctuations,
disturbances, imbalances – are the primary sources of creativity.
Margaret J. Wheatley *(1934-)*
American organization expert

Many people are inventive, sometimes cleverly so. But real
creativity begins with the drive to work on and on and on.
Margueritte Harmon Bro *(1894-1977)*
English writer

No artist is ahead of their time. They are their time. It
is just that others are behind the time.
Martha Graham *(1894-1991)*
American dancer, choreographer

Creativity is inventing, experimenting, growing, taking risks,
breaking rules, making mistakes, and having fun.
Mary Lou Cook *(1910-)*
American community activist

Stop the habit of wishful thinking and start the habit of thoughtful wishes.
Mary Martin *(1913-1990)*
American actress

Cease to be a drudge, seek to be an artist.
Mary McLeod Bethune *(1875-1955)*
American educator

*Imitation is for shirkers, like-minded-ness for the
comfort lovers, unifying for the creators.*
Mary Parker Follett *(1868-1933)*
American management consultant

*Invention, it must be humbly admitted, does not consist
in creating out of voice, but out of chaos.*
Mary Shelley *(1797-1851)*
British novelist

*I think there are two keys to being creatively productive. One is not being
daunted by one's fear of failure, the second is sheer perseverance.*
Mary-Claire King *(1946-)*
American geneticist

Exchange is creation.
Muriel Rukeyser *(1913-1980)*
American poet, activist

Responsibility is what awaits outside the Eden of Creativity.
Nadine Gordimer *(1923-)*
South African novelist, activist

*In this country we encourage creativity among the
mediocre, but real bursting creativity appalls us. We put
it down as undisciplined, as somehow too much.*
Pauline Kael *(1919-2001)*
American film critic

*The truly creative mind in any field is no more than this: a human
creature born abnormally, inhumanly sensitive. To them, a touch is a
blow, a sound is a noise, a misfortune is a tragedy, a joy is an ecstasy, a
friend is a lover, a lover is a god, and failure is death. Add to this cruelly
delicate organism the overpowering necessity to create, create, create ...
They must create, must pour out creation. By some strange, unknown,
inward urgency they are not really alive unless they are creating.*
Pearl S. Buck *(1892-1973)*
American writer

*Creativity comes from trust. Trust your instincts.
And never hope more than you work.*
Rita Mae Brown *(1944-)*
American novelist

Creativity is a lot like looking at the world through a kaleidoscope. You look at a set of elements, the same ones everyone else sees, but then reassemble those floating bits and pieces into an enticing new possibility.
Rosabeth Moss Kanter *(1943-)*
American academic, author

Putting a stamp on things just helps you say, 'Hey, yesterday I was there, and today I'm here.' It's another step forward, and it feels like another turning point and an unleashing of creativity....
Shania Twain *(1965-)*
Canadian musician

Make-believe colors the past with innocent distortion, and it swirls ahead of us in a thousand ways – in science, in politics, in every bold intention. It is part of our collective lives, entwining our past and our future...a particularly rewarding aspect of life itself.
Shirley Temple Black *(1928-)*
American actress

There is a fountain of youth: it is your mind, your talents, the creativity you bring to your life and the lives of people you love. When you learn to tap this source, you will truly have defeated age.
Sophia Loren *(1934-)*
Italian actress

I remember asking my dear friend Tom Petty to work with me on some songs. He said, No. You're a premier songwriter. You don't need anyone to help you with your songs. Do it yourself. It was the jolt I needed.
Stevie Nicks *(1948-)*
American songwriter, singer

In human life, art may arise from almost any activity, and once it does so, it is launched on a long road of exploration, invention, freedom to the limits of extravagance, interference to the point of frustration, finally discipline, controlling constant change and growth.
Susanne Langer *(1895-1985)*
American philosopher

What I really need is for people to know that I don't just do this, I do this and this and this and this. We all have creativity in us and we all are multi-dimensional and we are all interested in a lot of things ...We can handle a lot of things.
Suzanne Somers *(1946-)*
American actress

There is only one answer to destructiveness and that is creativity.
Sylvia Ashton-Warner *(1908-1984)*
New Zealand writer, poet

Sometimes you've got to let everything go – purge yourself.
If you are unhappy with anything . . . whatever is bringing
you down, get rid of it. Because you'll find that when you're
free, your true creativity, your true self comes out.
Tina Turner *(1939-)*
American singer

Early in my career I felt that organization would destroy
my creativity. Whereas now, I feel the opposite. Discipline
is the concrete that allows you to be creative.
Verna Gibson *(1946-)*
American business executive

Normal is nothing more than a cycle on a washing machine.
Whoopi Goldberg *(1955-)*
American actress, comedian

Curiosity

I am one of the people who love the why of things.
Catherine the Great *(1729-1796)*
Russian royalty

Perhaps the only misplaced curiosity is that which persists in trying
to find out here, on this side of death, what lies beyond the grave.
Colette *(1873-1954)*
French novelist

If I were just curious, it would be very hard to say to someone,
"I want to come to your house and have you talk to me and
tell me the story of your life." I mean people are going to say,
"You're crazy." ...But the camera is a kind of license.
Diane Arbus *(1923-1971)*
American photographer

I don't know what tree we're barking up.
Dianne Feinstein *(1933-)*
American politician

Believe only half of what you see and nothing that you hear.
Dinah Mulock Craik *(1826-1887)*
English novelist, poet

The cure for boredom is curiosity. There is no cure for curiosity.
Dorothy Parker *(1893-1967)*
American writer, satirist

In spite of illness, in spite even of the archenemy sorrow, one can remain alive long past the usual date of disintegration if one is unafraid of change, insatiable in intellectual curiosity, interested in big things, and happy in small ways.
Edith Wharton *(1862-1937)*
American novelist

One thing life has taught me: If you are interested, you never have to look for new interests. They come to you. When you are genuinely interested in one thing, it will always lead to something else.
Eleanor Roosevelt *(1884 - 1962)*
American First Lady

Curiosity is the one thing invincible in nature.
Freya Stark *(1893-1993)*
French-born travel writer, explorer

There is nothing so carking as the pangs of unsatisfied curiosity.
Gertrude Atherton *(1857-1948)*
American writer

Some men and women are inquisitive about everything, they are always asking, if they see any one with anything they ask what is that thing, what is it you are carrying, what are you going to be doing with that thing, why have you that thing, where did you get that thing, how long will you have that thing, there are very many men and women who want to know about anything about everything.
Gertrude Stein *(1874-1946)*
American writer

The curious are always in some danger. If you are curious you might never come home.
Jeanette Winterson *(1959-)*
British novelist

As long as one keeps searching the answers come.
Joan Baez *(1941-)*
American folksinger, songwriter

Faith and doubt both are needed not as antagonists but working side by side to take us around the unknown curve.
Lillian Smith *(1729-1796)*
American author

Nothing attracts me like a closed door. I cannot let my camera rest until I have pried it open.
Margaret Bourke-White *(1906-1971)*
American photojournalist

The world can forgive practically anything except people who mind their own business.
Margaret Mitchell *(1900-1949)*
American novelist

Question everything.
Maria Mitchell *(1818-1889)*
American scientist

Be less curious about people and more curious about ideas.
Marie Curie *(1867-1934)*
Polish-French physicist

I'm curious about other people. That's the essence of my acting. I'm interested in what it would be like to be you.
Meryl Streep *(1949-)*
American actress

Even cowards can endure hardship; only the brave can endure suspense.
Mignon McLaughlin *(1913-1983)*
American journalist

The greatest gift is not being afraid to question.
Ruby Dee *(1924-)*
American actress

Curiosity is one of those insatiable passions that grow by gratification.
Sarah Scott *(1720-1795)*
English novelist

Don't be curious of matters that don't concern you;
never speak of them and don't ask about them.
Teresa of Avila *(1515-1582)*
Spanish Roman Catholic nun, saint

Research is formalized curiosity. It is poking and prying with
a purpose. It is a seeking that they who wish may know the
cosmic secrets of the world and they that dwell therein.
Zora Neale Hurston *(1891-1960)*
American dramatist

Customers

I feel I'm able to serve my customer by knowing what she or he wants.
...people give me great ideas, tell me what they want, what they don't want.
Kathy Ireland *(1963-)*
American entrepreneur

The critical element in selling a service comes in providing support
after the sale, because, unlike other types of marketing, the customer
can't really try the product until he's already bought it.
Kay Knight Clarke *(1947-)*
Chairman, Templeton, Inc.

Business is not financial science, it's about trading... buying and selling.
It's about creating a product or service so good that people will pay for it.
Anita Roddick *(1942-2007)*
English entrepreneur, activist

The principle was right there – you couldn't miss it. The more
you did for your customers the more they did for us.
Debbi Fields *(1956-)*
American entrepreneur

Repetition makes reputation and reputation makes customers.
Elizabeth Arden *(1884-1966)*
Canadian-American entrepreneur

My take: the basics of business is to stay as close as
possible to your customers, understand their behavior,
their preferences, their purchasing patterns, etc.
Indra Nooyi *(1955-)*
Indian, CEO of Pepsico

*At the end of the day I think the single biggest thing that
will set Kraft apart as we are successful will be our ability to
understand our consumers better than anybody else.*
Irene Rosenfeld *(1953-)*
American, CEO Kraft Foods

*We don't want to push our ideas on to customers,
we simply want to make what they want.*
Laura Ashley *(1925-)*
British designer

*When you are skinning your customers, you should leave some
skin on to grow again so that you can skin them again.*
Nikki Giovanni *(1943-)*
American poet, author

*Marketing is trying to figure out what people
want so you can give it to them.*
Shelley Lazarus *(1947-)*
American advertising executive

Decisions

*No trumpets sound when the important decisions of our
life are made. Destiny is made known silently.*
Agnes De Mille *(1905-1993)*
American dancer

*The most difficult thing is the decision to act, the rest is merely
tenacity. The fears are paper tigers. You can do anything
you decide to do. You can act to change and control your life;
and the procedure, the process is its own reward.*
Amelia Earhart *(1897-1937)*
American aviator

The cards are on the table. The choices are clear.
Angela Merkel *(1954-)*
German Chancellor

*I think that was the hardest decision I've ever made in my life. It was
also the right decision, but having it be right did not make it easy.*
Ann Bancroft *(1955-)*
American adventurer

It is better to arm and strengthen your hero,
than to disarm and enfeeble your foe.
Anne Bronte *(1820-1849)*
British novelist, poet

People died all the time. ... Parts of them died when they made the
wrong kinds of decisions – decisions against life. Sometimes they
died bit by bit until finally they were just living corpses walking
around. If you were perceptive you could see it in their eyes; the fire
had gone out ... you always knew when you made a decision against
life. ... The door clicked and you were safe inside – safe and dead.
Anne Morrow Lindbergh *(1906-2001)*
American aviator, author

The percentage of mistakes in quick decisions is no greater than
in long-drawn-out vacillation, and the effect of decisiveness
itself 'makes things go' and creates confidence.
Anne O'Hare McCormick *(1882-1954)*
American journalist

It is possible to be different and still be all right. There can be two
– or more – answers to the same question, and all can be right.
Anne Wilson Schaef *(1947-)*
American psychotherapist

Contradictions do not exist. Whenever you think you are facing a
contradiction, check your premises. You will find that one of them is wrong.
Ayn Rand *(1905-1982)*
Russian-American novelist

I could never tell where inspiration begins and impulse leaves off. I suppose
the answer is in the outcome. If your hunch proves a good one, you were
inspired; if it proves bad, you are guilty of yielding to thoughtless impulse.
Beryl Markham *(1874-1946)*
English-born Kenyan pilot

Forty pictures I was in, and all I remember is 'What kind
of bra will you be wearing today, honey?' That was always
the area of big decision – from the neck to the navel.
Donna Reed *(1921-1986)*
American actress

That would be a good thing for them to cut on my tombstone: Wherever she went, including here, it was against her better judgment.
Dorothy Parker *(1893-1967)*
American writer, satirist

Somehow we learn who we really are and then live with that decision.
Eleanor Roosevelt *(1884 - 1962)*
American First Lady

I believe that we are solely responsible for our choices, and we have to accept the consequences of every deed, word, and thought throughout our lifetime.
Elisabeth Kübler-Ross *(1926-2004)*
Swiss psychiatrist

Take your life in your own hands and what happens? A terrible thing: no one to blame.
Erica Jong *(1942-)*
American writer

Decide on what you think is right, and stick to it.
George Eliot *(1819-1880)*
English novelist

We cannot freely and wisely choose the right way for ourselves unless we know both good and evil.
Helen Keller *(1880-1968)*
American author, educator

Do not wait for ideal circumstances, nor the best opportunities; they will never come.
Janet Erskine Stuart *(1857-1914)*
English, Roman Catholic nun

I made the decision. I'm accountable.
Janet Reno *(1938-)*
American Attorney General

I have a theory that every time you make an important choice, the part of you left behind continues the other life you could have had.
Jeanette Winterson *(1959-)*
British novelist

What one decides to do in crisis depends on one's philosophy of
life and that philosophy cannot be changed by an incident. If one
hasn't any philosophy, in crises others make the decision.
Jeannette Rankin *(1880-1973)*
American, first Congresswoman

It's very easy to make certain decisions that affect
your life that you have no perspective on.
Jena Malone *(1984-)*
American actress

I invented this rule for myself. I would sort out all the arguments
and see which belonged to fear and which to creativeness,
and other things being equal I would make the decision which
had the larger number of creative reasons on its side.
Katharine Butler Hathaway *(1890-1942)*
American writer

I don't believe in intuition. When you get sudden flashes of perception, it is
just the brain working faster than usual. But you've been getting ready to
know it for a long time, and when it comes, you feel you've known it always.
Katherine Anne Porter *(1890-1980)*
American journalist

I have made it a rule of my life never to regret and never
to look back. Regret is an appalling waste of energy...
you can't build on it; it's only good for wallowing in.
Katherine Mansfield *(1888 - 1923)*
New Zealand-born writer

Too great a preoccupation with motives (especially one's own
motive) is lia ble to lead to too little concern for consequences.
Katherine Whitehorn *(1914-1956)*
British columnist

The decision to speak out is the vocation and lifelong
peril by which the intellectual must live.
Kay Boyle *(1902-1992)*
American writer, activist

Sometimes it's the smallest decisions that can change your life forever.
Keri Russell *(1976-)*
American actress, dancer

Decisions, particularly important ones, have always made me sleepy, perhaps because I know that I will have to make them by instinct, and thinking things out is only what other people tell me I should do.
Lillian Hellman *(1905-1984)*
American playwright

Throughout my political career, I've believed in the concept of home rule. Some call it local control. Whichever phrase you use, the concept is the same – the best decisions are those made closest to those who will be impacted by the decisions.
Linda Lingle *(1953-)*
American politician

Choice is the essence of what I believe it is to be human.
Liv Ullmann *(1938-)*
Norwegian actress, director

When choosing between two evils, I always like to try the one I've never tried before.
Mae West *(1892-1980)*
American actress

Standing in the middle of the road is very dangerous; you get knocked down by traffic from both sides.
Margaret Thatcher *(1925-)*
English Prime Minister

The difference between weakness and wickedness is much less than people suppose; and the consequences are nearly always the same.
Marguerite Blessington *(1789-1849)*
Irish-born English writer

Ever notice that 'what the hell' is always the right decision?
Marilyn Monroe *(1926-1962)*
American actress

If your head tells you one thing and your heart tells you another, before you do anything you should first decide whether you have a better head or a better heart.
Marilyn vos Savant *(1946-)*
American writer

*I have made the choices that work best for me. I know
I cannot please everyone, and that's fine.*
Marlee Matlin *(1965-)*
American actress

*There are two ways for a painter: the broad and
easy one or the narrow and hard one.*
Mary Cassatt *(1844-1926)*
American impressionist artist

*If someone tells you they are going to make a 'realistic decision', you
immediately understand they have resolved to do something bad.*
Mary McCarthy *(1912-1989)*
American writer

*You can't make decisions based on fear and the possibility of
what might happen. We just weren't raised that way.*
Michelle Obama *(1964-)*
American First Lady

*Yesterday is gone. Tomorrow has not yet come.
We only have today. Let us begin.*
Mother Teresa *(1910-1997)*
Albanian Roman Catholic nun

*I think there is a choice possible to us at any moment....
But there is no sacrifice. There is a choice, and the rest
falls away. Second choice does not exist.*
Muriel Rukeyser *(1913-1980)*
American poet, activist

*One of the biggest lessons I've learned recently is that when you don't
know what to do, you should do nothing until you figure out what to do...*
Oprah Winfrey *(1954-)*
American media mogul

*Once the what is decided, the how always follows. We must not
make the how an excuse for not facing and accepting the what.*
Pearl S. Buck *(1892-1973)*
American writer

*I made decisions that I regret, and I took them as learning
experiences... I'm human, not perfect, like anybody else.*
Queen Latifa *(1970-)*
American singer, actress

We stand now where two roads diverge. But unlike the roads in Robert Frost's familiar poem, they are not equally fair. The road we have long been traveling is deceptively easy, a smooth superhighway on which we progress with great speed, but at its end lies disaster. The other fork of the road – the one less traveled by – offers our last, our only chance to reach a destination that assures the preservation of the earth.
Rachel Carson *(1907-1964)*
American environmentalist

I choose things by how they resonate in my heart.
Rita Coolidge *(1944-)*
American musician

A peacefulness follows any decision, even the wrong one.
Rita Mae Brown *(1944-)*
American novelist

The two important things I did learn were that you are as powerful and strong as you allow yourself to be, and that the most difficult part of any endeavour is taking the first step, making the first decision.
Robyn Davidson *(1950-)*
Australian writer

I'd rather be strongly wrong than weakly right.
Tallulah Bankhead *(1902-1968)*
American actress

In Iroquois society, leaders are encouraged to remember seven generations in the past and consider seven generations in the future when making decisions that affect the people.
Wilma Pearl Mankiller *(1945-2010)*
American Cherokee leader

Determination

I want to walk through life instead of being dragged through it.
Alanis Morisette *(1974-)*
Canadian singer

Most of us who aspire to be tops in our fields don't really consider the amount of work required to stay tops.
Althea Gibson *(1927-2003)*
American tennis player

Use your fear...it can take you to the place where you store your courage.
Amelia Earhart *(1897-1937)*
American aviator

Maturity is the ability to do a job whether or not you are supervised, to carry money without spending it and to bear an injustice without wanting to get even.
Ann Landers *(1918-2002)*
American advice columnist

The thing that is really hard, and really amazing, is giving up on being perfect and beginning the work of becoming yourself.
Anna Quindlen *(1952-)*
American journalist

I was asked to act when I couldn't act. I was asked to sing 'Funny Face' when I couldn't sing, and dance with Fred Astaire when I couldn't dance – and do all kinds of things I wasn't prepared for. Then I tried like mad to cope with it.
Audrey Hepburn *(1929-1993)*
Belgian-born actress

All my life I've been competing—and competing to win. I came to realize that in this way this cancer was the toughest competition I had faced yet. I made up my mind that I was going to lick it all the way. I not only wasn't going to let it kill me I wasn't even going to let it put me on the shelf.
Babe Didrikson Zaharias *(1911-1956)*
American golfer

I will fight for what I believe in until I drop dead. And that's what keeps you alive.
Barbara Castle *(1910-2002)*
British politician

If you know you are on the right track, if you have this inner knowledge, then nobody can turn you off...regardless of what they say.
Barbara McClintock *(1902- 1992)*
American scientist

I survived because I was tougher than anybody else.
Bette Davis *(1908-1989)*
American actress

You don't always get what you ask for, but you never get what you don't ask for... unless it's contagious!
Beverly Sills *(1929-2007)*
American operatic soprano

Ask Nureyev to stop dancing, ask Sinatra to stop singing, then you can ask me to stop playing.
Billie Jean King *(1934-)*
American tennis player

I have willpower and determination. I am very resilient, like rock.
Carnie Wilson *(1968-)*
American musician

I didn't try to put any pressure on me by setting high goals or anything, I just want to make sure that every single time I'm out there on the court I do my best, I give 100%, and see where it's going to end up next year.
Daniela Hantuchova *(1983-)*
Slovakian tennis player

I'm a Salieri not a Mozart, a Damon Hill not a Michael Schumacher. I wouldn't flounce away from the track muttering about the engine letting me down. ...I'd stay and help the mechanics push it clear.
Deborah Mansfield *(1963-)*
English ballet dancer

You can't just sit there and wait for people to give you that golden dream. You've got to get out there and make it happen for yourself.
Diana Ross *(1944-)*
American singer, actress

Razors pain you; rivers are damp; acids stain you; and drugs cause cramp. Guns aren't lawful; nooses give; gas smells awful; you might as well live.
Dorothy Parker *(1893-1967)*
American writer, satirist

You've just got to do the best that you can.
Drew Barrymore *(1975-)*
American actress

To be able to look life in the face: that's worth living in a garret for, isn't it?
Edith Wharton *(1862-1937)*
American novelist

I was trained by my husband. He said, If you want a thing done – go. If not – send. I belong to that group of people who move the piano themselves.
Eleanor Robson Belmont *(1878-1979)*
English actress

It's not the having, it's the getting.
Elizabeth Taylor *(1932-2011)*
British-born actress

There is no chance, no destiny, no fate, that can circumvent or hinder or control the firm resolve of a determined soul.
Ella Wheeler Wilcox *(1850-1919)*
American poet

I would be so exhausted by my determination that I had no strength left to do the actual work.
Esther Etty Hillesum *(1914-1943)*
Netherlands, Jewish prisoner at Auschwitz

Keep your dreams alive. Understand to achieve anything requires faith and belief in yourself, vision, hard work, determination, and dedication. Remember all things are possible for those who believe.
Gail Devers *(1966-)*
American Olympic medalist track and field

It's them as take advantage that get advantage i' this world.
George Eliot *(1819-1880)*
English novelist

I've been absolutely terrified every moment of my life – and I've never let it keep me from doing a single thing I wanted to do.
Georgia O'Keeffe *(1887-1986)*
American painter

The goal is to live a full, productive life even with all that ambiguity. No matter what happens, whether the cancer never flares up again or whether you die, the important thing is that the days that you have had you will have lived.
Gilda Radner *(1946-1989)*
American comedian

Nobody gets anything for nothing.
Gloria Swanson *(1899-1983)*
American actress

What really distinguishes this generation in all countries from earlier generations... is its determination to act, its joy in action, the assurance of being able to change things by one's own efforts.
Hannah Arendt *(1906-1975)*
German philosopher

You had better live your best and act your best and think your best today; for today is the sure preparation for tomorrow and all the other tomorrows that follow.
Harriet Martineau *(1802-1876)*
English social theorist

Even if I died in the service of the nation, I would be proud of it. Every drop of my blood, I am sure, will contribute to the growth of this nation and make it strong and dynamic.
Indira Gandhi *(1917-1984)*
Indian Prime Minister

I am prepared to sacrifice every so-called privilege I possess in order to have a few rights.
Inez Milholland *(1886-1916)*
American suffragist

I have no regrets. I wouldn't have lived my life the way I did if I was going to worry about what people were going to say.
Ingrid Bergman *(1915-1982)*
Swedish-born, American actress

In my experience there is only one motivation and that is desire. No reasons or principle contain it or stand against it.
Jane Smiley *(1949-)*
American novelist

The bear is what we all wrestle with. Everybody has their bear in life. It's about conquering that bear and letting him go.
Jennifer Lopez *(1970-)*
American musician

There seemed to be endless obstacles – it seemed that the root cause of them all was fear.
Joanna Field *(1900-1998)*
British psychoanalyst

*In each of us are places where we have never gone. Only
by pressing the limits do you ever find them.*
Joyce Brothers *(1927-)*
American psychologist

*It was good to learn so early. They're not going to be kind to you.
You have to do it and get on, and then gulp down and get better.*
Judi Dench *(1934-)*
English actress

People can only do what they are ready to do when they are ready to do it.
Judith Light *(1949-)*
American actress

*I have learned, as a rule of thumb, never to ask whether you
can do something. Say, instead, that you are doing it. Then
fasten your seat belt. The most remarkable things follow.*
Julia Cameron *(1948-)*
American teacher, author

*Some people regard discipline as a chore. For me it
is a kind of order that sets me free to fly.*
Julie Andrews *(1935-)*
British film, stage actress

*I never expected in a million years that I would have the honor to become
an advocate of women's health care and education, and I'd dive on a
live grenade to get this message out, so thank you for this forum.*
Karen Duffy *(1962-)*
American actress

*I used to want the words 'She tried' on my
tombstone. Now I want 'She did it.'*
Katherine Dunham *(1912-2006)*
American actress

If I'd been easily discouraged, I could have been a one-hit wonder.
Laurell K. Hamilton *(1963-)*
American writer

*If you want it you've got to go for it, so I just kept saying to myself
'work, work, work'. I proved I wanted it more than anyone else.*
Liz McColgan *(1964-)*
Scottish Olympic medalist

Anyone who has gumption knows what it is, and anyone who hasn't can never know what it is. So there is no need of defining it.
Lucy Maud Montgomery *(1874-1942)*
Canadian writer

Determination, energy, and courage appear spontaneously when we care deeply about something. We take risks that are unimaginable in any other context.
Margaret J. Wheatley *(1934-)*
American organization expert

There ain't nothing from the outside that can lick any of us.
Margaret Mitchell *(1900-1949)*
American novelist

No person has the right to rain on your dreams.
Marian Wright Edelman *(1939-)*
American, founder Children's Defense Fund

Never face facts; if you do you'll never get up in the morning.
Marlo Thomas *(1937-)*
American actress

Some people have thousands of reasons why they cannot do what they want to, when all they need is one reason why they can.
Martha Graham *(1894-1991)*
American dancer, choreographer

Just go out there and do what you have to do.
Martina Navratilova *(1956-)*
Czech American tennis player

Determination and perseverance move the world; thinking that others will do it for you is a sure way to fail.
Marva Collins *(1936-)*
American educator

If you think you can, you can. If you think you can't, you're right.
Mary Kay Ash *(1918-2001)*
American entrepreneur

Nothing contributes so much to tranquilize the mind as a steady purpose – a point on which the soul may fix its intellectual eye.
Mary Shelley *(1797-1851)*
British novelist

True champions aren't always the ones that
win, but those with the most guts.
Mia Hamm *(1972-   )*
American soccer player

I wanted to express myself. I wanted to be creative and I
didn't want to worry about someone bossing me around in
the process. You have to struggle no matter where you are to
get to where you're going, so I'm like, working it honey!
Michelle Rodriguez *(1978-   )*
American actress

As a mother and grandmother, I think 'lioness.'
You come near the cubs, you're dead.
Nancy Pelosi *(1940-   )*
American politician

It is so much easier sometimes to sit down and be
resigned than to rise up and be indignant.
Nellie McClung *(1873-1951)*
Canadian activist

No one can figure out your worth but you.
Pearl Bailey *(1918-1990)*
American entertainer

I think exercise tests us in so many ways – our skills, our hearts, our
ability to bounce back after setbacks. This is the inner beauty of sports
and competition and it can serve us all well as adult athletes.
Peggy Fleming *(1948-   )*
American Olympic skater

I declare before you that my whole life, whether it be long
or short, shall be devoted to your service and the service of
our great Imperial family to which we all belong.
Queen Elizabeth II *(1926-   )*
English royalty

I will be good.
Queen Victoria *(1819-1901)*
English royalty

The only tired I was, was tired of giving in.
Rosa Parks *(1949-   )*
American Civil Rights Activist

We must believe in ourselves or no one else will believe in us; we must match our aspirations with the competence, courage, and determination to succeed.
Rosalind Sussman Yalow *(1921-)*
American physicist

You just try to do everything that comes up. Get up an hour earlier, stay up an hour later, make the time. Then you look back and say, Well, that was a neat piece of juggling there – school, marriage, babies, career. The enthusiasms took me through the action, not the measuring of it or the reasonableness.
Ruby Dee *(1924-)*
American actress

Slaying the dragon of delay is no sport for the short-winded.
Sandra Day O'Connor *(1930-)*
American Supreme Court Justice

Other people may not have had high expectations for me... but I had high expectations for myself.
Shannon Miller *(1977-)*
American gymnast

There is something in me even now that would push a peanut all the way down a street just to see if I could do it.
Shirley MacLaine *(1934-)*
American actress

We must remember that one determined person can make a significant difference, and that a small group of determined people can change the course of history.
Sonia Johnson *(1936-)*
American activist, writer

I knew I was going to be a journalist, and that was it... full stop.
Suzie Wetlaufer Welch *(1959-)*
American journalist

I never deviated from my grim determination to someday have all the money I needed and wanted.
Taylor Caldwell *(1900-1985)*
American author

The stalwart soul has the will to live and is eager for the race.
Taylor Caldwell *(1900-1985)*
American author

Pain is never permanent.
Teresa of Avila *(1515-1582)*
Spanish Roman Catholic nun, saint

You have to lift your head up out of the mud and just do it.
Teri Garr *(1944-)*
American actress

I didn't have anybody, really, no foundation in life, so I had to make my own way. Always, from the start. I had to go out in the world and become strong, to discover my mission in life.
Tina Turner *(1939-)*
American singer

For a gallant spirit there can never be defeat.
Wallis Simpson *(1895-1986)*
American royalty

I grew up in a time when it would never have occurred to anyone to tell me there was anything I couldn't do.
Whoopi Goldberg *(1955-)*
American actress, comedian

I ran and ran and ran every day, and I acquired this sense of determination, this sense of spirit that I would never, never give up, no matter what else happened.
Wilma Rudolph *(1940-1994)*
American Olympic runner

You must have discipline to have fun.
Julia Child *(1912-2004)*
American cookbook author

Diversity

I think we have to own the fears that we have of each other, and then, in some practical way, some daily way, figure out how to see people differently than the way we were brought up to.
Alice Walker *(1944-)*
American writer

I know there is strength in the differences between us.
I know there is comfort where we overlap.
Ani DiFranco *(1970-)*
American singer, guitarist

It is the curse of minorities in this power-worshipping world that either
from fear or from an uncertain policy of expedience they distrust their
own standards and hesitate to give voice to their deeper convictions,
submitting supinely to estimates and characterizations of themselves
as handed down by a not unprejudiced dominant majority.
Anna Julia Cooper *(1858-1964)*
American educator

Differences challenge assumptions.
Anne Wilson Schaef *(1947-)*
American psychotherapist

I deplore any action which denies artistic talent an opportunity
to express itself because of prejudice against race origin.
Bess Truman *(1885-1982)*
American First Lady

The fact is that the diversity in this political class serves the same
interest as diversity in any arena, which is it stirs the competitive pot.
Carol Moseley Braun *(1947-)*
American politician, author

Let me say that I am incredibly proud that in the most diverse city in
the world, diversity is seen as a strength, and not an impediment.
Christine Quinn *(1966-)*
American politician

Diversity on the bench is critical. We need judges who understand
what discrimination feels like. We need judges who understand what
inequality feels like. We need judges who understand the subtleties of
unfair treatment and who are willing to call it out when they see it!
Debbie Wasserman Schultz *(1966-)*
American politician

I don't judge people by their sexual orientation or the color of their
skin, so I find it really hard to identify someone by saying that
they're a gay person or a black person or a Jewish person.
Diana Ross *(1944-)*
American singer, actress

We must develop a deeper interest and greater understanding of the people we meet here or abroad. Like us, they are passengers on board that mysterious ship called life.
Ella Maillart *(1903-1997)*
Swiss writer

Every effort for progress, for enlightenment, for science, for religious, political, and economic liberty, emanates from the minority, and not from the mass.
Emma Goldman *(1869-1940)*
Russian-born, American activist

What we have to do…is to find a way to celebrate our diversity and debate our differences without fracturing our communities
Hillary Rodham Clinton*(1947-)*
American, Secretary of State

Mankind will endure when the world appreciates the logic of diversity.
Indira Gandhi *(1917-1984)*
Indian Prime Minister

Whatever is not commonly seen is condemned as alien.
Iris Chang *(1968-2004)*
Chinese historian

I think this feeling that I have for people and the importance of behaving in a way which is respectful to people of all colours, shapes, sizes and religions goes back a very long way… possibly to my mother and father in very early stages of childhood.
Janet Holmes à Court *(1943-)*
Australian business woman

I'd be stupid not to take into consideration that there are certain things people will not consider me for because my name is Lopez. And I know I can do any kind of role. I don't want anybody to say, Oh, she can't pull this off. So those are barriers that you have to overcome.
Jennifer Lopez *(1970-)*
American musician

You know, gay, lesbian, bisexual, transgender – people are people.
Judith Light *(1949-)*
American actress

*Diversity is the most basic principle of creation. No two
snowflakes, blades of grass, or people are alike.*
Lynn Maria Laitala *(1868-1933)*
American writer

*I hope that people will finally come to realize that there is only one
race – the human race – and that we are all members of it.*
Margaret Atwood *(1939-)*
Canadian poet, novelist

*If we are to achieve a richer culture, rich in contrasting values,
we must recognize the whole gamut of human potentialities,
and so weave a less arbitrary social fabric, one in which
each diverse human gift will find a fitting place.*
Margaret Mead *(1901-1978)*
American cultural anthropologist

*Every one of us is different in some way, but for those of us who are
more different, we have to put more effort into convincing the less
different that we can do the same thing they can, just differently.*
Marlee Matlin *(1965-)*
American actress

Labels are for filing. Labels are for clothing. Labels are not for people.
Martina Navratilova *(1956-)*
Czech American tennis player

*Insight, I believe, refers to the depth of understanding that comes by
setting experiences, yours and mine, familiar and exotic, new and
old, side by side, learning by letting them speak to one another.*
Mary Catherine Bateson *(1939-)*
American anthropologist

*What people often mean by getting rid of conflict is
getting rid of diversity, and it is of the utmost importance
that these should not be considered the same.*
Mary Parker Follett *(1868-1933)*
American management consultant

*We all should know that diversity makes for a rich tapestry,
and we must understand that all the threads of the tapestry
are equal in value no matter what their color*
Maya Angelou *(1928-)*
American poet, memoirist

*I feel my heart break to see a nation ripped apart by
it's own greatest strength – it's diversity.*
Melissa Etheridge *(1961-)*
American musician

*Racism is an ism to which everyone in the world today is exposed;
for or against, we must take sides. And the history of the future
will differ according to the decision which we make.*
Ruth Benedict *(1887-1948)*
American scientist

*The fact that we are human beings is infinitely more important than all
the peculiarities that distinguish human beings from one another.*
Simone de Beauvoir *(1908-1986)*
French writer, philosopher

*Everybody is sitting around saying, 'Well, jeez, we need
somebody to solve this problem of bias.' That somebody is us.
We all have to try to figure out a better way to get along.*
Wilma Pearl Mankiller *(1945-2010)*
American Cherokee leader

Drive

If you do things well, do them better. Be daring, be first, be different, be just.
Anita Roddick *(1942-2007)*
English entrepreneur

*You can't just beat a team, you have to leave a lasting impression
in their minds so they never want to see you again.*
Mia Hamm *(1972-)*
American soccer player

*Getting ahead in a difficult profession requires avid faith in yourself.
That is why some people with mediocre talent, but with great inner
drive, go much further than people with vastly superior talent.*
Sophia Loren *(1934-)*
Italian film actress

I was resolved to sustain and preserve in my college the bite of the mind, the chance to stand face to face with truth, the good life lived in a small, various, highly articulate and democratic society.
Virginia Crocheron Gildersleeve *(1877-1965)*
American educator

Empathy

How sick one gets of being 'good,' how much I should respect myself if I could burst out and make everyone wretched for twenty-four hours.
Alice James *(1848-1892)*
American diarist

I hope to leave my children a sense of empathy and pity and a will to right social wrongs.
Anita Roddick *(1942-2007)*
English entrepreneur

When you have nobody you can make a cup of tea for, when nobody needs you, that's when I think life is over.
Audrey Hepburn *(1929-1993)*
Belgian-born actress

Don't confuse being stimulating with being blunt.
Barbara Walters *(1929-)*
American broadcast journalist, author

But you can't realize, you can't know what another person goes through.
Beatrice Wood *(1893-1998)*
American artist

I praise loudly, I blame softly.
Catherine the Great *(1729-1796)*
Russian royalty

It is a curious thing that people only ask if you are enjoying yourself when you aren't.
Edith Nesbitt *(1858-1924)*
English poet, author

Empathy, the least comfortable of human emotions.
Frances Gray Patton *(1906-2000)*
American short story writer

We want people to feel with us more than to act for us.
George Eliot *(1819-1880)*
English novelist

People genuinely happy in their choices seem less often tempted to force them on other people than those who feel martyred and broken by their lives.
Jane Rule *(1931-2007)*
Canadian writer

Human altruism is thought to be based, in part, on empathy. To be empathetic, you need to understand the thoughts and desires of others.
Joan Silk *(1953-)*
American scientist

It's odd that you can get so anesthetized by your own pain or your own problem that you don't quite fully share the hell of someone close to you.
Lady Bird Johnson *(1912-2007)*
American First Lady

There will always be someone else with a different view than you. I appreciate them and would never say that they are wrong. I hope that they would give me that courtesy also.
Melissa Etheridge *(1961-)*
American musician

The great gift of human beings is that we have the power of empathy.
Meryl Streep *(1949-)*
American actress

I think empathy is a beautiful thing. I think that's the power of film though. We have one of the most powerful, one of the greatest communicative tools known to anyone.
Michelle Rodriguez *(1978-)*
American actress

I am continually fascinated at the difficulty intelligent people have in distinguishing what is controversial from what is merely offensive.
Nora Ephron *(1941-)*
American director, screenwriter

Nobody likes having salt rubbed into their wounds even if it is the salt of the earth.
Rebecca West *(1892-1983)*
Irish-born, British writer

I've always had a really developed sense of justice. As a child, I would rotate my dolls' dresses for fear that they might come alive at midnight and one of them would always have the best dress on. Whatever it was that made me worry about my dolls I suppose has paid off in my career because, really, an actor is all about empathy and imagination. And those are the cornerstones of activism.

Susan Sarandon *(1946-   )*
American actress

I consider myself more exportant than important.

Vanna Bonta *(1958-   )*
American novelist, poet

When you are kind to someone in trouble, you hope they'll remember and be kind to someone else. And it'll become like a wildfire.

Whoopi Goldberg *(1955-   )*
American actress, comedian

Entrepreneurs

Nobody talks of entrepreneurship as survival, but that's exactly what it is and what nurtures creative thinking.

Anita Roddick *(1942-2007)*
English entrepreneur

There is a fine line between the delinquent mind of an entrepreneur and that of a crazy person. The entrepreneur's dream is almost a kind of madness, and is almost as isolating. When you see something new, your vision usually isn't shared by others... the difference between a crazy person and the successful entrepreneur is that the latter can convince others to share the vision. That force of will is fundamental to entrepreneurship.

Anita Roddick *(1942-2007)*
English entrepreneur

I've never felt like I was in the cookie business. I've always been in a feel good feeling business. My job is to sell joy. My job is to sell happiness. My job is to sell an experience.

Debbi Fields *(1956-   )*
American entrepreneur

*It's a given that if you start your own business, you're going
to be (1) in control of your destiny, and (2) real busy.*
Georgette Mosbacher *(1947-)*
American, CEO of Borghese

Entrepreneurship is the last refuge of the trouble making individual.
Natalie Clifford Barney *(1876-1972)*
French writer

*Going into business for yourself, becoming an entrepreneur, is
the modern-day equivalent of pioneering on the old frontier.*
Paula Nelson *(1893-1967)*
American economist

Ethics

*When a Carl Sagan appears – someone who really has that
astonishing combination of poetry, of knowledge, of ethics,
of vision – that's the person I want to work with and do that
new 'Cosmos.' I haven't found that person quite yet.*
Ann Druyan *(1949-)*
American author, producer

*Every aspect of Western culture needs a new code of ethics
– a rational ethics – as a precondition of rebirth.*
Ayn Rand *(1905-1982)*
Russian-American novelist

*To act without rapacity, to use knowledge with wisdom,
to respect interdependence, to operate without hubris and
greed, are not simply moral imperatives. They are an accurate
scientific description of the means of survival.*
Barbara Ward *(1914-1981)*
British economist, writer

*It is no wonder we behave badly, we are literally ignorant of the laws of
ethics, which is the simplest of sciences, the most necessary, the most
continuously needed. The childish misconduct of our revolted youth is
quite equaled by that of older people, and neither young nor old seem to
have any understanding of the reasons why conduct is good or bad.*
Charlotte Perkins Gilman *(1860-1935)*
American sociologist, novelist

*Nothing is less important than which fork you use. Etiquette is the
science of living. It embraces everything. It is ethics. It is honor.*
Emily Post *(1872-1960)*
American author on etiquette

*Stripped of ethical rationalizations and philosophical pretensions,
a crime is anything that a group in power chooses to prohibit.*
Freda Adler *(1934-)*
American criminologist, educator

*I don't think we are doing well in detecting, investigating
and responding to ethics violations when they occur.*
Heather Wilson *(1960-)*
American politician

*I do believe that it is extremely important that each one of us is a
participant in life and what's going on around us rather than being a
spectator to it and if you do that, if you participate in the world, in your
community, your school, your company, or your country, whatever...
then you will be useful and hopefully leave the planet a little better.*
Janet Holmes à Court *(1943-)*
Australian business woman

A person educated in mind and not in morals is a menace to society.
Juanita Kidd Stout *(1919-1998)*
American judge

Did I violate journalistic ethics by not disclosing it? I don't know. You tell me.
Maggie Gallagher *(1960-)*
American writer

*The real nature of an ethic is that it does not become
an ethic unless and until it goes into action.*
Margaret Halsey *(1910-1997)*
American writer

*One of the most marked characteristics of our day is a reckless
neglect of principles, and a rigid adherence to their semblance.*
Marguerite Blessington *(1789-1849)*
Irish-born English writer

*English literature is a kind of training in social ethics. English trains you
to handle a body of information in a way that is conducive to action.*
Marilyn Butler *(1937-)*
British literary critic

*Hollywood is a place where they'll pay you a thousand
dollars for a kiss and fifty cents for your soul.*
Marilyn Monroe *(1926-1962)*
American actress

*Since when do grown men and women, who presume to hold
high government office and exercise what they think of as
moral leadership, require ethics officers to tell them whether
it is or isn't permissible to grab the secretary's behind or
redirect public funds to their own personal advantage?*
Meg Greenfield *(1930-1999)*
American journalist

Today we live in a society suffering from ethical rickets.
Rita Mae Brown *(1944-)*
American novelist

Excellence

To try to be better is to be better.
Charlotte Cushman *(1816-1776)*
American stage actress

*I've spent my life pursing excellence as an artist, which
is what I always wanted to do anyhow.*
Claire Bloom *(1931-)*
British actress

We only do well the things we like doing.
Colette *(1873-1954)*
French novelist

*It is more to my personal happiness and advantage to indulge the love
and admiration of excellence, than to cherish a secret envy of it.*
Elizabeth Montagu *(1718-1800)*
British social reformer

Striving for excellence motivates you; striving for perfection is demoralizing.
Harriet Beryl Braiker *(1948-2004)*
American psychologist, writer

I have been a waitress, and I was a damn fine waitress too, let me tell you.
Jessica Lange *(1949-)*
American actress

*Persistence is the twin sister of excellence. One is a
matter of quality, the other a matter of time.*
Marabel Morgan *(1937-)*
American author

The only sin is mediocrity.
Martha Graham *(1894-1991)*
American dancer, choreographer

*Excellence is not an act but a habit. The things you
do the most are the things you will do best.*
Marva Collins *(1936-)*
American educator

Excellence costs a great deal.
May Sarton *(1912-1995)*
American poet, novelist

*Everything we say signifies; everything counts that we put out into the
world. It impacts on kids, it impacts on the zeitgeist of the time.*
Meryl Streep *(1949-)*
American actress

*My parents always told me that people will never know how long it
takes you to do something. They will only know how well it is done.*
Nancy Hanks *(1927-1983)*
American, Chair National Endowment for the Arts

The good is the greatest rival of the best.
Nellie McClung *(1873-1951)*
Canadian activist

*I had spent many years pursuing excellence, because that
is what classical music is all about... Now it was dedicated
to freedom, and that was far more important.*
Nina Simone *(1933-2003)*
American musician

Excellence is the best deterrent to racism or sexism.
Oprah Winfrey *(1954-)*
American media mogul

The secret of joy in work is contained in one word – excellence.
To know how to do something well is to enjoy it.
Pearl S. Buck *(1892-1973)*
American writer

I don't believe in perfection. I don't think there is such a thing. But
the energy of wanting things to be great is a perfectionist energy.
Reese Witherspoon *(1976-)*
American actress

I don't know that there are any short cuts to doing a good job.
Sandra Day O'Connor *(1930-)*
American Supreme Court Justice

The sad truth is that excellence makes people nervous.
Shana Alexander *(1925-2005)*
American journalist

Experience

If we could sell our experiences for what they cost us we'd be millionaires.
Abigail Van Buren *(1918-2002)*
American advice columnist

My path has not been determined. I shall have more
experiences and pass many more milestones.
Agnetha Faltskog *(1950-)*
Swedish musician

My experiences have taught me a lot and I'm happy with my
learnings, if not with what I went through to learn.
Ally Sheedy *(1962-)*
American actress

The fruit of life is experience, not happiness.
Amelia E. Barr *(1831-1919)*
British novelist

If what Proust says is true, that happiness is the absence of
fever, then I will never know happiness. For I am possessed
by a fever for knowledge, experience, and creation.
Anais Nin *(1902-1977)*
French author, diarist

Fate did not leave anything out for me. Everything anyone could possibly experience fell to my lot.
Anna Akhmatova *(1889-1966)*
Russian poet

I go by instinct. ... I don't worry about experience.
Barbara Streisand *(1942-)*
American singer, actor, producer

I don't care how smart a kid you are. The only way you learn what's not right is from experience.
Cameron Diaz *(1972-)*
American actress

What matters most is that we learn from living.
Doris Lessing *(1919-)*
Persian-born British writer

And I think that's important, to know how the water's gone over the dam before you start to describe it. It helps to have been over the dam yourself.
E. Annie Proulx *(1935-)*
American author

Life is long enough but not quite broad enough. Things crowd in so thickly and it takes time for experience to become clarified.
Edith Evans *(1888-1976)*
English actress

Experience shows that exceptions are as true as rules.
Edith Ronald Mirrielees *(1878-1962)*
American educator

When I am told by the left-wing boys that I can't write poetry because I have no proletarian experiences, I often wonder how many of them, at the age of 17, have been sent to pawn false teeth – parental false teeth
Edith Sitwell *(1902-1986)*
British poet, critic

Life is the only real counselor, wisdom unfiltered through personal experience does not become a part of the moral tissue.
Edith Wharton *(1862-1937)*
American novelist

Experience isn't interesting until it begins to repeat itself,
in fact, till it does that, it hardly is experience.
Elizabeth Bowen *(1899-1973)*
Irish novelist

The soul should always stand ajar, ready to welcome the ecstatic experience.
Emily Dickinson *(1830-1886)*
American poet

One is taught by experience to put a premium on those few
people who can appreciate you for what you are.
Gail Godwin *(1937-)*
American short story writer

When I was born and how I have lived is unimportant. It is what
I have done with where I have been that should be of interest.
Georgia O'Keeffe *(1887-1986)*
American artist

Life is what we make it, always has been, always will be.
Grandma Moses *(1860-1961)*
American folk artist

For the things we have to learn before we can
do them, we learn by doing them.
Hannah Arendt *(1906-1975)*
German philosopher

I long to put the experience of fifty years at once into your young lives,
to give you at once the key to that treasure chamber every gem of which
has cost me tears and struggles and prayers, but you must work for
these inward treasures yourselves. [said to her twin daughters]
Harriet Beecher Stowe *(1811-1896)*
American writer

The marvelous richness of human experience would lose something of
rewarding joy if there were no limitations to overcome. The hilltop hour
would not be half so wonderful if there were no dark valleys to traverse.
Helen Keller *(1880-1968)*
American author, educator

The follies which a person regrets most in their life are those
which they didn't commit when they had the opportunity.
Helen Rowland *(1875-1950)*
American writer

Everything you experience is what constitutes you as a human being, but the experience passes away and the person's left. The person is the residue.
Ilka Chase *(1900-1978)*
American actress, novelist

What one has not experienced, one will never understand in print.
Isadora Duncan *(1878-1927)*
American dancer

What is it which is bought dearly, offered for nothing, and then most often refused? Experience.
Isak Dineson *(1885-1962)*
Danish writer

A rattlesnake that doesn't bite teaches you nothing.
Jessamyn West *(1902-1984)*
American writer

I believe that being an actress or being involved in a movie has to be a life experience, otherwise why go for it? I have to change me, and I have to learn things, and I have to push me and my limits. By acting, I find a freedom inside of a prison in a way.
Juliette Binoche *(1964-)*
French actress

Experience is what really happens to you in the long run; the truth that finally overtakes you.
Katherine Anne Porter *(1890-1980)*
American journalist

Fear nothing for every renewed effort raises all former failures into lessons, all sins into experience.
Katherine Tingley *(1847-1929)*
Swedish theosophist

Experience teaches, it is true; but she never teaches in time.
Letitia Landon *(1802-1838)*
English poet, novelist

There is a large stock on hand; but somehow or other, nobody's experience ever suits us except our own.
Letitia Landon *(1802-1838)*
English poet, novelist

*Experience suggests it doesn't matter so much how
you got here, as what you do after you arrive.*
Lois McMaster Bujold *(1949-)*
American author

Life is my college. May I graduate well, and earn some honors!
Louisa May Alcott *(1832-1888)*
American author

We are each responsible for all of our experiences.
Louise L. Hay *(1926-)*
American author, publisher

*Experience is by far the best teacher. You know, ever since I
was a little girl I knew that if you look both ways when you
cross the street, you'll see a lot more than traffic.*
Mae West *(1892-1980)*
American actress

Pain is no longer pain when it is past.
Margaret Junkin Preston *(1820-1897)*
American poet, author

*But there are roughly two sorts of informed people, aren't there?
People who start off right by observing the pitfalls and mistakes and
going round them, and the people who fall into them and get out
and know they're there because of that. They both come to the same
conclusions but they don't have quite the same point of view.*
Margery Allingham *(1904-1966)*
English crime writer

*None are so eager to gain new experience as those who
don't know how to make use of the old ones.*
Marie von Ebner-Eschenbach *(1830-1916)*
Austrian writer

*Fame will go by and so long I've had you fame. If it
goes by I've always known it was fickle. So at least it's
something I experience but that's not where I live.*
Marilyn Monroe *(1926-1962)*
American actress

I am still determined to be cheerful and happy, in whatever situation I may be for I have also learned from experience that the greater part of our happiness or misery depends upon our dispositions, and not upon our circumstances.
Martha Washington *(1731-1802)*
American First Lady

There is no such thing as vicarious experience.
Mary Parker Follett *(1868-1933)*
American management consultant

I'm an experienced woman; I've been around... well, alright, I might not've been around, but I've been... nearby.
Mary Tyler Moore *(1936-)*
American actress

Experience has no text books nor proxies. She demands that her pupils answer to her roll-call personally.
Minna Thomas Antrim *(1861-1950)*
American writer

Experience is a good teacher, but she sends in terrific bills.
Minna Thomas Antrim *(1861-1950)*
American writer

The journey is my home.
Muriel Rukeyser *(1913-1980)*
American poet, activist

I've got my whole life. There's a lifetime of experience, a lifetime of experiencing the road and the music and different players. It makes me a richer human being. I have a greater source of information to tap into, a wealth of life.
Rita Coolidge *(1944-)*
American musician

Good judgment comes from experience, and often experience comes from bad judgment.
Rita Mae Brown *(1944-)*
American novelist

Every theory is a self-fulfilling prophecy that orders experience into the framework it provides.
Ruth Hubbard *(1924-)*
American academic,

Each of us brings to our job, whatever it is, our
lifetime of experience and our values.
Sandra Day O'Connor *(1930-)*
American Supreme Court Justice

Why is it that when people have no capacity for private
usefulness they should be so anxious to serve the public?
Sara Jeannette Duncan *(1861-1922)*
Canadian journalist

The real stuff of life was experience, in which sorrow and fear and
disaster had as important a part to play as beauty and joy.
Sheila Kaye Smith *(1887-1956)*
English writer

I think on-stage nudity is disgusting, shameful and damaging to
all things American. But if I were 22 with a great body, it would be
artistic, tasteful, patriotic and a progressive religious experience.
Shelley Winters *(1920-2006)*
American actress

What a wonderful life I've had! I only wish I'd realized it sooner.
Sidonie-Gabrielle Colette *(1873-1954)*
French novelist

To reach something good it is very useful to have
gone astray, and thus acquire experience.
Teresa of Avila *(1515-1582)*
Spanish Roman Catholic nun, saint

We are volcanoes. When we offer our experience as our truth, as
human truth, all the maps change. There are new mountains.
Ursula K. LeGuin *(1929-)*
American novelist

Never regret. If it's good, it's wonderful. If it's bad, it's experience.
Victoria Holt *(1906-1993)*
English author

One never believes other people's experience, and one
is only very gradually convinced by one's own.
Vita Sackville-West *(1892-1962)*
English author

A person's life can really be a succession of lives, each revolving around some emotionally compelling situation or challenge, and each marked off by some intense experience.
Wallis Simpson *(1895-1986)*
American royalty

It is better to take experience, to suffer, to love, and to remember than to walk unscathed between the fires...The two fires of poverty and passion have never burned me, and I am a lesser person for my safety.
Winifred Holtby *(1898-1935)*
English novelist

Failure

The happy people are failures because they are on such good terms with themselves that they don't give a damn.
Agatha Christie *(1890-1976)*
English detective novelist

Failure must be but a challenge to others.
Amelia Earhart *(1897-1937)*
American aviator

I didn't fear failure. I expected failure.
Amy Tan *(1952-)*
American writer (Chinese descent)

Life is a process of becoming, a combination of states we have to go through. Where people fail is that they wish to elect a state and remain in it. This is a kind of death.
Anais Nin *(1902-1977)*
French author, diarist

I believe in recovery, and I believe that as a role model I have the responsibility to let young people know that you can make a mistake and come back from it.
Ann Richards *(1933-2006)*
American politician

I'm sure not afraid of success and I've learned not to be afraid of failure. The only thing I'm afraid of now is of being someone I don't like much.
Anna Quindlen *(1952-)*
American journalist

It's best to have failure happen early. It wakes up the
Phoenix bird in you so you rise from the ashes.
Anne Baxter *(1923-1985)*
American actress

It takes as much courage to have tried and failed
as it does to have tried and succeeded.
Anne Morrow Lindbergh *(1906-2001)*
American aviator, author

There is no human failure greater than to launch a profoundly
important endeavor and then leave it half done. This is what
the West has done with its colonial system. It shook all the
societies in the world loose from their old moorings. But it seems
indifferent whether or not they reach safe harbor in the end.
Barbara Ward *(1914-1981)*
British economist, writer

The love of nature is consolation against failure.
Berthe Morisot *(1841-1895)*
French impressionist painter

Who thinks it just to be judged by a single error?
Beryl Markham *(1874-1946)*
English-born Kenyan pilot

Victory is fleeting, but losing is forever.
Billie Jean King *(1934-)*
American tennis player

It's how you deal with failure that determines how you achieve success.
Charlotte Whitton *(1896-1975)*
Canadian politician

The greatest failure is not to try. Had I listened to all the people
during the course of my life who said, You can't. You'll fail. It
won't work. You don't have…, I wouldn't be here today.
Debbi Fields *(1956-)*
American entrepreneur

Failure: Is it a limitation? Bad timing? It's a lot of things. It's
something you can't be afraid of, because you'll stop growing. The
next step beyond failure could be your biggest success in life.
Debbie Allen *(1950-)*
American actress, dancer

All that is necessary to break the spell of inertia and frustration is this:
Act as if it were impossible to fail. That is the talisman, the formula, the
command of right-about-face which turns us from failure towards success.
Dorothea Brande *(1893-1948)*
American writer, editor

The only difference between a rut and a grave is their dimensions.
Ellen Glasgow *(1873-1945)*
American novelist

I've probably earned the right to screw up a few times. I don't want
the fear of failure to stop me from doing what I really care about.
Emma Watson *(1990-)*
British actress

It is better to be young in your failures than old in your successes.
Flannery O'Connor *(1925-1964)*
American writer

Apparent failure may hold in its rough shell the germs of a success
that will blossom in time, and bear fruit throughout eternity.
Frances Ellen Watkins Harper *(1825-1911)*
American, 19th century abolitionist

There's folks 'ud stand on their heads and then
say the fault was i' their boots.
George Eliot *(1819-1880)*
English novelist

What separates the winners from the losers is that winners are
able to handle problems and crises that they never imagined
would occur. You hit the floor, but what counts is how fast you can
get up and regroup. Failure is simply part of the equation.
Georgette Mosbacher *(1947-)*
American, CEO of Borghese

A real failure does not need an excuse. It is an end in itself.
Gertrude Stein *(1874-1946)*
American writer

A series of failures may culminate in the best possible result.
Gisela Richter *(1882-1972)*
English archaeologist

If you're 40 years old and you've never had a failure, you've been deprived.
Gloria Swanson *(1899-1983)*
American actress

Do not think of today's failures, but of the success that may come tomorrow. You have set yourselves a difficult task, but you will succeed if you persevere; and you will find a joy in overcoming obstacles. Remember, no effort that we make to attain something beautiful is ever lost.
Helen Keller *(1880-1968)*
American author, educator

While we are young the idea of death or failure is intolerable to us; even the possibility of ridicule we cannot bear.
Isak Dineson *(1885-1962)*
Danish writer

I make mistakes; I'll be the second to admit it.
Jean Kerr *(1923-2003)*
American author

If you sit down for 20 minutes in this business now it's a comeback.
Judy Garland *(1922-1969)*
American actress, singer

The only real stumbling block is fear of failure. In cooking you've got to have a 'What the hell?' attitude.
Julia Child *(1912-2004)*
American cookbook author

Mine was a life of failure – one thing after another – like most lives…but that is all right, it is universal, it is the great human experience to fail.
Katharine Butler Hathaway *(1890-1942)*
American writer

When we begin to take our failures so seriously, it means we are ceasing to be afraid of them. It is of immense importance to learn to laugh at ourselves.
Katherine Mansfield *(1888 - 1923)*
New Zealand-born writer

If we do not always see our own mistakes and omissions we can always see those of our neighbors.
Kathleen Norris *(1880-1966)*
American poet, novelist

*I've learned so many things and a lot of things I've learned the hard way.
I look at failure as education...in that respect I'm very well educated.*
Kathy Ireland *(1963-)*
American entrepreneur

*Success and failure are not true opposites and they're not even
in the same class; they're not even a couch and a chair.*
Lillian Hellman *(1905-1984)*
American playwright

Thank goodness all flops aren't failures.
Lillian Vernon *(1929-)*
German entrepreneur

*Don't be afraid of missing opportunities. Behind every failure
is an opportunity somebody wishes they had missed.*
Lily Tomlin *(1939-)*
American actress, comedian

Sometimes what you want to do has to fail so you won't.
Margueritte Harmon Bro *(1894-1977)*
English writer

Failure is just another way to learn how to do something right.
Marian Wright Edelman *(1939-)*
American, founder Children's Defense Fund

*There is nothing in the universe that I fear but that I
shall not know all my duty or fail to do it.*
Mary Lyon *(1797-1849)*
American educator

In a total work, the failures have their not unimportant place.
May Sarton *(1912-1995)*
American poet, novelist

We may encounter many defeats but we must not be defeated.
Maya Angelou *(1928-)*
American poet, memoirist

*Failure happens all the time. It happens every day in practice.
What makes you better is how you react to it.*
Mia Hamm *(1972-)*
American soccer player

I walked along that slippery slope where if you fail through lack of faith, you sell your soul to the devil.
Michelle Shocked *(1962-)*
American musician

One of the greatest diseases is to be nobody to anybody.
Mother Teresa *(1910-1997)*
Albanian Roman Catholic nun

It is nothing to succeed if one has not taken great trouble, and it is nothing to fail if one has done the best one could.
Nadia Boulanger *(1887-1979)*
French composer

I would never think of crying about any loss of an office, because that's always a possibility, and if you're professional, then you deal with it professionally.
Nancy Pelosi *(1940-)*
American politician

I really don't think life is about the I-could-have-beens. Life is only about the I-tried-to-do. I don't mind the failure but I can't imagine that I'd forgive myself if I didn't try.
Nikki Giovanni *(1943-)*
American poet, author

Failure is defined by our reaction to it.
Oprah Winfrey *(1954-)*
American media mogul

Some of the biggest failures I ever had were successes.
Pearl S. Buck *(1892-1973)*
American writer

Nothing fails like success; nothing is so defeated as yesterday's triumphant cause.
Phyllis Mcginley *(1905-1978)*
American writer

Nothing succeeds like failure.
Rebecca West *(1892-1983)*
Irish-born, British writer

Flops are a part of life's menu and I've never been
a girl to miss out on any of the courses.
Rosalind Russell *(1907-1976)*
American actress

Failure is impossible.
Susan B. Anthony *(1820-1906)*
American activist

Any critic is entitled to wrong judgments, of course. But certain lapses
of judgment indicate the radical failure of an entire sensibility.
Susan Sontag *(1933-2004)*
American activist, writer

To think of losing is to lose already.
Sylvia Townsend Warner *(1893-1978)*
English novelist, poet

There is no such thing as failing. Failing is when you
give up. Just move on and try something else.
Tara Vanderveer *(1953-)*
American basketball coach

The dream is real, my friends. The failure to realize it is the only unreality.
Toni Cade Bambara *(1939-1995)*
American author, filmmaker

Fame

I don't mind if my skull ends up on a shelf as long as it's got my name on it.
Debbie Harry *(1945-)*
American singer, songwriter

In the final analysis, it's true that fame is unimportant. No matter how
great a person is, the size of the funeral usually depends on the weather.
Rosemary Clooney *(1928-2002)*
American singer, actress

Generosity

You cannot give to people what they are not capable of receiving.
Agatha Christie *(1890-1976)*
English detective novelist

I postpone death by living, by suffering, by error,
by risking, by giving, by losing.
Anais Nin *(1902-1977)*
French author, diarist

We are rich only through what we give, and
poor only through what we refuse.
Anne Sophie Swetchine *(1752-1857)*
Russian mystic

Ask yourself: Have you been kind today? Make kindness
your daily modus operandi and change your world.
Annie Lennox *(1954-)*
Scottish singer-songwriter

Some people give time, some money, some their skills and connections, some
literally give their life's blood . . . but everyone has something to give.
Barbara Bush *(1925-)*
American First Lady

To the wrongs that need resistance, To the right that needs
assistance, To the future in the distance, Give yourselves.
Carrie Chapman Catt *(1859-1947)*
American activist

Life appears to me too short to be spent in nursing
animosity or registering wrongs.
Charlotte Bronte *(1816-1855)*
English novelist

When we grow old, there can only be one regret –
not to have given enough of ourselves.
Eleonora Duse *(1858-1924)*
Italian actress

Giving opens the way for receiving.
Florence Scovel Shinn *(1871-1940)*
American artist, book illustrator

*This idea of selfishness as a virtue, as opposed to
generosity: That, to me, is unnatural.*
Jessica Lange *(1949-   )*
American actress

*Holding on to anger, resentment and hurt only gives you tense muscles,
a headache and a sore jaw from clenching your teeth. Forgiveness
gives you back the laughter and the lightness in your life.*
Joan Lunden *(1950-   )*
American journalist

*We are here to add to the sum of human goodness. To prove the thing
exists. And however futile each individual act of courage or generosity,
self-sacrifice or grace – it still proves the thing exists. Each act adds to the
fund. It needs replenishment. Not only because evil flourishes, and is, most
indefensibly, defended. But because goodness is no longer a respectable
aim in life. The hound of hell, envy, has driven it from the house.*
Josephine Hart *(1942-2011)*
Irish-born British writer

*I have come to believe that giving and receiving are really the
same. Giving and receiving – not giving and taking.*
Joyce Grenfell *(1910-1979)*
English actress, comedian

*I feel that if you are blessed, or lucky enough, to
be doing well, you should help others.*
Laurell K. Hamilton *(1963-   )*
American writer

*Enthusiasm is the divine particle in our composition: with it we are
great, generous, and true; without it, we are little, false, and mean.*
Letitia Landon *(1802-1838)*
English poet, novelist

It was easier to do a friendly thing than it was to stay and be thanked for it.
Louisa May Alcott *(1832-1888)*
American author

*Sometimes when we are generous in small, barely detectable
ways it can change someone else's life forever.*
Margaret Cho *(1968-   )*
American comedian, actress

Service is the rent we pay to be living. It is the very purpose
of life and not something you do in your spare time.
Marian Wright Edelman *(1939-)*
American, founder Children's Defense Fund

My father said there were two kinds of people in the world: givers
and takers. The takers may eat better, but the givers sleep better.
Marlo Thomas *(1937-)*
American actress

It was dangerous to praise or even to approve of any thing belonging to
herself in her hearing; if it had been the carpet under her feet or the shawl
on her shoulders, either would instantly have been stripped off to offer.
Mary Russell Mitford *(1787-1855)*
English playwright

Generosity with strings is not generosity; it is a deal.
Marya Mannes *(1904-1990)*
American author, critic

If you only have one smile in you, give it to the people you
love. Don't be surly at home, then go out in the street and
start grinning Good Morning at total strangers.
Maya Angelou *(1928-)*
American poet, memoirist

We'd all like a reputation for generosity and we'd all like to buy it cheap.
Mignon McLaughlin *(1913-1983)*
American journalist

I believe that as much as you take, you have to give back.
It's important not to focus on yourself too much.
Nicole Kidman *(1967-)*
Australian actress

Those who have suffered understand suffering
and therefore extend their hand.
Patti Smith *(1946-)*
American musician

Service is the rent that you pay for room on this earth.
Shirley Chisholm *(1924-2005)*
American politician

That's what I consider true generosity. You give your all,
and yet you always feel as if it costs you nothing.
Simone de Beauvoir *(1908-1986)*
French writer, philosopher

In this world people have to pay an extortionate
price for any exceptional gift whatever.
Willa Cather *(1873-1947)*
American writer

Goals

To tend, unfailingly, unflinchingly, towards a goal, is the secret of success.
Anna Pavlova *(1881-1931)*
Russian ballerina

People thought I was ruthless, which I was. I didn't give a darn who was
on the other side of the net. I'd knock you down if you got in my way.
Althea Gibson *(1927-2003)*
American tennis player

Please know that I am aware of the hazards. I
want to do it because I want to do it.
Amelia Earhart *(1897-1937)*
American aviator

What we truly and earnestly aspire to be, that in some sense we are.
Anna Jameson *(1794-1860)*
British writer

There are two ways of attaining an important end, force and perseverance;
the silent power of the latter grows irresistible with time.
Anne Sophie Swetchine *(1752-1857)*
Russian mystic

Before I was even in my teens, I knew exactly what I wanted to be when
I grew up. My goal was to be the greatest athlete that ever lived.
Babe Didrikson Zaharias *(1911-1956)*
American golfer

*Set goals for yourself and work your hardest to achieve them.
Some goals you will achieve and others you won't, but at least you
will have the satisfaction of knowing where you were going.*
Beth Daniel *(1956-)*
American golfer

*I am doomed to an eternity of compulsive work. No set
goal achieved satisfies. Success only breeds a new goal.
The golden apple devoured has seeds. It is endless.*
Bette Davis *(1908-1989)*
American actress

I've always tried to go a step past wherever people expected me to end up.
Beverly Sills *(1929-2007)*
American operatic soprano

*No matter what the competition is I try to find
a goal that day and better that goal.*
Bonnie Blair *(1964- (*
American Olympic speed skater

*We are always afraid to start something that we
want to make very good, true, and serious.*
Brenda Ueland *(1891-1985)*
American journalist

*There's only so much you can do, but if somebody doesn't
give you a chance there is nothing you can do.*
Charlize Theron *(1975-)*
South African actress

*Find something that you're really interested in doing in your life. Pursue
it, set goals, and commit yourself to excellence. Do the best you can.*
Chris Evert *(1954-)*
American tennis player

There are several paths one can take, but not every path is open to you.
Claire Bloom *(1931-)*
British actress

*I knew all these people had the same goals I did, but the one that worked
the hardest would come out on top. That's what drove me all the time.
But I had fun. I did better every day, and that's what made it fun.*
Debbie Meyer *(1952-)*
American Olympic swimmer

If you want to touch the other shore badly enough,
barring an impossible situation, you will. If your desire
is diluted for any reason, you'll never make it.
Diana Nyad *(1949-)*
American distance swimmer

I don't want to get to the end of my life and find that I lived just
the length of it. I want to have lived the width of it as well.
Diane Ackerman *(1948-)*
American poet, naturalist

My favorite thing is to go where I've never been.
Diane Arbus *(1923-1971)*
American photographer

I never wanted to set the world on fire. So I never
had to burn any bridges behind me.
Dinah Shore *(1916-1994)*
American actress

The way I see it, if you want the rainbow, you gotta put up with the rain.
Dolly Parton *(1946-)*
American singer-songwriter

There is only one real sin and that is to persuade oneself
that the second best is anything but second best.
Doris Lessing *(1919-)*
Persian-born British writer

The fresh start is always an illusion but a necessary one.
Eleanor Clark *(1913-1996)*
American writer

I love to fly. I always wanted to fly. It's been one of my dreams since
I was 3 years old. I remember saying to my mom, 3 years old, every
day, 'I can fly!' Living on the ninth floor, it was dangerous.
Elena Anaya *(1975-)*
Spanish actress

One ship drives east and another drives west,
With the selfsame winds that flow.
'Tis the set of sails and not the gales, Which tells us the way to go.
Ella Wheeler Wilcox *(1850-1919)*
American poet

*I wanted so badly to study ballet, but it was
really all about wearing the tutu.*
Elle Macpherson *(1964-)*
Australian model

*My expectations – which I extended whenever I came close to accomplishing
my goals – made it impossible ever to feel satisfied with my success.*
Ellen Sue Stern *(1943-1976)*
American political activist

The brain is wider than the sky.
Emily Dickinson *(1830-1886)*
American poet

*I'm incredibly impressed by people who organize to achieve
a goal, and believe that they can make a difference and then
go ahead and do just that. I think it's incredible.*
Fiona Apple *(1977-)*
American musician

*The best antidote I have found is to yearn for something. As long as
you yearn you can't congeal: there is a forward motion to yearning.*
Gail Godwin *(1937-)*
American short story writer

*There is no sorrow I have thought more about than that – to
love what is great, and try to reach it, and yet to fail.*
George Eliot *(1819-1880)*
English novelist

*Maybe I'm not going to be Meryl Streep, but I think I can do something
honest and that the audience will leave the cinema feeling filled up.*
Geri Halliwell *(1972-)*
English pop singer

*Obstacles are those frightful things you see
when you take your eyes off the goal.*
Hannah More *(1745-1833)*
English writer, philanthropist

*One of the sources of pride in being a human being is the ability to
bear present frustrations in the interests of longer purposes.*
Helen Merrell Lynd *(1896-1982)*
American sociologist, philosopher

*If a young female sees my dreams and goals come true, they
will realize their dreams and goals might also come true.*
Jackie Joyner-Kersee *(1962-)*
American Olympic athlete

*I might have been born in a hovel but I am determined
to travel with the wind and the stars.*
Jacqueline Cochran *(1910-1980)*
American aviator

An aim in life is the only fortune worth finding.
Jacqueline Kennedy Onassis *(1929-1994)*
American First Lady

I always say don't make plans, make options.
Jennifer Aniston *(1969-)*
American actress

My current goal is to place a moratorium on goals.
Jessica Savitch *(1947-1983)*
American journalist

*No matter how many goals you have achieved, you
must set your sights on a higher one.*
Jessica Savitch *(1947-1983)*
American journalist

*A fulfilling life is different to each person. You have to
acknowledge your dreams, and not just wait for life to happen,
and opportunities to come knocking at your door.*
Joan Lunden *(1950-)*
American journalist

*I knew I could live no other way, that the one thing
I wanted was to act and do it well.*
Juliette Lewis *(1973-)*
American actress

*I can remember walking as a child. It was not customary to say you were
fatigued. It was customary to complete the goal of the expedition.*
Katharine Hepburn *(1907-2003)*
American actress

No first step can be really great; it must of necessity possess more of prophecy than of achievement; nevertheless it is by the first step that a person marks the value not only of their cause but of themself.
Katherine Cecil Thurston *(1875-1911)*
Irish novelist

Before you begin a thing, remind yourself that difficulties and delays quite impossible to foresee are ahead. If you could see them clearly, naturally you could do a great deal to get rid of them but you can't. You can only see one thing clearly and that is your goal. Form a mental vision of that and cling to it through thick and thin.
Kathleen Norris *(1880-1966)*
American poet, novelist

I definitely wanted to be an actor. I didn't want to be on TV, I didn't want to be famous, I didn't want to be anyone in particular; I just wanted to do it. I see young people now who look at magazines, or American Idol and their goal is to have that lifestyle – to have good handbags, or go out with cute guys from shows, or whatever. But I definitely wanted to be an actor.
Lauren Graham *(1967-)*
American actress

You can only bite off so much, so you gotta know what you want to do.
Lesley Gore *(1946-)*
American singer, musician

Begin somewhere; you can't build a reputation on what you intend to do.
Liz Smith *(1923-)*
American gossip columnist

Far away there in the sunshine are my highest aspirations. I may not reach them, but I can look up and see their beauty, believe in them and try to follow where they lead.
Louisa May Alcott *(1832-1888)*
American author

What had seemed easy in imagination was rather hard in reality.
Lucy Maud Montgomery *(1874-1942)*
Canadian writer

I have the same goal I've had ever since I was a girl. I want to rule the world.
Madonna Ciccone *(1958-)*
American recording artist

There must be a goal at every stage of life! There must be a goal!
Maggie Kuhn *(1905-1995)*
American activist

To get anywhere, strike out for somewhere, or you'll get nowhere.
Martha Lipton *(1913-2006)*
American operatic mezzo-soprano

Goals too clearly defined can become blinkers.
Mary Catherine Bateson *(1939-)*
American anthropologist

*Our ultimate goal is to stay in business. We are not here
with a specific plan. That's kind of how our entire career has
evolved. We will figure things out as we go along.*
Mary-Kate Olsen *(1986-)*
American actress, entrepreneur

*My dreams were all my own; I accounted for them to nobody; they
were my refuge when annoyed – my dearest pleasure when free.*
Mary Shelley *(1797-1851)*
British novelist

*I am building a fire, and everyday I train, I add more
fuel. At just the right moment, I light the match.*
Mia Hamm *(1972-)*
American soccer player

*I've worked too hard and too long to let anything stand in the way of my
goals. I will not let my teammates down and I will not let myself down.*
Mia Hamm *(1972-)*
American soccer player

*One of the lessons I grew up with was to always stay true to
yourself and never let what somebody else says distract you from
your goals. So when I hear about negative and false attacks, I really
don't invest any energy in them, because I know who I am.*
Michelle Obama *(1964-)*
American First Lady

If people would forget about utopia! When rationalism destroyed heaven and decided to set it up here on earth, that most terrible of all goals entered human ambition. It was clear there'd be no end to what people would be made to suffer for it.
Nadine Gordimer *(1923-)*
South African novelist, activist

It's hard to stay committed...to stay in touch with the goal without saying there's something wrong with myself, my goal, the world.
Nancy Hogshead-Makar *(1962-)*
American Olympic swimmer

How high I aim, how much I see, how far I reach, depends on me.
Nancy Kerrigan *(1969-)*
American Olympic skater

I would like to do what I want to do. I don't want to do what you tell me to do.
Olga Korbut *(1955-)*
Soviet Olympic gymnast

To have realized your dream makes you feel lost.
Oriana Fallaci *(1929-2006)*
Italian journalist, writer

The ultimate goal should be doing your best and enjoying it.
Peggy Fleming *(1948-)*
American Olympic skater

Aim high, and you won't shoot your foot off.
Phyllis Diller *(1917-)*
American comedian

The goal of winning is not losing two times in a row.
Rosabeth Moss Kanter *(1943-)*
American academic, author

I'm coming up on 30. There are other things that I want to pursue outside of just performing.
Shannon Miller *(1977-)*
American gymnast

I don't set goals for myself too much, but I'm always trying to write that one great song.
Sheryl Crow *(1962-)*
American musician

Secretly, I had always wanted to go to Vegas,
and have my own really bad act!
Sigourney Weaver *(1949-)*
American actress

Sooner or later we all discover that the important moments in life are not
the advertised ones, not the birthdays, the graduations, the weddings,
the great goals achieved. The real milestones are less prepossessing. They
come to the door of memory unannounced, stray dogs that amble in, sniff
around a bit and simply never leave. Our lives are measured by these.
Susan B. Anthony *(1820-1906)*
American activist

I wanted to acquire an education, work extremely hard
and never deviate from my goal, to make it.
Taylor Caldwell *(1900-1985)*
American author

It is good to have an end to journey toward; but it
is the journey that matters, in the end.
Ursula K. LeGuin *(1929-)*
American novelist *The end is nothing, the road is all.*
Willa Cather *(1873-1947)*
American writer

I want a busy life, a just mind and a timely death.
Zora Neale Hurston *(1891-1960)*
American dramatist

Honesty

The whore is despised by the hypocritical world because she has made a
realistic assessment of her assets and does not have to rely on fraud to make
a living. In an area of human relations where fraud is regular practiced
between the sexes, her honesty is regarded with a mocking wonder.
Angela Carter *(1940-1992)*
English novelist, journalist

If one cannot invent a really convincing lie, it
is often better to stick to the truth.
Angela Thirkell *(1890-1961)*
English-Australian novelist

One must be frank to be relevant.
Corazon Aquino *(1933-2009)*
Philippine president

I would seriously question whether anybody is foolish enough to really say what they mean. Sometimes I think civilization as we know it would kind of break down if we all were completely honest.
Elizabeth Hurley *(1965-)*
English model, actress

Unless I am what I am and feel what I feel – as hard as I can and as honestly and truly as I can – then I am nothing.
Elizabeth Janeway *(1913-2005)*
American author, critic

Truth is so rare that it is delightful to tell it.
Emily Dickinson *(1830-1886)*
American poet

A liar did ought to have a good memory.
Flora Thompson *(1876-1947)*
English novelist

The main thing in acting is honesty, to feel the humanity and get to the essence of the character. You can't put anything into a character that you haven't got within you.
Genevieve Bujold *(1942-)*
Canadian actress

I've done more harm by the falseness of trying to please than by the honesty of trying to hurt.
Jessamyn West *(1902-1984)*
American writer

I think I have come to a place where I'm able to feel more comfortable about being honest.
June Jordan *(1936-2002)*
American writer

Maybe half a lie is worse than a real lie.
Lillian Hellman *(1905-1984)*
American playwright

If you can't be direct, why be?
Lily Tomlin *(1939-)*
American actress, comedian

Honesty is the only way with anyone, when you'll be so
close as to be living inside each other's skins.
Lois McMaster Bujold *(1949-)*
American author

What I would like my legacy to be is that of a person who took good care of
her family and sang some songs that made a difference in some way. I hope
I'll be remembered as somebody who was always down to earth and who
handled her career and other people with honesty, integrity and class.
Martina McBride *(1966-)*
American singer

In order to be profoundly dishonest, a person must have
one of two qualities – either they are unscrupulously
ambitious, or they are unswervingly egocentric.
Maya Angelou *(1928-)*
American poet, memoirist

That inner voice has both gentleness and clarity. So to get
to authenticity, you really keep going down to the bone,
to the honesty, and the inevitability of something.
Meredith Monk *(1942-)*
American composer

I always like to reveal the fact that the emperor has no clothes.
And children are best at that. They teach us how to see the
world in that sense. They are without artifice; they see it
for what it is. I am drawn to that ruthless honesty.
Mira Nair *(1957-)*
Indian director

Honesty and transparency make you vulnerable.
Be honest and transparent anyway.
Mother Teresa *(1910-1997)*
Albanian Roman Catholic nun

The first and worst of all frauds is to cheat
one's self. All sin is easy after that.
Pearl Bailey *(1918-1990)*
American entertainer

Candor is a compliment; it implies equality. It's how true friends talk.
Peggy Noonan *(1950-)*
American author, columnist

When a contradiction is impossible to resolve except
by a lie, then we know that it is really a door.
Simone Weil *(1909-1943)*
French philosopher

Nobody can boast of honesty till they are tried.
Susannah Centilivre *(1667-1723)*
English poet

Lies are often imbued with transcendent instrumental value by the
individuals and institutions that utter them. Sometimes the lies are self-
serving, of course, but the tendency – or temptation – to lie in service of
justice makes it virtually impossible to condemn all lying categorically.
Wendy Kaminer *(1949-)*
American writer, social critic

Honor

There could be no honor in a sure success, but much
might be wrested from a sure defeat.
Ann Landers *(1918-2002)*
American advice columnist

You have chosen me, from a low estate, to be your queen and your
companion, far beyond my desert or desire. If then, you find me
worthy of such honour, good your Grace, let not any light fancy, or bad
counsel of mine enemies, withdraw your princely favour from me.
Anne Boleyn *(1501-1536)*
English, Queen of England

To mention honor was to suggest its opposite.
Dorothy L. Sayers *(1893-1957)*
English crime writer

Civilization...is a matter of imponderables, of delight in the thins of the
mind, of love, of beauty, of honor, grace, courtesy, delicate feeling.
Edith Hamilton *(1867-1963)*
American educator

Wounded vanity knows when it is mortally hurt and limps off the field, piteous, all disguises thrown away. But pride carries its banner to the last and fast as it is driven from one field unfurls it in another, never admitting that there is a shade less honor in the second field than in the first, or in the third than in the second.
Helen Hunt Jackson *(1830-1885)*
American writer

We would rather starve than sell our national honor.
Indira Gandhi *(1917-1984)*
Indian Prime Minister

It is a full time job being honest one moment at a time, remembering to love, to honor, to respect. It is a practice, a discipline, worthy of every moment.
Jasmine Guy *(1964-)*
American actress

Reputation is what other people know about you, honor is what you know about yourself.
Lois McMaster Bujold *(1949-)*
American author

Would that the simple maxim, that honesty is the best policy, might be laid to heart; that a sense of the true aim of life might elevate the tone of politics and trade till public and private honor become identical.
Margaret Fuller *(1810-1850)*
American journalist, author

A woman of honor should not suspect another of things she would not do herself.
Marguerite de Valois *(1553-1615)*
French, Queen of France, Navarre

We treat our people like royalty. If you honor and serve the people who work for you they will honor and serve you.
Mary Kay Ash *(1918-2001)*
American entrepreneur

Humility

I have been guilty of wrong thinking.
Anne Hutchinson *(1591-1643)*
American religious leader

I never think of myself as an icon. What is in other people's minds is not in my mind. I just do my thing.
Audrey Hepburn *(1929-1993)*
Belgian-born actress

The second sweetest set of three words in English is I don't know.
Carol Tavris *(1944-)*
American social psychologist

In Wales it's brilliant. I go to the pub and see everybody who I went to school with. And everybody goes 'So what you doing now?' And I go, 'Oh, I'm doing a film with Antonio Banderas and Anthony Hopkins.' And they go, 'Ooh, good.' And that's it.
Catherine Zeta-Jones *(1969-)*
Welsh actress

I have often wished I had time to cultivate modesty... But I am too busy thinking about myself.
Edith Sitwell *(1887-1964)*
British poet, critic

I find it's as hard to live down an early triumph as an early indiscretion.
Edna Saint Vincent Millay *(1892-1950)*
American poet, playwright

There are times when there is nothing more humiliating in life than the knowledge of being inferior to one's reputation.
Eleonora Duse *(1858-1924)*
Italian actress

I'm on the patch right now. Where it releases small dosages of approval until I no longer crave it, and then I'm gonna rip it off.
Ellen DeGeneres *(1958-)*
American comedian, television host

I'm not a braggart, but when I was a little girl people used to come from all over Hollywood to hear me sing.
Etta James *(1938-)*
American musician

Humility is no substitute for a good personality.
Fran Lebowitz *(1950-)*
American writer

*No sooner do we think we have assembled a comfortable life
than we find a piece of ourselves that has no place to fit in.*
Gail Sheehy *(1937-)*
American writer, lecturer

*I know I'm only one human being and I'm only making one
tiny contribution and it's nothing more than that.*
Halle Berry *(1969-)*
American actress

Humility is like underwear; essential, but indecent if it shows.
Helen Nielsen *(1919-1992)*
American mystery writer

*If arrogance is the heady wine of youth then
humility must be its eternal hangover.*
Helen Van Slyke *(1919-1979)*
American author

*Nothing is more deceitful than the appearance of humility. It is often
only carelessness of opinion, and sometimes an indirect boast.*
Jane Austen *(1775-1817)*
English novelist

*I feel for eight minutes on screen, I should only get a little bit of
him. [regarding her Oscar for her role as Queen Elizabeth]*
Judi Dench *(1934-)*
English actress

*Being a famous actress may give you a sense of being
important, but believe me, it's just an illusion.*
Juliette Binoche *(1964-)*
French actress

*Humility is not my forte, and whenever I dwell for any length
of time on my own shortcomings, they gradually begin to
seem mild, harmless, rather engaging little things, not at all
like the staring defects in other people's characters.*
Margaret Halsey *(1910-1997)*
American writer

*Our humility rests upon a series of learned behaviors, woven together
into patterns that are infinitely fragile and never directly inherited.*
Margaret Mead *(1901-1978)*
American cultural anthropologist

You can't get spoiled if you do your own ironing.
Meryl Streep *(1949-)*
American actress

The proud person can learn humility, but they will be proud of it.
Mignon McLaughlin *(1913-1983)*
American journalist

*I'm definitely happy with the way my career has gone, the success; but
I even feel glad that I've experienced some failure in my life. That gives
you perspective and humility about this business; it's good to realize that
you're always just one movie away from not being in Vogue anymore.*
Reese Witherspoon *(1976-)*
American actress

*In the intellectual order, the virtue of humility is nothing
more nor less than the power of attention.*
Simone Weil *(1909-1943)*
French philosopher

*I believe that to be with people who are suffering,
whoever they are, makes one humble.*
Sue Ryder *(1923-2000)*
English philanthropist

Humility is the ability to give up your pride and still retain your dignity.
Vanna Bonta *(1958-)*
American novelist, poet

Humor

*Humor brings insight and tolerance. Irony brings a
deeper and less friendly understanding.*
Agnes Repplier *(1855-1950)*
American essayist

*The essence of humor is that it should be unexpected, that it should
embody an element of surprise, that it should startle us out of that
reasonable gravity which, after all, must be our habitual frame of mind.*
Agnes Repplier *(1855-1950)*
American essayist

Keep your sense of humor. There's enough stress in the rest of your life to let bad shots ruin a game you're supposed to enjoy.
Amy Alcott *(1956-)*
American golfer

Nobody says you must laugh, but a sense of humor can help you overlook the unattractive, tolerate the unpleasant, cope with the unexpected, and smile through the day.
Ann Landers *(1918-2002)*
American advice columnist

I have often been downcast, but never in despair; I regard our hiding as a dangerous adventure, romantic and interesting at the same time. In my diary I treat all the privations as amusing. I have made up my mind now to lead a different life from other girls and, later on, different from ordinary housewives. My start has been so very full of interest, and that is the sole reason why I have to laugh at the humorous side of the most dangerous moments.
Anne Frank *(1929-1945)*
German writer, holocaust victim

I realize that humor isn't for everyone. It's only for people who want to have fun, enjoy life, and feel alive.
Anne Wilson Schaef *(1947-)*
American psychotherapist

I love people who make me laugh. I honestly think it's the thing I like most, to laugh. It cures a multitude of ills. It's probably the most important thing in a person.
Audrey Hepburn *(1929-1993)*
Belgian-born actress

A good laugh makes any interview or any conversation so much better.
Barbara Walters *(1929-)*
American broadcast journalist, author

Happiness for the average person may be said to flow largely from common sense – adapting one-self to circumstances – and a sense of humor.
Beatrice Lillie *(1894-1989)*
British actress

If someone makes me laugh, I'm their slave for life.
Bette Midler *(1945-)*
American actress

I think we're losing our sense of humor instead of being able to relax and laugh at ourselves. I don't care whether it's ethnicity, age, sexual orientation, or whose ox is being gored.
Betty White *(1922-)*
American actress, comedian

Total absence of humor renders life impossible.
Colette *(1873-1954)*
French novelist

Humor has been a fashioning instrument in America, cleaving its way through the national life, holding tenaciously to the spread elements of that life. Its mode has often been swift and coarse and ruthless, beyond art and beyond established civilization.
Constance Rourke *(1885-1941)*
American author, educator

A lot of my humor does come from anger. It's like, you're not gonna pull one over on me – which is pretty much my motto anyway.
Courteney Cox *(1964-)*
American actress

Laughter is by definition healthy.
Doris Lessing *(1919-)*
Persian-born British writer

I had thought, on starting this composition, that I should define what humor means to me. However, every time I tried to, I had to go and lie down with a cold wet cloth on my head.
Dorothy Parker *(1893-1967)*
American writer, satirist

There's a hell of a distance between wisecracking and wit. Wit has truth in it; wisecracking is simply calisthenics with words.
Dorothy Parker *(1893-1967)*
American writer, satirist

Good humor like the jaundice makes every one of its own complexion.
Elizabeth Inchbald *(1784-1810)*
British dramatist

Humor is an antidote to isolation.
Elizabeth Janeway *(1913-2005)*
American author, critic

Laugh and the world laughs with you; Weep, and you weep alone.
Ella Wheeler Wilcox *(1850-1919)*
American poet

The first person I learned I could make happy with laughter was my mother, whom I idolize. It was a powerful thing to realize. I knew I had found my life's work.
Ellen DeGeneres *(1958-)*
American comedian, television host

Don't try for wit. Settle for humor. You'll last longer.
Elsa Maxwell *(1883-1963)*
American gossip columnist

Humor is a spontaneous, wonderful bit of an outburst that just comes. It's unbridled, its unplanned, it's full of surprises.
Erma Bombeck *(1927-1966)*
American writer, humorist

Laughter rises out of tragedy; when you need it the most, it rewards you for your courage.
Erma Bombeck *(1927-1966)*
American writer, humorist

When humor goes, there goes civilization.
Erma Bombeck *(1927-1966)*
American writer, humorist

There's nothing like a gleam of humor to reassure you that a fellow human being is ticking inside a strange face.
Eva Hoffman *(1945-)*
Polish writer, academic

Delicate humor is the crowning virtue of the saints.
Evelyn Underhill *(1875-1941)*
English writer

A difference of taste in jokes is a great strain on the affections.
George Eliot *(1819-1880)*
English novelist

I haven't lost my sense of humour or my tolerance of dreadful behaviour.
Germaine Greer *(1939-)*
Australian-born writer

It is a difficult thing to like anybody else's ideas of being funny.
Gertrude Stein *(1874-1946)*
American writer

You feel completely in control when you hear a wave of laughter coming back at you that you have caused.
Gilda Radner *(1946-1989)*
American comedian

It's dreadful when two people's senses of humor are antagonistic. I don't believe there's any bridging that gulf!
Jean Webster *(1876-1917)*
American writer

If you could choose one characteristic that would get you through life, choose a sense of humor.
Jennifer Jones *(1919-)*
American actress

A taste for irony has kept more hearts from breaking than a sense of humor, for it takes irony to appreciate the joke which is on oneself.
Jessamyn West *(1902-1984)*
American writer

Show me a person who doesn't like to laugh and I'll show you a person with a toe tag.
Julia Roberts *(1967-)*
American actress

Life can be wildly tragic at times, and I've had my share. But whatever happens to you, you have to keep a slightly comic attitude. In the final analysis, you have got to not forget to laugh.
Katharine Hepburn *(1907-2003)*
American actress

It is of immense importance to learn to laugh at ourselves.
Katherine Mansfield *(1888 - 1923)*
New Zealand-born writer

Humor has been the balm of my life, but it's been reserved for those close to me, not part of the public Lana.
Lana Turner *(1920-1995)*
American actress

Humor tells me where the trouble is.
Louise Bernikow *(1940-)*
American writer

Wit consists in seeing the resemblance between things which differ, and the difference between things which are alike.
Madame de Stael *(1766-1817)*
French writer

I now know all the people worth knowing in America, and I find no intellect comparable to my own.
Margaret Fuller *(1810-1850)*
American journalist, author

The announcement that you are going to tell a good story (and the chuckle that precedes it) is always a dangerous opening.
Margot Asquith *(1864-1945)*
Anglo-Scottish socialite

A sense of humor is a major defense against minor troubles.
Mignon McLaughlin *(1913-1983)*
American journalist

Perhaps one has to be very old before one learns to be amused rather than shocked.
Pearl S. Buck *(1892-1973)*
American writer

Wit penetrates; humor envelops. Wit is a function of verbal intelligence; humor is imagination operating on good nature.
Peggy Noonan *(1950-)*
American author, columnist

I love humor. I always will fall back on humor. That's something I think you can't ever get enough of and, if it's done well, it's great. When it's bad, it's horrible.
Sandra Bullock *(1964-)*
American actress

The ability to laugh at life is right at the top, with love and communication, in the hierarchy of our needs. Humour has much to do with pain; it exaggerates the anxieties and absurdities we feel, so that we gain distance and through laughter, relief.
Sara Davidson *(1943-)*
American author

One loses so many laughs by not laughing at oneself.
Sara Jeannette Duncan *(1861-1922)*
Canadian journalist

Blessed are they who have learned to laugh at themselves
for they shall never cease to be entertained.
Shirley MacLaine *(1934-)*
American actress

Total absence of humor renders life impossible.
Sidonie-Gabrielle Colette *(1873-1954)*
French novelist

It is often a sign of wit not to show it, and not to see that others want it.
Suzanne Necker *(1739-1794)*
French patroness

Whatever you have read I have said is almost certainly untrue,
except if it is funny, in which case I definitely said it.
Tallulah Bankhead *(1902-1968)*
American actress

I learned very early that an audience would relax and look at things
differently if they felt they could laugh with you from time to time. There's
an energy that comes through the release of tension that is laughter.
Twyla Tharp *(1941-)*
American dancer

Humor is the first of the gifts to perish in a foreign tongue.
Virginia Woolf *(1882-1941)*
English author

Ideas

Ideas are like pizza dough, made to be tossed around.
Anna Quindlen *(1952-)*
American journalist

There are no new ideas. There are only new ways of making them felt.
Audre Lorde *(1934-1992)*
Caribbean-American writer

Paris is always a good idea.
Audrey Hepburn *(1929-1993)*
Belgian-born actress

Beware of people carrying ideas. Beware of ideas carrying people.
Barbara Grizzuti Harrison *(1934-2002)*
American journalist, essayist

There are no original ideas. There are only original people.
Barbara Grizzuti Harrison *(1934-2002)*
American journalist, essayist

We live in an epoch in which the solid ground of our
preconceived ideas shakes daily under our certain feet.
Barbara Ward *(1914-1981)*
British economist, writer

You can imprison a person, but not an idea. You can exile a person,
but not an idea. You can kill a person, but not an idea.
Benazir Bhutto *(1953-2007)*
Pakistani Prime Minister

They think they can make fuel from horse manure – Now,
I don't know if your car will be able to get 30 miles to the
gallon, but it's sure gonna put a stop to siphoning.
Billie Holiday *(1915-1959)*
American jazz singer

These people who are always briskly doing something and
as busy as waltzing mice, they have little, sharp, staccato
ideas, such as: I see where I can make an annual cut of $3.47
in my meat budget. But they have no slow, big ideas.
Brenda Ueland *(1891-1985)*
American journalist

My mother...taught me about the power of inspiration and courage, and
she did it with a strength and a passion that I wish could be bottled.
Carly Fiorina *(1954-)*
American, Former HP CEO

Ideas move rapidly when their time comes.
Carolyn Heilbrun *(1926-2003)*
American academic, author

Night time is really the best time to work. All the ideas are there to be yours because everyone else is asleep.
Catherine O'Hara *(1954-)*
Canadian-American actress

Our world has changed over the years because new ideas were acted upon. People may not have had all the answers, but as they began to take action, the answers became clear!
Catherine Pulsifer *(1957-)*
American glass artist, author

Fashion is not something that exists in dresses only. Fashion is in the sky, in the street, fashion has to do with ideas, the way we live, what is happening.
Coco Chanel *(1883-1971)*
French fashion designer

I'm not afraid of facts, I welcome facts but a congeries of facts is not equivalent to an idea. This is the essential fallacy of the so-called scientific mind. People who mistake facts for ideas are incomplete thinkers; they are gossips.
Cynthia Ozick *(1929-)*
American novelist

There are well-dressed foolish ideas just as there are well-dressed fools.
Diane Ackerman *(1948-)*
American poet, author, naturalist

The Wright brothers flew through the smoke screen of impossibility.
Dorothea Brande *(1893-1948)*
American writer, editor

You need to be open to improvisation, you need to appreciate serendipity.
Drew Gilpin Faust *(1947-)*
American, first woman president, Harvard

The air of ideas is the only air worth breathing.
Edith Wharton *(1862-1937)*
American novelist

Great minds discuss ideas; Average minds discuss events; Small minds discuss people.
Eleanor Roosevelt *(1884 - 1962)*
American First Lady

If a theme or idea is too near the surface, the novel
becomes simply a tract illustrating an idea.
Elizabeth Bowen *(1899-1973)*
Irish novelist

No idea is so antiquated that it was not once modern. No idea
is so modern that it will not someday be antiquated.
Ellen Glasgow *(1873-1945)*
American novelist

I've dreamt in my life dreams that have stayed with me ever after,
and changed my ideas: they've gone through and through me,
like wine through water, and altered the colour of my mind.
Emily Brontë *(1818-1848)*
English author

One must marry one's feelings to one's beliefs and ideas. That is
probably the only way to achieve a measure of harmony in one's life.
Esther Etty Hillesum *(1914-1943)*
Netherlands, Jewish prisoner at Auschwitz

Great people talk about ideas, average people talk about
things, and small people talk about wine.
Fran Lebowitz *(1950-   )*
American writer

I said to myself, I have things in my head that are not like what anyone
has taught me – shapes and ideas so near to me – so natural to my
way of being and thinking that it hasn't occurred to me to put them
down. I decided to start anew, to strip away what I had been taught.
Georgia O'Keeffe *(1887-1986)*
American artist

Tyranny cannot defeat the power of ideas.
Helen Keller *(1880-1968)*
American author, educator

I had never been as resigned to ready-made ideas as I was to ready-
made clothes; perhaps because, although I couldn't sew, I could think.
Jane Rule *(1931-2007)*
Canadian writer

Being an intellectual creates a lot of questions and no answers. You can fill your life up with ideas and still go home lonely. All you really have that really matters are feelings. That's what music is to me.
Janis Joplin *(1943-1970)*
American singer

I think it would be very foolish not to take the irrational seriously.
Jeanette Winterson *(1959-)*
British novelist

People who think in absolutes usually don't listen to anyone but themselves. They resist new ideas and try to preserve the status quo... People who think they know usually stopped thinking long ago.
Jennifer James *(1977-)*
English actress

Nothing dies harder than a bad idea.
Julia Cameron *(1948-)*
American teacher, author

The clash of ideas is the sound of freedom.
Lady Bird Johnson *(1912-2007)*
American First Lady

The toughest question has always been, How do you get your ideas? How do you answer that? It's like asking runners how they run, or singers how they sing. They just do it!
Lynn Johnston *(1947-)*
Canadian cartoonist

I have always fought for ideas – until I learned that it isn't ideas but grief, struggle, and flashes of vision which enlighten.
Margaret Anderson *(1886-1973)*
American publisher

If you have one good idea, people will lend you twenty.
Marie von Ebner-Eschenbach *(1830-1916)*
Austrian writer

A good idea will keep you awake during the morning, but a great idea will keep you awake during the night.
Marilyn vos Savant *(1946-)*
American writer

When you stop having dreams and ideas – well,
you might as well stop altogether.
Marian Anderson *(1897-1993)*
American singer

A mediocre idea that generates enthusiasm will go
further than a great idea that inspires no one.
Mary Kay Ash *(1918-2001)*
American entrepreneur

General notions are generally wrong.
Mary Wortley Montagu *(1689-1762)*
British author, poet

No matter how brilliantly an idea is stated, we will not really be
moved unless we have already half-thought of it ourselves.
Mignon McLaughlin *(1913-1983)*
American journalist

We are governed not by armies but by ideas.
Mona Caird *(1854-1932)*
Scottish novelist, essayist

If we keep an open mind, too much is likely to fall into it.
Natalie Clifford Barney *(1876-1972)*
French writer

Never, never rest contented with any circle of ideas, but
always be certain that a wider one is still possible.
Pearl Bailey *(1918-1990)*
American entertainer

It's very good for an idea to be commonplace. The important thing is that a
new idea should develop out of what is already there so that it soon becomes
an old acquaintance. Old acquaintances aren't by any means always
welcome, but at least one can't be mistaken as to who or what they are.
Penelope Fitzgerald *(1916-2000)*
English novelist

After years of telling corporate citizens to trust the system,
many companies must relearn instead to trust their people – and
encourage their people to use neglected creative capacities in order
to tap the most potent economic stimulus of all: idea power.
Rosabeth Moss Kanter *(1943-)*
American academic, author

*You don't make progress by standing on the sidelines, whimpering
and complaining. You make progress by implementing ideas.*
Shirley Chisholm *(1924-2005)*
American politician

Inspiration always arrives unannounced.
Vanna Bonta *(1958-)*
American novelist, poet

Ridicule has historically proven itself a rickety fence for great ideas.
Vanna Bonta *(1958-)*
American novelist, poet

*I like going from one lighted room to another,
such is my brain to me; lighted rooms.*
Virginia Woolf *(1882-1941)*
English author

Imagination

As soon as we left the ground, I knew I had to fly.
Amelia Earhart *(1897-1937)*
American aviator

Memory feeds imagination.
Amy Tan *(1952-)*
American writer (Chinese descent)

*Appealing workplaces are to be avoided. One wants a room with
no view, so imagination can meet memory in the dark.*
Annie Dillard *(1945-)*
American author

*It could be that our faithlessness is a cowering cowardice born of our very
smallness, a massive failure of imagination... If we were to judge nature
by common sense or likelihood, we wouldn't believe the world existed.*
Annie Dillard *(1945-)*
American author

*Kindness and intelligence don't always deliver us from the pitfalls
and traps: there are always failures of love, of will, of imagination.
There is no way to take the danger out of human relationships.*
Barbara Grizzuti Harrison *(1934-2002)*
American journalist, essayist

The imagination needs moodling – long, inefficient,
happy idling, dawdling, and puttering.
Brenda Ueland *(1891-1985)*
American journalist

Death? Why this fuss about death? Use your imagination, try to visualize
a world without death! Death is the essential condition of life, not an evil.
Charlotte Perkins Gilman *(1860-1935)*
American sociologist, novelist

Dreaming is not enough. You have to go a step further and use
your imagination to visualize, with intent! Forget everything
you've ever been taught, and believe it will happen, just as you
imagined it. That is the secret. That is the mystery of life.
Christine Anderson *(1983-)*
American musician

In order to be irreplaceable one must always be different.
Coco Chanel *(1883-1971)*
French fashion designer

Imagination, like memory, can transform lies to truths.
Cristina Garcia *(1958-)*
Cuban-born journalist

To imagine the unimaginable is the highest use of the imagination.
Cynthia Ozick *(1929-)*
American novelist

There are moments when a person's imagination so easily
subdued to what it lives in, suddenly rises above its daily
level and surveys the long windings of destiny.
Edith Wharton *(1862-1937)*
American novelist

Imagination, industry, and intelligence – the three I's – are all indispensable
to the actress, but of these three the greatest is, without doubt, imagination.
Ellen Terry *(1847-1928)*
English Shakespearean actress

The Possible's slow fuse is lit by the Imagination.
Emily Dickinson *(1830-1886)*
American poet

Imagination took the reins, and Reason, slow-paced, though surefooted, was unequal to a race with so eccentric and flighty a companion.
Fanny Burney *(1752-1840)*
English novelist, diarist

Only in your imagination can you revise.
Fay Wray *(1907-2004)*
American actress

This is a great moment, when you see, however distant, the goal of your wandering. The thing which has been living in your imagination suddenly become part of the tangible world. It matters not how many ranges, rivers or parching dusty ways may lie between you; it is yours now forever.
Freya Stark *(1893-1993)*
French-born travel writer, explorer

Without imagination nothing is dangerous.
Georgette Leblanc *(1875-1941)*
French operatic soprano

The curse of human nature is imagination. When a long anticipated moment comes, we always find it pitched a note too low.
Gertrude Atherton *(1857-1948)*
American writer

Without leaps of imagination, or dreaming, we lose the excitement of possibilities. Dreaming, after all, is a form of planning.
Gloria Steinem *(1934-)*
American activist, writer, publisher

Imagination frames events unknown. In wild fantastic shapes of hideous ruin. And what it fears creates.
Hannah More *(1745-1833)*
English writer, philanthropist

It is our imagination that transforms itself into reality, through our physical strength and endeavours.
Helen Araromi *(1987-)*
Nigerian musician

Imagination has always had powers of resurrection that no science can match.
Ingrid Benqis *(1944-)*
American essayist

*What wild imaginations one forms where dear self
is concerned! How sure to be mistaken!*
Jane Austen *(1775-1817)*
British novelist

*The key to life is imagination. If you don't have that, no
matter what you have, it's meaningless. If you do have
imagination... you can make a feast of straw.*
Jane Stanton Hitchcock *(1946-)*
American author

*They say every snowflake is different. If that were true, how
could the world go on? How could we ever get up off our knees?
How could we ever recover from the wonder of it?*
Jeanette Winterson *(1959-)*
British novelist

*We cast away priceless time in dreams, born of imagination,
fed upon illusion, and put to death by reality.*
Judy Garland *(1922-1969)*
American actress, singer

Imagination is the highest kite one can fly.
Lauren Bacall *(1924-)*
American actress

*To believe in something not yet proved and to underwrite it with
our lives: it is the only way we can leave the future open. People,
surrounded by facts, permitting themselves no surmise, no
intuitive flash, no great hypothesis, no risk, are in a locked cell.
Ignorance cannot seal the mind and imagination more surely.*
Lillian Smith *(1729-1796)*
American author

Sometimes I feel like a figment of my own imagination.
Lily Tomlin *(1939-)*
American actress, comedian

*There are so many unpleasant things in the world already
that there is no use in imagining any more.*
Lucy Maud Montgomery *(1874-1942)*
Canadian writer

Imagination is much harder to face than reality.
Mabel Seeley *(1903-1991)*
American mystery writer

*An opera begins long before the curtain goes up and ends long after
it has come down. It starts in my imagination, it becomes my life,
and it stays part of my life long after I've left the opera house.*
Maria Callas *(1923-1977)*
American-born Greek soprano

We especially need imagination in science.
Maria Mitchell *(1818-1889)*
American scientist

*We especially need imagination in science. It is not all mathematics,
nor all logic, but it is somewhat beauty and poetry.*
Maria Montessori *(1870-1952)*
Italian educator

Without imagination, there is no goodness, no wisdom.
Marie von Ebner-Eschenbach *(1830-1916)*
Austrian writer

*We all use our imagination every day. However, most of
us are unaware that what we envision affects every cell of
our bodies and every aspect of our performance.*
Marilyn King *(1949-)*
American Olympic athlete

*When you stop having dreams and ideals – well,
you might as well stop altogether.*
Marion Anderson *(1902-1993)*
American singer

*It would be a bitter cosmic joke if we destroy ourselves
due to atrophy of the imagination.*
Martha Gellhorn *(1908-1998)*
American journalist

*I believe in imagination. I did Kramer vs. Kramer before I had
children. But the mother I would be was already inside me.*
Meryl Streep *(1949-)*
American actress

Censorship is never over for those who have experienced it. It is a brand on the imagination that affects the individual who has suffered it, forever.

Nadine Gordimer *(1923-)*
South African novelist, activist

Imagination is new reality in the process of being created. It represents the part of the existing order that can still grow.

Nancy Hale *(1908-1989)*
American writer

Even the wildest dreams have to start somewhere. Allow yourself the time and space to let your mind wander and your imagination fly.

Oprah Winfrey *(1954-)*
American media mogul

With our progress we have destroyed our only weapon against tedium: that rare weakness we call imagination.

Oriana Fallaci *(1929-2006)*
Italian journalist, writer

Imagination must be visited constantly, or else it begins to become restless and emit strange bellows at embarrassing moments; ignoring it only makes it grow larger and noisier.

Patricia McKillip *(1948-)*
American author science fiction, fantasy

Inside myself is a place where I live all alone and that's where you renew your springs that never dry up.

Pearl S. Buck *(1892-1973)*
American writer

You have to imagine it possible before you can see something. You can have the evidence right in front of you, but if you can't imagine something that has never existed before, it's impossible.

Rita Dove *(1952-)*
American poet

If you believe, then you hang on. If you believe, it means you've got imagination, you don't need stuff thrown out for you in a blueprint, you don't face facts – what can stop you. If I don't make it today, I'll come in tomorrow.

Ruth Gordon *(1896-1985)*
American actress, writer

222

The faculty of imagination is both the rudder and the bridle of the senses.
Simone de Beauvoir *(1908-1986)*
French writer, philosopher

Imagination and fiction make up more than three quarters of our real life.
Simone Weil *(1909-1943)*
French philosopher

Many who have had an opportunity of knowing any more about mathematics confuse it with arithmetic, and consider it an arid science. In reality, however, it is a science which requires a great amount of imagination.
Sofia Kovalevskaya *(1850-1891)*
Russian mathematician

So long as we think dugout canoes are the only possibility – all that is real or can be real – we will never see the ship, we will never feel the free wind blow.
Sonia Johnson *(1936-)*
American activist, writer

You see, my good friend, how much we are the creatures of situation and circumstance, and with what pliant servility the mind resigns itself to the impressions of the senses, or the illusions of the imagination.
Sydney Morgan *(1776-1859)*
Irish novelist

Everything in life is writable about if you have the outgoing guts to do it and the imagination to improvise.
Sylvia Plath *(1932-1963)*
American writer

My imagination makes me human and makes me a fool; it gives me all the world and exiles me from it.
Ursula K. LeGuin *(1929-)*
American novelist

I used my imagination to make the grass whatever color I wanted it to be.
Whoopi Goldberg *(1955-)*
American actress, comedian

Innovation

*I don't think necessity is the mother of invention. Invention,
in my opinion, arises directly from idleness, possibly
also from laziness – to save oneself trouble.*
Agatha Christie *(1890-1976)*
English detective novelist

Innovation! One cannot be forever innovating. I want to create classics.
Coco Chanel *(1883-1971)*
French fashion designer

*I'm really an experimentalist. I used to say, I think with my hands. I just like
manipulation. I began to like it as a child and it's continued to be a pleasure.*
Dorothy Hodgkin *(1910-1994)*
British chemist

*Look to the past to help create the future. Look to science and
to poetry. Combine innovation and interpretation. We need the
best of both. And it is universities that best provide them.*
Drew Gilpin Faust *(1947-)*
American, first woman president, Harvard

Innovators are inevitably controversial.
Eva Le Gallienne *(1899-1991)*
English-American actress, director

*At first people refuse to believe that a strange new thing can be done,
then they hope it can be done, then they see it can be done – then it is
done and the whole world wonders why it was not done centuries ago.*
Frances Hodgson Burnett *(1849-1924)*
English playwright, author

*Imagination is not only the uniquely human capacity to envision
that which is not, and therefore the fount of all invention and
innovation. In its arguably most transformative and revelatory
capacity, it is the power that enables us to empathize with
humans whose experiences we have never shared.*
J. K. Rowling *(1965-)*
English writer

Innovation, creativity, and enthusiasm are all linked. When you walk into a warehouse and the manager can't wait to show you what the staff has accomplished, you can feel the enthusiasm, excitement, and pride. When that energy doesn't exist, there probably isn't much innovation or creativity going on.
Judith Anderson *(1897-1992)*
Australian-born actress

I don't know what your story will be, but if you don't find a way to talk about innovation, it's distinct or extinct.
Julie Andrews *(1935-)*
British film, stage actress

It would be a terrific innovation if you could get your mind to stretch a little further than the next wisecrack.
Katharine Hepburn *(1907-2003)*
American actress

I think all great innovations are built on rejections.
Louise Nevelson *(1899-1988)*
American sculptor, painter

Innovation is fostered by information gathered from new connections; from insights gained by journeys into other disciplines or places; from active, collegial networks and fluid, open boundaries. Innovation arises from ongoing circles of exchange, where information is not just accumulated or stored, but created. Knowledge is generated anew from connections that weren't there before.
Margaret J. Wheatley *(1934-)*
American organization expert

Mindless habitual behavior is the enemy of innovation.
Rosabeth Moss Kanter *(1943-)*
American academic, author

We have a desire to do things at scale, and by scale we mean the kinds of things that can touch not just millions, but hundreds of millions of people, and an approach that combines real innovation, technically and otherwise.
Sheryl Sandberg *(1969-)*
American, Google VP of Sales

It is human nature to instinctively rebel at obscurity or ordinariness.
Taylor Caldwell *(1900-1985)*
American author

Integrity

The true measure of a person is how they treat someone
who can do them absolutely no good.
Ann Landers *(1918-2002)*
American advice columnist

Morality is judgment to distinguish right and wrong, vision
to see the truth, courage to act upon it, dedication to that
which is good, and integrity to stand by it at any price.
Ayn Rand *(1905-1982)*
Russian-American novelist

In all things preserve integrity.
Barbara Babe Paley *(1915-1978)*
American socialite

The imperative is to define what is right and do it.
Barbara Jordan *(1936-1996)*
American politician

A guilty conscience is the mother of invention.
Carolyn Wells *(1862-1942)*
American author, poet

I am most proud of my integrity and least proud of my cynicism.
Chloe Sevigny *(1974-)*
American actress

My virtue's still far too small, I don't trot it out and about yet.
Colette *(1873-1954)*
French novelist

There is...nothing greater than touching the shore after crossing some great
body of water knowing that I've done it with my own two arms and legs.
Diana Nyad *(1949-)*
American distance swimmer

Do what you feel in your heart to be right – for you'll be criticized
anyway. You'll be damned if you do, and damned if you don't.
Eleanor Roosevelt *(1884-1962)*
American First Lady

Values are not trendy items that are casually traded in.
Ellen Goodman *(1950-)*
American journalist

*What I believe is a process rather than a finality. Finalities are
for gods and governments, not for the human intellect.*
Emma Goldman *(1869-1940)*
Russian-born, American activist

*Integrity can be neither lost nor concealed nor faked nor quenched nor
artificially come by nor outlived, nor, I believe, in the long run denied.*
Eudora Welty *(1909-2001)*
American writer

If you don't stand for something, you will stand for anything.
Ginger Rogers *(1911-1995)*
American actress, dancer

*Brains, integrity, and force may be all very well, but what you
need today is Charm. Go ahead and work on your economic
programs if you want to, I'll develop my radio personality.*
Gracie Allen *(1906-1964)*
American actress, comedian

*The hypocrite's crime is that they bear false witness against themself.
What makes it so plausible to assume that hypocrisy is the vice of
vices is that integrity can indeed exist under the cover of all other vices
except this one. ...only the hypocrite is really rotten to the core.*
Hannah Arendt *(1906-1975)*
German philosopher

*Probably my worst quality is that I get very
passionate about what I think is right.*
Hillary Rodham Clinton *(1947-)*
American, Secretary of State

*Our intent is not to just beat our chests and try to take credit for what
we're doing ... we're just quietly doing it because it's the right thing to do.*
Irene Rosenfeld *(1953-)*
American, CEO Kraft Foods

*It is as easy for most of us to keep from stealing our dinners
as it is to digest them, and there is quite as much voluntary
morality involved in one process as the other.*
Jane Addams *(1860-1935)*
American activist

*The most important thing is to actually think about what you do. To
become aware and actually think about the effect of what you do on the
environment and on society. That's key, and that underlies everything else.*
Jane Goodall *(1934-)*
English, chimpanzee researcher

*If somebody thinks I have an integrity problem, then the honest
thing to do is to tell me what they think it is and let me address it.*
Janet Reno *(1938-)*
American Attorney General

We can love an honest rogue, but what is more offensive than a false saint?
Jessamyn West *(1902-1984)*
American writer

I want to be inspiring to myself, to my kids, my family, and my friends.
Jodie Foster *(1962-)*
American actress

*There is only one history of any importance and it is the history of what
you once believed in and the history of what you came to believe in.*
Kay Boyle *(1902-1992)*
American writer, activist

*The reward for doing right is mostly an internal phenomenon:
self-respect, dignity, integrity, and self-esteem.*
Laura Schlessinger *(1947-)*
American talk radio host

I cannot and will not cut my conscience to fit this year's fashions.
Lillian Hellman *(1905-1984)*
American playwright

*I do not hold with those who think it is all right to do whatever you
want so long as it doesn't hurt anyone. Who's to be the judge of that?*
Loretta Young *(1913-2000)*
American actress

It's so easy to be wicked without knowing it, isn't it?
Lucy Maud Montgomery *(1874-1942)*
Canadian writer

The voice of conscience is so delicate that it is easy to stifle it;
but it is also so clear that it is impossible to mistake it.
Madame de Stael *(1766-1817)*
French writer

Virtue has its own reward, but has no sale at the box office.
Mae West *(1892-1980)*
American actress

Conscience as I understand it is the impulse to do the right thing
because it is right regardless of personal ends and has nothing whatever
to do with the ability to distinguish between right and wrong.
Margaret Collier Graham *(1850-1910)*
American writer

There isn't any virtue where there has never been any
temptation. Virtue is just temptation, overcome.
Margaret Deland *(1857-1945)*
American short story writer

When I'm not doing something that comes deeply from me, I get bored.
When I get bored I get distracted and when I get distracted, I become
depressed. It's a natural resistance, and it insures your integrity.
Maria Irene Fornes *(1930-)*
Cuban-American playright

We must Think what we Say, and Mean what we Profess.
Mary Astell *(1666-1731)*
English writer

Is it really so difficult to tell a good action from a bad one? I think one
usually knows right away or a moment afterward, in a horrid flash of regret.
Mary McCarthy *(1912-1989)*
American writer

Real integrity is doing the right thing, knowing that
nobody's going to know whether you did it or not.
Oprah Winfrey *(1954-)*
American media mogul

You cannot make yourself feel something you do not feel, but you can make yourself do right in spite of your feelings.
Pearl S. Buck *(1892-1973)*
American writer

It is queer how it is always one's virtues and not one's vices that precipitate one into disaster.
Rebecca West *(1892-1983)*
Irish-born, British writer

No one ever confides a secret to one person only. No one destroys all copies of a document.
Renata Adler *(1938-)*
American journalist, critic

That disturbs people when they know they didn't have the guts or integrity to stick to their dreams.
Sandra Bernhard *(1955-)*
American actress

There's a lot of integrity with musicians; you really still aspire to grow, and be great, to be the best version of yourself you can be.
Sheryl Crow *(1962-)*
American musician

If you come back from the dead, you don't have the same value system, I think.
Sigourney Weaver *(1949-)*
American actress

I ran the wrong kind of business, but I did it with integrity.
Sydney Biddle Barrows *(1952-)*
American businesswoman, aka Mayflower Madam

Integrity is so perishable in the summer months of success.
Vanessa Redgrave *(1937-)*
English actress

Intelligence

*I've always felt that a person's intelligence is directly
reflected by the number of conflicting points of view they
can entertain simultaneously on the same topic.*
Abigail Adams *(1744-1818)*
American First Lady

*We owe most of our great inventions and most of the achievements
of genius to idleness – either enforced or voluntary.*
Agatha Christie *(1890-1976)*
English detective novelist

*One has a greater sense of intellectual degradation after an
interview with a doctor than from any human experience.*
Alice James *(1848-1892)*
American diarist

I am never afraid of what I know.
Anna Sewell *(1820-1878)*
English novelist

True genius doesn't fulfill expectations, it shatters them.
Arlene Croce *(1934-)*
American journalist

A great many people think that polysyllables are a sign of intelligence.
Barbara Walters *(1929-)*
American broadcast journalist

*I have two brain cells left, and one of them is
busy reminding me to buy toilet paper.*
Diana Gabaldon *(1952-)*
American author

It is quite hard at times to distinguish a genius from a lunatic.
Dorothy Thompson *(1893-1961)*
American journalist

Since when was genius found respectable?
Elizabeth Barrett Browning *(1806-1861)*
English poet

*We use 10 percent of our brains. Imagine how much we
could accomplish if we used the other 60 percent.*
Ellen DeGeneres *(1958-)*
American comedian, television host

*Scheherazade is the classical example of a
woman saving her head by using it.*
Esme Wynne-Tyson *(1898-1972)*
English actress

You may lead an ass to knowledge but you cannot make them think.
Ethel Watts Mumford *(1876-1940)*
American author

*It takes a clever person to turn cynic and a wise
person to be clever enough not to.*
Fannie Hurst *(1889-1968)*
American novelist

I think the reason I am important is that I know everything.
Gertrude Stein *(1874-1946)*
American writer

To think and to be fully alive are the same.
Hannah Arendt *(1906-1975)*
German philosopher

*Although intelligence tests are usually speed tests for the
sake of convenience, it is debatable whether speed has any
rightful place in the basic concept of intelligence.*
Isabel Briggs Myers *(1897-1980)*
American psychological theorist

*I feel like a baited bull and look a wreck, and as for my unfortunate
brain well I saw it neatly described yesterday on an automatic
thing in the tube: This machine is EMPTY till further notice.*
Jean Rhys *(1890-1979)*
British novelist

Genius is an infinite capacity for taking life by the scruff of the neck.
Katharine Hepburn *(1907-2003)*
American actress

Teflon brain – nothing sticks.
Lily Tomlin *(1939-)*
American actress, comedian

*I happen to think that the degree of a person's intelligence
is directly reflected by the number of conflicting attitudes
they can bring to bear on the same topic.*
Lisa Alther *(1944-)*
American author

Stupidity always accompanies evil. Or evil, stupidity.
Louise Bogan *(1897-1970)*
American critic, poet

For precocity some great price is always demanded sooner or later in life.
Margaret Fuller *(1810-1850)*
American journalist, author

*One sees intelligence far more than one hears it. People
do not always say transcendental things but if they are
capable of saying them it is always visible.*
Marie Leneru *(1875-1918)*
French diarist, playwright

*Making mental connections is our most crucial learning
tool, the essence of human intelligence: to forge links; to go
beyond the given; to see patterns, relationship, context.*
Marilyn Ferguson *(1938-2008)*
American author

*In our society those who are in reality superior in intelligence can
be accepted by their fellows only if they pretend they are not.*
Marya Mannes *(1904-1990)*
American author, critic

*The sign of intelligent people is their ability to control
emotions by the application of reason.*
Marya Mannes *(1904-1990)*
American author, critic

*Being a Southern person and a blonde, it's not a good combination.
Immediately, when people meet you, they think of you as not being smart.*
Reese Witherspoon *(1976-)*
American actress

Intelligence is really a kind of taste: taste in ideas.
Susan Sontag *(1933-2004)*
American activist, writer

*The art of leadership is one which the wicked, as a
rule, learn more quickly than the virtuous.*
Agnes E. Meyer *(1933-)*
American journalist

The clear sighted do not rule the world, but they sustain and console it.
Agnes Repplier *(1855-1950)*
American essayist

Leadership

*I need to be able to look at myself in the mirror and know that tough
decisions are made with a balance of commercial considerations and
those arising from a deep inner faith. If you can't say this out loud,
I believe you are missing an important element of leadership.*
Ann Iverson *(1944-)*
American-born, British-based executive

*I'm really glad that our young people missed the Depression, and missed
the great big war. But I do regret that they missed the leaders that I knew.
Leaders who told us when things were tough, and that we would have to
sacrifice, and these difficulties might last awhile. They didn't tell us things
were hard for us because we were different, or isolated, or special interests.
They brought us together and they gave us a sense of national purpose.*
Ann Richards *(1933-2006)*
American politician

Leadership comes in small acts as well as bold strokes.
Carly Fiorina *(1954-)*
American, Former HP CEO

If you can't be a good example, at least you can be a horrible warning.
Catherine Aird *(1930-)*
English writer, crime fiction

*In my position you have to read when you want to
write and to talk when you would like to read.*
Catherine the Great *(1729-1796)*
Russian royalty

People learn to lead because they care about something.
Charlotte Bunch *(1944-)*
American author, activist

In the final analysis there is no other solution to a person's progress but the day's honest work, the day's honest decision, the day's generous utterances, and the day's good deed.
Clare Boothe Luce *(1903 - 1987)*
American playwright, diplomat

It's okay to be the first. If you constantly look for role models like you, then there won't be any firsts.
Condoleezza Rice *(1954-)*
American, Secretary of State

Ninety percent of leadership is the ability to communicate something people want.
Dianne Feinstein *(1933-)*
American politician

If your actions create a legacy that inspires others to dream more, learn more, do more, and become more, then you are an excellent leader.
Dolly Parton *(1946-)*
American singer-songwriter

That is what leadership is all about: staking your ground ahead of where opinion is and convincing people, not simply following the popular opinion of the moment.
Doris Kearns Goodwin *(1943-)*
American historian

It is the mark of great people to treat trifles as trifles and important matters as important.
Doris Lessing *(1919-)*
Persian-born British writer

I want to be remembered as someone who used herself and anything she could touch to work for justice and freedom.... I want to be remembered as one who tried.
Dorothy Height *(1912-2010)*
American activist

The leadership instinct you are born with is the backbone. You develop the funny bone and the wishbone that go with it.
Elaine Agather *(1956-)*
American, CEO, JP Morgan Chase

I have always thought that what is needed is the development of people who are interested not in being leaders as much as in developing leadership in others.
Ella J. Baker *(1943-)*
American Civil Rights activist

The only safe ship in a storm is leadership.
Faye Wattleton *(1880-1973)*
American activist

It doesn't happen by itself, it needs focus, it needs energy, it needs leadership, it needs direction, it needs follow-up, it needs commitment, it needs all the hard yards.
Gail Kelly *(1956-)*
American, CEO Westpac

The secret of a leader lies in the tests they have faced over the whole course of their life and the habit of action they develop in meeting those tests.
Gail Sheehy *(1937-)*
American writer, lecturer

A leader who doesn't hesitate before they send their nation into battle is not fit to be a leader.
Golda Meir *(1898-1978)*
Ukrainian-born Israeli leader

Leadership is a two-way street, loyalty up and loyalty down. Respect for one's superiors; care for one's crew.
Grace Murray Hopper *(1906-1992)*
American Rear Admiral, U.S. Navy

Leadership is hard to define and good leadership even harder. But if you can get people to follow you to the ends of the earth, you are a great leader.
Indra Nooyi *(1955-)*
Indian, CEO of Pepsico

The one thing I have learned as a CEO is that leadership at various levels is vastly different. When I was leading a function or a business, there were certain demands and requirements to be a leader. As you move up the organization, the requirements for leading that organization don't grow vertically; they grow exponentially.
Indra Nooyi *(1955-)*
Indian, CEO of Pepsico

I believe very strongly in the concept of servant leadership and I would tell you that the people that work with me understand... I am there to help them not for them to help me.
Irene Rosenfeld *(1953-)*
American, CEO Kraft Foods

To my mind, you cannot speak about the need for leadership within our communities without being prepared to take on responsibility yourself. It's not enough to point the finger at those who have let us down and to expect others to come forward and fix our problems. Nor can anyone afford to call themselves a leader unless they truly have the interests of our community at heart. Too many people like to think they are leaders and too many are identified by the media as leaders who are not really leaders at all.
Jackie Huggins *(1956-)*
Australian author, historian

Now we've got around seven thousand people working, and that to me is fantastically satisfying... more than dollars and cents, because I just believe that the greatest thing you can give someone is a job.
Janet Holmes à Court *(1943-)*
Australian business woman

You take people as far as they will go not as far as you would like them to go.
Jeannette Rankin *(1880-1973)*
American, first Congresswoman

If you don't like bad news, you should get out of the leadership business. Your job is to hear as much bad news as there is out there and to figure out ways of dealing with it.
Kim Campbell *(1947-)*
Canadian politician

I believe that the capacity that any organization needs is for leadership to appear anywhere it is needed, when it is needed.
Margaret J. Wheatley *(1934-)*
American organization expert

Being prime minister is a lonely job. . . You cannot lead from the crowd.
Margaret Thatcher *(1925-)*
English Prime Minister

The first element of greatness is fundamental humbleness (this should not be confused with servility); the second is freedom from self; the third is intrepid courage, which, taken in its widest interpretation, generally goes with truth.
Margot Asquith *(1864-1945)*
Anglo-Scottish socialite

Leadership should be born out of the understanding of the needs of those who would be affected by it.
Marian Anderson *(1897-1993)*
American singer

The future of dance? If I knew, I'd want to do it first.
Martha Graham *(1894-1991)*
American dancer, choreographer

None of us whether Men or Women but have so good an Opinion of our own Conduct as to believe we are fit, if not to direct others, at least to govern our selves.
Mary Astell *(1666-1731)*
English writer

The speed of the leader is the speed of the gang.
Mary Kay Ash *(1918-2001)*
American entrepreneur

The insight to see possible new paths, the courage to try them, the judgment to measure results – these are the qualities of a leader.
Mary Parker Follett *(1868-1933)*
American management consultant

People ask me, how is managing in the New Economy different from managing in the Old Economy? Actually, it's a lot the same. It's about the financial discipline of the bottom line, understanding your customers, segmenting your customers by their needs, and building a world-class management team.
Meg Whitman *(1956-)*
American, Former eBay CEO

Do not wait for leaders; do it alone, person to person.
Mother Teresa *(1910-1997)*
Albanian Roman Catholic nun

I am your anointed Queen. I will never be by violence constrained to do anything. I thank God that I am embued with such qualities that if I were turned out of the Realm in my petticoat, I were able to live in any place in Christome.
Queen Elizabeth I *(1533-1603)*
English royalty

Leaders must wake people out of inertia. They must get people excited about something they've never seen before, something that does not yet exist.
Rosabeth Moss Kanter *(1943-)*
American academic, author

A leader takes people where they want to go. A great leader takes people where they don't necessarily want to go, but ought to be.
Rosalynn Carter *(1927-)*
American First Lady

Times of upheaval require not just more leadership but more leaders. People at all organizational levels, whether anointed or self-appointed, must be empowered to share leadership responsibilities.
Rosalynn Carter *(1927-)*
American First Lady

She had observed that it was from those who had never sailed stormy waters, came the quickest and harshest judgments on bad seamanship in heavy seas.
Susan Glaspell *(1876-1948)*
American playwright

The hunger for leadership in times of crisis is always unsettling and afflicts nearly everyone.
Wendy Kaminer *(1949-)*
American writer, social critic

I want to be remembered as the person who helped us restore faith in ourselves.
Wilma Pearl Mankiller *(1945-2010)*
American Cherokee leader

The stakes...are too high for government to be a spectator sport.
Barbara Jordan *(1936-1996)*
American politician

Learning

*Learning is not attained by chance, it must be sought
for with ardor and attended to with diligence.*
Abigail Adams *(1744-1818)*
American First Lady

*I learned three important things in college – to use a library,
to memorize quickly and visually, to drop asleep at any
time given a horizontal surface and fifteen minutes. What
I could not learn was to think creatively on schedule.*
Agnes De Mille *(1905-1993)*
American dancer

*It is as impossible to withhold education from the receptive
mind, as it is impossible to force it upon the unreasoning.*
Agnes Repplier *(1855-1950)*
American essayist

You live, you learn.
Alanis Morisette *(1974-)*
Canadian singer

*I wonder whether if I had an education I should
have been more or less a fool that I am.*
Alice James *(1848-1892)*
American diarist

*I imagine good teaching as a circle of earnest people sitting
down to ask each other meaningful questions. I don't see it
as the handing down of answers. So much of what passes for
teaching is merely a pointing out of what items to want.*
Alice Walker *(1944-)*
American writer

*You know, if you really want to fiddle the old-time way, you've got
to learn the dance. The contra-dances, hoedowns. It's all in the
rhythm of the bow. The great North Carolina fiddle player Tommy
Jarrell said, 'If a feller can't bow, he'll never make a fiddler. He
might make a violin player, but he'll never make no fiddler.'*
Alison Krauss *(1971-)*
American musician

...the less you look back, the better. If you do look back, then it can only be to learn for yourself through the events that have taken place.
Angela Merkel *(1954-)*
German Chancellor

Knowledge is essential to conquest; only according to our ignorance are we helpless. Thought creates character. Character can dominate conditions. Will creates circumstances and environment.
Annie Besant *(1847-1933)*
British writer, activist

I would like to learn, or remember, how to live.
Annie Dillard *(1945-)*
American author

Everything I learned I learned from the movies.
Audrey Hepburn *(1929-1993)*
Belgian-born actress

When I disagree with a rational person, I let reality be our final arbiter; if I am right, they will learn; if I am wrong, I will; one of us will win, but both will profit.
Ayn Rand *(1905-1982)*
Russian-American novelist

Whether you know the shape of a pebble or the structure of a solar system, the axioms remain the same; that it exists and that you know it.
Ayn Rand *(1905-1982)*
Russian-American novelist

You can learn new things at any time in your life if you're willing to be a beginner. If you actually learn to like being a beginner, the whole world opens up to you.
Barbara Sher *(1869-1942)*
American writer

I have always grown from my problems and challenges, from the things that don't work out, that's when I've really learned.
Carol Burnett *(1933-)*
American actress, comedian

We should live and learn; but by the time we've learned it's too late to live.
Carolyn Wells *(1862-1942)*
American author, poet

*It seems that we learn lessons when we least expect them
but always when we need them the most and the true 'gift' in
these lessons always lies in the learning process itself.*
Cathy Lee Crosby *(1946-)*
American actress

I learned from watching and I learned from doing.
Claire Bloom *(1931-)*
British actress

*I try to extract something positive from every situation even
if it's just learning not to make the same mistake twice.*
Claudia Schiffer *(1970-)*
American supermodel

*The thing that's important to know is that you never
know. You're always sort of feeling your way.*
Diane Arbus *(1923-1971)*
American photographer

*I think the one lesson I have learned is that there
is no substitute for paying attention.*
Diane Sawyer *(1945-)*
American broadcast journalist

*Learning to live with what you're born with is the
process, the involvement, the making of a life.*
Diane Wakoski *(1937-)*
American poet

*This is what learning is. You suddenly understand something
you've understood all your life, but in a new way.*
Doris Lessing *(1919-)*
Persian-born British writer

You can't teach an old dogma new tricks.
Dorothy Parker *(1893-1967)*
American writer, satirist

*We've got to learn hard things in our lifetime, but it's love that gives
you the strength. It's being nice to people and having a lot of fun and
laughing harder than anything, hopefully every single day of your life.*
Drew Barrymore *(1975-)*
American actress

I think you should learn, of course, and some days you must learn a great deal. But you should also have days when you allow what is already in you to swell up inside of you until it touches everything. And you can feel it inside you. If you never take time out to let that happen, then you just accumulate facts, and they begin to rattle around inside of you. You can make noise with them, but never really feel anything with them.

E. L. Konigsburg *(1930-)*
American illustrator children's books

I am learning all the time. The tombstone will be my diploma.

Eartha Kitt *(1927-2008)*
American actress, singer

It has always seemed strange to me that in our endless discussions about education so little stress is laid on the pleasure of becoming an educated person, the enormous interest it adds to life. To be able to be caught up into the world of thought – that is to be educated.

Edith Hamilton *(1867-1963)*
American educator

Pity me that the heart is slow to learn / What the swift mind beholds at every turn.

Edna Saint Vincent Millay *(1892-1950)*
American poet, playwright

There are no mistakes, no coincidences. All events are blessings given to us to learn from.

Elisabeth Kübler-Ross *(1926-2004)*
Swiss psychiatrist

We learn nothing by being right.

Elizabeth Bibesco *(1918-1999)*
English writer

You must learn day by day, year by year to broaden your horizon. The more things you love, the more you are interested in, the more you enjoy, the more you are indignant about, the more you have left when anything happens.

Ethel Barrymore *(1879-1959)*
American actress

I hardly teach. It's more like a gathering of minds looking at one subject and learning from each other. I enjoy the process.

Fay Godwin *(1931-2005)*
British photographer

Love of learning is a pleasant and universal bond, since
it deals with what one is and not what one has.
Freya Stark *(1893-1993)*
French-born travel writer, explorer

Do you know because I tell you so, or do you know, do you know?
Gertrude Stein *(1874-1946)*
American writer

Acting is not about dressing up. Acting is about stripping bare.
The whole essence of learning lines is to forget them so you can
make them sound like you thought of them that instant.
Glenda Jackson *(1936-)*
English actress

I used to believe that anything was better than nothing.
Now I know that sometimes nothing is better.
Glenda Jackson *(1936-)*
English actress

The first problem for all of us… is not to learn, but to unlearn.
Gloria Steinem *(1934-)*
American activist, writer, publisher

It is not so important to know everything as to know the exact value of
everything, to appreciate what we learn and to arrange what we know.
Hannah More *(1745-1833)*
English writer, philanthropist

The most beautiful thing in the world is, precisely,
the conjunction of learning and inspiration.
Hazel Henderson *(1933-)*
English futurist

Have you ever been at sea in a dense fog, when it seemed as if a tangible
white darkness shut you in, and the great ship, tense and anxious,
groped her way toward the shore with plummet and sounding-line,
and you waited with beating heart for something to happen? I was like
that ship before my education began, only I was without compass or
sounding-line, and had no way of knowing how near the harbor was.
Helen Keller *(1880-1968)*
American author, educator

The highest result of education is tolerance.
Helen Keller *(1880-1968)*
American author, educator

The thing about anything in life is you have to get ready for it. Study, learn.
Jacqueline Bisset *(1944-)*
English actress

*Being away from home gave me the chance to look at myself with
a jaundiced eye. I learned not to be ashamed of a real hunger
for knowledge, something I had always tried to hide.*
Jacqueline Kennedy Onassis *(1929-1994)*
American First Lady

There are no regrets in life, just lessons.
Jennifer Aniston *(1969-)*
American actress

Teaching is the royal road to learning.
Jessamyn West *(1902-1984)*
American writer

*The growth of understanding follows an ascending
spiral rather than a straight line.*
Joanna Field *(1900-1998)*
British psychoanalyst

Lack of education is an extraordinary handicap when one is being offensive.
Josephine Tey *(1896-1952)*
Scottish mystery writer

It's what you learn after you know it all that counts.
Judith Kelman *(1927-2008)*
American writer

*I thought I was learning about show business. The more painful
it was, the more important I thought the experience must be.
Hating it, I convinced myself it must be invaluable.*
Judy Holliday *(1921-1965)*
American actress

Knowledge...always imposes responsibility.
Julia Louisa M. Woodruff *(1833-1909)*
American writer

Bromidic though it may sound, some questions don't have answers, which is a terribly difficult lesson to learn.
Katharine Graham *(1917-2001)*
American publisher

When you stop learning, stop listening, stop looking and asking questions, then it is time to die.
Lillian Smith *(1729-1796)*
American author

I ain't got much education, but I got some sense.
Loretta Lynn *(1935-)*
American musician

Nearly everyone I met, worked with, or read about was my teacher, one way or another.
Loretta Young *(1913-2000)*
American actress

I am not afraid of storms for I am learning to sail my ship.
Louisa May Alcott *(1832-1888)*
American author

Isn't it splendid to think of all the things there are to find out about? It just makes me feel glad to be alive – it's such an interesting world.
Lucy Maud Montgomery *(1874-1942)*
Canadian writer

That's the way things come clear. All of a sudden. And then you realize how obvious they've been all along.
Madeleine L'Engle *(1918-)*
American novelist

I think a major act of leadership right now, call it a radical act, is to create the places and processes so people can actually learn together, using our experiences.
Margaret J. Wheatley *(1934-)*
American organization expert

Learning is always rebellion...Every bit of new truth discovered is revolutionary to what was believed before.
Margaret Lee Runbeck *(1905-1956)*
American author

The best way to learn is to learn from the best.
Margaret Mead *(1901-1978)*
American cultural anthropologist

We have a hunger of the mind which asks for knowledge of all around us, and the more we gain, the more is our desire; the more we see, the more we are capable of seeing.
Maria Mitchell *(1818-1889)*
American scientist

And so we discovered that education is not something which the teacher does, but that it is a natural process which develops spontaneously in the human being.
Maria Montessori *(1870-1952)*
Italian educator

In youth we learn; in age we understand.
Marie von Ebner-Eschenbach *(1830-1916)*
Austrian writer

To acquire knowledge, one must study; but to acquire wisdom, one must observe.
Marilyn vos Savant *(1946-)*
American writer

What is important is to keep learning, to enjoy challenge, and to tolerate ambiguity. In the end there are no certain answers.
Marina Horner *(1939-)*
American academic

Learn by practice.
Martha Graham *(1894-1991)*
American dancer, choreographer

The essence of teaching is to make learning contagious, to have one idea spark another.
Marva Collins *(1936-)*
American educator

We are not what we know but what we are willing to learn.
Mary Catherine Bateson *(1939-)*
American anthropologist

From the first, I made my learning, what little
it was, useful every way I could.
Mary McLeod Bethune *(1875-1955)*
American educator

I've learned that you shouldn't go through life with a catcher's mitt
on both hands; you need to be able to throw something back.
Maya Angelou *(1928-)*
American poet, memoirist

If we don't rededicate ourselves to education with the same attitude
Americans have applied to going to the moon and fighting wars, the
results will be profound. We will gradually lose our successful workforce.
Meg Whitman *(1956-)*
American, Former eBay CEO

Learning too soon our limitations, we never learn our powers.
Mignon McLaughlin *(1913-1983)*
American journalist

Real education should educate us out of self into something far
finer; into a selflessness which links us with all humanity.
Nancy Astor *(1879-1964)*
American born, British politician

As far as the education of the children is concerned I think they
should be taught not the little virtues but the great ones. Not
thrift but generosity and an indifference to money; not caution but
courage and a contempt for danger; not shrewdness but frankness
and a love of truth; not tact but love for one's neighbor and self-
denial; not a desire for success but a desire to be and to know.
Natalia Ginzburg *(1916-1991)*
Italian author

I don't love studying. I hate studying. I like learning. Learning is beautiful.
Natalie Portman *(1981-)*
American actress

I studied the classics and was filled with integrity.
Pam Grier *(1949-)*
American actress

If I had influence with the good fairy who is supposed to preside over the christening of all children, I should ask that her gift to each child in the world be a sense of wonder so indestructible that it would last throughout life.

Rachel Carson *(1907-1964)*
American environmentalist

The excitement of learning separates youth from old age. As long as you're learning you're not old.

Rosalind Sussman Yalow *(1921-)*
American physicist

If you are not educated – if you can't write clearly, speak articulately, think logically – you have lost control of your own life.

Sadie Delaney *(1877-1965)*
American educator

Learn everything you can, anytime you can, from anyone you can – there will always come a time when you will be grateful you did.

Sarah Caldwell *(1924-2006)*
American opera conductor

We learn and grow and are transformed not so much by what we do but by why and how we do it.

Sharon Salzberg *(1952-)*
American author

The joy of learning is as indispensable in study as breathing is in running. Where it is lacking there are no real students, but only poor caricatures of apprentices who, at the end of their apprenticeship, will not even have a trade.

Simone Weil *(1909-1943)*
French philosopher

It's a mistake to think that once you're done with school you need never learn anything new.

Sophia Loren *(1934-)*
Italian actress

If your mind isn't open, keep your mouth shut too.

Sue Grafton *(1940-)*
American author detective novels

*If we would have new knowledge, we must get
a whole world of new questions.*
Susanne Langer *(1895-1985)*
American philosopher

*I read Shakespeare and the Bible and I can shoot
dice. That's what I call a liberal education.*
Tallulah Bankhead *(1902-1968)*
American actress

*I've learned the most from other people. Buy yourself
a brain picker – ask a lot of questions.*
Tara Vanderveer *(1953-)*
American basketball coach

*Learning should be a joy and full of excitement. It is life's greatest adventure;
it is an illustrated excursion into the minds of the noble and the learned.*
Taylor Caldwell *(1900-1985)*
American author

*Don't be afraid to take time to learn. It's good to work for other
people. I worked for others for 20 years. They paid me to learn.*
Vera Wang *(1949-)*
American designer

We can learn something new anytime we believe we can.
Virginia Satir *(1916-1988)*
American author, psychotherapist

*The first duty of a lecturer – to hand you after an hour's
discourse a nugget of pure truth to wrap up between the pages
of your notebooks and keep on the mantelpiece forever.*
Virginia Woolf *(1882-1941)*
English author

*Only people who die very young learn all they
really need to know in kindergarten.*
Wendy Kaminer *(1949-)*
American Law Professor

There are some things you learn best in calm and some in storm.
Willa Cather *(1873-1947)*
American writer

Sometimes it takes years to really grasp what has happened to your life.
Wilma Rudolph *(1940-1994)*
American Olympic runner

Learning without wisdom is a load of books on a donkey's back.
Zora Neale Hurston *(1891-1960)*
American dramatist

Listening

The less you talk, the more you are listened to.
Abigail Van Buren *(1918-2002)*
American advice columnist

*A person who listens because they have nothing to say can hardly
be a source of inspiration. The only listening that counts is that
of the talker who alternately absorbs and expresses ideas.*
Agnes Repplier *(1855-1950)*
American essayist

*Listening is not merely not talking though even that is beyond most of our
powers; it means taking a vigorous human interest in what is being told us.*
Alice Duer Miller *(1874-1942)*
American writer, poet

*The longer we listen to one another – with real attention – the more
commonality we will find in all our lives. That is, if we are careful to
exchange with one another life stories and not simply opinions.*
Barbara Deming *(1917-1984)*
American author

*Listening is a magnetic and strange thing, a creative force. When we really
listen to people there is an alternating current, and this recharges us so
that we never get tired of each other. We are constantly being re-created.*
Brenda Ueland *(1891-1985)*
American journalist

With the gift of listening comes the gift of healing.
Catherine de Hueck *(1896-1985)*
American activist

I give credit for that to all my teachers and all my choreographers, but also to myself – for listening to them.
Chita Rivera *(1933-)*
American (Hispanic) musical theater actress

The biggest mistake is believing there is one right way to listen, to talk, to have a conversation – or a relationship.
Deborah Tannen *(1945-)*
American academic, linguist

It takes a disciplined person to listen to convictions which are different from their own.
Dorothy Fuldheim *(1928-)*
American broadcast journalist

Make sure you have finished speaking before your audience has finished listening.
Dorothy Sarnoff *(1917-)*
American stage actress

My personal hobbies are reading, listening to music, and silence.
Edith Sitwell *(1887-1964)*
British poet, critic

Silences have a climax, when you have got to speak.
Elizabeth Bowen *(1899-1973)*
Irish novelist

Why should I pay strangers to listen to me talk when I can get strangers to pay to listen to me talk?
Ellen DeGeneres *(1958-)*
American comedian, television host

Any problem, big or small, within a family, always seems to start with bad communication. Someone isn't listening.
Emma Thompson *(1959-)*
British actress

Listening to other companies' customers is the best way to gain market share, while listening to the visionaries is the best way to create new markets.
Esther Dyson *(1951-)*
American commentator

When anyone tells me I can't do anything. I'm just not listening any more.
Florence Griffith Joyner *(1959-1998)*
American track and field star

The opposite of talking isn't listening. The opposite of talking is waiting.
Fran Lebowitz *(1950-)*
American writer

Let me listen to me and not to them.
Gertrude Stein *(1874-1946)*
American writer

She's descended from a long line her mother listened to.
Gypsy Rose Lee *(1914-1970)*
American burlesque entertainer

*I get so tired listening to one million dollars here,
one million dollars there, it's so petty.*
Imelda Marcos *(1929-)*
Filipino politician

*My first 100 days as CEO were spent on a listening tour to find out what
was on people's minds. I had town hall sessions and spent time with board
members, customers and suppliers. I wanted to learn what was working and
what wasn't, which informed everything I've done since becoming CEO.*
Irene Rosenfeld *(1953-)*
American, CEO Kraft Foods

*You need to become a good listener. As you're working, you hear
someone else's lines and how you absorb them becomes your acting.*
Jacqueline Bisset *(1944-)*
English actress

Everything in writing begins with language. Language begins with listening.
Jeanette Winterson *(1959-)*
British novelist

*Writers have to have a knack for listening. I need to be able
to hear what is being said to me by the voices I create.*
Jeanette Winterson *(1959-)*
British novelist

*So, yes, there's nothing I love more than listening
to directors talk about their movies.*
Jodie Foster *(1962-)*
American actress

Listening, not imitation, my be the sincerest form of flattery.
Joyce Brothers *(1927-)*
American psychologist

*You really have to listen to yourself and know if
what someone is saying is true for you.*
Judith Light *(1949-)*
American actress

You can learn so much just by doing, not by listening to anybody.
Juliana Hatfield *(1967-)*
American musician

*A good listener is not someone with nothing to say. A
good listener is a good talker with a sore throat.*
Katherine Whitehorn *(1914-1956)*
British columnist

It's no secret that I love to talk, but the real secret is I love to listen, too.
Kathie Lee Gifford *(1953-)*
American entertainer

*When you least expect it, someone may actually
listen to what you have to say.*
Maggie Kuhn *(1905-1995)*
American activist

*Listening is such a simple act. It requires us to be present, and that takes
practice, but we don't have to do anything else. We don't have to advise,
or coach, or sound wise. We just have to be willing to sit there and listen.*
Margaret J. Wheatley *(1934-)*
American organization expert

*There are many benefits to this process of listening. The first is that good
listeners are created as people feel listened to. Listening is a reciprocal
process – we become more attentive to others if they have attended to us.*
Margaret J. Wheatley *(1934-)*
American organization expert

It you want to be listened to, you should put in time listening.
Marge Piercy *(1936-)*
American novelist, poet

You seldom listen to me, and when you do you don't hear, and when you do hear you hear wrong, and even when you hear right you change it so fast that it's never the same.
Marjorie Kellogg *(1922-2005)*
American author

No one really listens to anyone else, and if you try it for a while you'll see why.
Mignon McLaughlin *(1913-1983)*
American journalist

Listening to someone talk isn't at all like listening to their words played over on a machine. What you hear when you have a face before you is never what you hear when you have before you a winding tape.
Oriana Fallaci *(1929-2006)*
Italian journalist, writer

To talk to someone who does not listen is enough to tense the devil.
Pearl Bailey *(1918-1990)*
American entertainer

I took advice from none but the best. I listened, how I listened!
Peggy Guggenheim *(1898-1979)*
American art collector

There was a definite process by which one made people into friends, and it involved talking to them and listening to them for hours at a time.
Rebecca West *(1892-1983)*
Irish-born, British writer

The will to be totally rational is the will to be made out of glass and steel: and to use others as if they were glass and steel.
Marge Piercy *(1936-)*
American novelist, poet

You manage things, you lead people. We went overboard on management and forgot about leadership. It might help if we ran the MBAs out of Washington.
Grace Murray Hopper *(1906-1992)*
American Rear Admiral, U.S. Navy

Mistakes

Know when to tune out, if you listen to too much advice
you may wind up making other peoples mistakes.
Ann Landers *(1918-2002)*
American advice columnist

My life is full of mistakes. They're like pebbles that make a good road.
Beatrice Wood *(1893-1998)*
American artist

Do not be afraid to make decisions, do not be afraid to make mistakes.
Carly Fiorina *(1954-)*
American, Former HP CEO

We have to keep trying things we're not sure we can pull off. If we
just do the things we know we can do ... you don't grow as much.
You gotta take those chances on making those big mistakes.
Cybill Shepherd *(1950-)*
American actress, former model

Those who don't know the mistakes of the past won't be able
to enjoy it when they make them again in the future.
Diane Elizabeth Duane *(1952-)*
American science fiction author

Having harvested all the knowledge and wisdom we can from our mistakes
and failures, we should put them behind us and go ahead, for vain
regretting interferes with the flow of power into our own personalities.
Edith Hamilton *(1867-1963)*
American educator

About mistakes, it's funny. You got to make your own; and not only
that, if you try to keep people from making theirs they get mad.
Edna Ferber *(1885-1968)*
American novelist

I wouldn't change one thing about my professional life,
and I make it a point not to dwell on my mistakes.
Ethel Merman *(1908-1984)*
American singer

Every minute you are thinking of evil, you might have been thinking of good instead. Refuse to pander to a morbid interest in your own misdeeds. Pick yourself up, be sorry, shake yourself, and go on again.
Evelyn Underhill *(1875-1941)*
English writer

I really don't think anything I do is a mistake.
It could be if I didn't learn from it.
Fiona Apple *(1977-)*
American musician

We are living in the Age of Human Error...Since we're all human, since anybody can make mistakes, since nobody's perfect, and since everybody is equal, a human error is Democracy in Action.
Florence King *(1936-)*
American novelist

I am not the kind of woman who excuses her mistakes while reminding us of what used to be.
Gene Tierney *(1920-1991)*
American actress

Just because you made a mistake doesn't mean you are a mistake.
Georgette Mosbacher *(1947-)*
American, CEO of Borghese

If you have to make mistakes, make them good and big, don't be middling in anything if you can help it.
Hildegard Knef *(1925-2002)*
German actress, singer

It is not easy but you have to be willing to make mistakes. And the earlier you make those mistakes the better.
Jane Cahill Pfeiffer *(1954-)*
American, former CEO NBC

I will go to my grave regretting the photograph of me on an anti-aircraft gun, which looks like I was trying to shoot at American planes. It galvanized hostility.
Jane Fonda *(1937-)*
American actress

It is very easy to forgive others their mistakes. It takes more gut and gumption to forgive them for having witnessed our own.
Jessamyn West *(1902-1984)*
American writer

Life is not life unless you make mistakes.
Joan Collins *(1933-)*
British actress

A mistake is simply another way of doing things.
Katharine Graham *(1917-2001)*
American publisher

I have many regrets, and I'm sure everyone does. The stupid things you do, you regret if you have any sense, and if you don't regret them, maybe you're stupid.
Katharine Hepburn *(1907-2003)*
American actress

We are a people who do not want to keep much of the past in our heads. It is considered unhealthy in America to remember mistakes, neurotic to think about them, psychotic to dwell on them.
Lillian Hellman *(1905-1984)*
American playwright

It doesn't matter if I don't succeed in something, what matters is that I learn from my mistakes.
Linda Evans *(1942-)*
American actress

Tomorrow is always fresh, with no mistakes in it.
Lucy Maud Montgomery *(1874-1942)*
Canadian writer

If you have made mistakes, even serious ones, there is always another chance for you. What we call failure is not the falling down but the staying down.
Mary Pickford *(1893-1979)*
Canadian-American actress

I'm a perfectionist, which I think is a mistake.
Michelle Shocked *(1962-)*
American musician

I'm an incredibly lucky girl. For someone who has made some very foolish mistakes and had some tough lessons to learn very quickly, I am still incredibly lucky.
Monica Lewinsky *(1973-)*
American celebrity

Mistakes are a fact of life. It is the response to error that counts.
Nikki Giovanni *(1943-)*
American poet, author

Every great mistake has a halfway moment, a split second when it can be recalled and perhaps remedied.
Pearl S. Buck *(1892-1973)*
American writer

There's nothing final about a mistake, except its being taken as final.
Phyllis Bottome *(1884-1963)*
British novelist

I've made mistakes, and I know why I made them, but I made that choice. Nobody's ever made a choice for me.
Sandra Bullock *(1964-)*
American actress

So many roads. So many detours. So many choices. So many mistakes.
Sarah Jessica Parker *(1965-)*
American actress

You can't be in the public eye without making mistakes and having some regrets and having people analyze everything you do.
Sheryl Crow *(1962-)*
American musician

Mistakes are part of the dues one pays for a full life.
Sophia Loren *(1934-)*
Italian actress

If I had to live my life again, I'd make the same mistakes, only sooner.
Tallulah Bankhead *(1902-1968)*
American actress

When you lose, you're more motivated. When you win, you fail to see your mistakes and probably no one can tell you anything.
Venus Williams *(1980-)*
American tennis player

*Feelings of worth can flourish only in an atmosphere where
individual differences are appreciated, mistakes are tolerated,
communication is open, and rules are flexible.*
Virginia Satir *(1916-1988)*
American author, psychotherapist

Morals

*Physical pain, however great, ends in itself and falls away like dry husks
from the mind, whilst moral discords and nervous horrors sear the soul.*
Alice James *(1848-1892)*
American diarist

*In morals what begins in fear usually ends in wickedness; in
religion what begins in fear usually ends in fanaticism. Fear,
either as a principle or a motive, is the beginning of all evil.*
Anna Jameson *(1794-1860)*
British writer

The foundation of the world will be shaky until the moral props are restored.
Anne O'Hare McCormick *(1882-1954)*
American journalist

*My philosophy, in essence, is the concept of people as heroic beings, with
their own happiness as the moral purpose of their life, with productive
achievement as their noblest activity, and reason as their only absolute.*
Ayn Rand *(1905-1982)*
Russian-American novelist

*The most painful moral struggles are not those between good
and evil, but between the good and the lesser good.*
Barbara Grizzuti Harrison *(1934-2002)*
American journalist, essayist

*There is no moral virtue in being endowed with genius rather
than talent: It is a gift of the gods or the luck of the genes.*
Dorothy Green *(1920-2008)*
American actress

Roast Beef, medium, is not only a food. It is a philosophy. Seated
at Life's Dining Table, with the menu of Morals before you, your
eye wanders a bit over the entrees, the hors d'oeuvres, though you
know that Roast Beef, medium, is safe and sane, and sure.
Edna Ferber *(1885-1968)*
American novelist

When the sun comes up, I have morals again.
Elayne Boosler *(1952-)*
American comedian

The idea of winning a doctor's degree gradually assumed the aspect of a great
moral struggle, and the moral fight possessed immense attraction for me.
Elizabeth Blackwell *(1821-1910)*
British, first U.S. woman doctor

It is wiser to be conventionally immoral than unconventionally
moral. It isn't the immorality they object to, but the originality.
Ellen Glasgow *(1873-1945)*
American novelist

I place a high moral value on the way people behave. I find it repellent to
have a lot, and to behave with anything other than courtesy in the old
sense of the word-politeness of the heart, a gentleness of the spirit.
Emma Thompson *(1959-)*
British actress

The act of acting morally is behaving as if everything we do matters.
Gloria Steinem *(1934-)*
American activist, writer, publisher

Almost all people have this potential for evil, which would be
unleashed only under certain dangerous social circumstances
Iris Chang *(1968-2004)*
Chinese historian

The essence of immorality is the tendency to make an exception of myself.
Jane Addams *(1860-1935)*
American activist

Morality is a test of our conformity rather than our integrity.
Jane Rule *(1931-2007)*
Canadian writer

I am still sure of absolute wrong but much less certain of absolute right.
Jill Tweedie *(1932-1993)*
American writer

Belief is a moral act for which the believer is to be held responsible.
Lillian Hellman *(1905-1984)*
American playwright

People want to be amused, not preached at, you know. Morals don't sell nowadays.
Louisa May Alcott *(1832-1888)*
American author

Scientific progress makes moral progress a necessity; for if a person's power is increased, the checks that restrain them from abusing it must be strengthened.
Madame de Stael *(1766-1817)*
French writer

I'm the girl who lost her reputation and never missed it.
Mae West *(1892-1980)*
American actress

Moral cowardice that keeps us from speaking our minds is as dangerous to this country as irresponsible talk. The right way is not always the popular and easy way. Standing for right when it is unpopular is a true test of moral character.
Margaret Chase Smith *(1897-1995)*
American politician

It has been my fate in a long life of production to be credited chiefly with the equivocal virtue of industry, a quality so excellent in morals, so little satisfactory in art.
Margaret Oliphant *(1828-1897)*
Scottish novelist

Morality did not keep well; it required stable conditions; it was costly; it was subject to variations, and the market for it was uncertain.
Mary McCarthy *(1912-1989)*
American writer

Integrate what you believe in every single area of your life. Take your heart to work and ask the most and best of everybody else, too.
Meryl Streep *(1949-)*
American actress

There is no moral authority like that of sacrifice.
Nadine Gordimer *(1923-)*
South African novelist, activist

The federal budget should be a statement of our values,
our national morals, and our priorities.
Nancy Pelosi *(1940-)*
American politician

When morality comes up against profit, it is seldom that profit loses.
Shirley Chisholm *(1924-2005)*
American politician

The day knowledge was preferred to wisdom and mere usefulness to
beauty... Only a moral revolution – not a social or a political revolution
– only a moral revolution would lead people back to their lost truth.
Simone de Beauvoir *(1908-1986)*
French writer, philosopher

Much of modern art is devoted to lowering the threshold of what is terrible.
By getting us used to what, formerly, we could not bear to see or hear,
because it was too shocking, painful, or embarrassing, art changes morals.
Susan Sontag *(1933-2004)*
American activist, writer

Morals are private. Decency is public.
Therese of Lisieux *(1873-1897)*
French carmelite nun

Negotiating

Who is apt on occasion to assign a multitude of reasons when
one will do? This is a sure sign of weakness in argument.
Harriet Martineau *(1802-1876)*
English social theorist

We'll hold out our hand; they have to unclench their fist.
Hillary Rodham Clinton *(1947-)*
American, Secretary of State

Opportunity

... you asked me one day if it seemed like giving up much for your sake. Only leave me free, as free as you are and everyone ought to be, and it is giving up nothing.
Antoinette Brown Blackwell *(1825-1921)*
American minister

Seize the moment. Remember all those women on the 'Titanic' who waved off the dessert cart.
Erma Bombeck *(1927-1966)*
American writer, humorist

Optimism

I have sometimes been wildly, despairingly, acutely, racked with sorrow, but through it all I still know quite certainly that just being alive is a grand thing.
Agatha Christie *(1890-1976)*
English detective novelist

Like simplicity, and candor, and other much-commended qualities, enthusiasm is charming until we meet it face to face, and cannot escape from its charm.
Agnes Repplier *(1855-1950)*
American essayist

The good old days. The only good days are ahead.
Alice Childress *(1920-1994)*
American playwright, author

Expect nothing. Live frugally on surprise.
Alice Walker *(1944-)*
American writer

In my life I had come to realize that when things were going very well indeed it was just the time to anticipate trouble. And, conversely, I learned from pleasant experience that at the most despairing crisis, when all looked sour beyond words, some delightful break was apt to lurk just around the corner.
Amelia Earhart *(1897-1937)*
American aviator

There are moments when you feel free, moments when you have energy, moments when you have hope, but you can't rely on any of these things to see you through. Circumstances do that.
Anita Brookner *(1938-)*
English historian

If we had no winter, the spring would not be so pleasant; if we did not sometimes taste of adversity, prosperity would not be so welcome.
Anne Bradstreet *(1612-1672)*
American, first published poet

... she knew in her heart that to be without optimism, that core of reasonless hope in the spirit rather than the brain, was a fatal flaw, the seed of death.
Anne Perry *(1938-)*
English author, detective fiction

I believe in pink. I believe that laughing is the best calorie burner. I believe in kissing, kissing a lot. I believe in being strong when everything seems to be going wrong. I believe that happy girls are the prettiest girls. I believe that tomorrow is another day and I believe in miracles.
Audrey Hepburn *(1929-1993)*
Belgian-born actress

If my world were to cave in tomorrow, I would look back on all the pleasures, excitements and worthwhilenesses I have been lucky enough to have had. Not the sadness, not my miscarriages or my father leaving home, but the joy of everything else. It will have been enough.
Audrey Hepburn *(1929-1993)*
Belgian-born actress

I live a day at a time. Each day I look for a kernel of excitement. In the morning, I say: What is my exciting thing for today? Then, I do the day. Don't ask me about tomorrow.
Barbara Jordan *(1936-1996)*
American politician

Developing a cheerful disposition can permit an atmosphere wherein one's spirit can be nurtured and encouraged to blossom and bear fruit. Being pessimistic and negative about our experiences will not enhance the quality of our lives. A determination to be of good cheer can help us and those around us to enjoy life more fully.
Barbara W. Winder *(1931-)*
American LDS president

I'm not happy, I'm cheerful. There's a difference. A happy woman has no cares at all. A cheerful woman has cares but has learned how to deal with them.
Beverly Sills *(1929-2007)*
American operatic soprano

I've never felt more comfortable in my skin, I've never enjoyed life as much and I feel so lucky.
Candace Bergen *(1946-)*
American actress

Happiness is the ability to recognize it.
Carolyn Wells *(1862-1942)*
American author, poet

I'm one of those people who figures that it will eventually sort itself out.
Daryl Hannah *(1960-)*
American actress

No one has a right to sit down and feel hopeless. There's too much work to do.
Dorothy Day *(1897-1980)*
American journalist, activist

Life is always a tightrope or a feather bed. Give me the tightrope.
Edith Wharton *(1862-1937)*
American novelist

It is the inalienable right of all to be happy.
Elizabeth Cady Stanton *(1815-1902)*
American reformist, writer

Good humor, like the jaundice, makes every one of its own complexion.
Elizabeth Inchbald *(1753-1821)*
English novelist

Hope is the thing with feathers that perches in the soul.
Emily Dickinson *(1830-1886)*
American poet

I tried to drown my sorrows, but the bastards learned how to swim, and now I am overwhelmed by this decent and good feeling.
Frida Kahlo *(1907-1954)*
Mexican artist

It's such an act of optimism to get through a day and enjoy it and laugh and do all that without thinking about death. What spirit human beings have!
Gilda Radner *(1948-1989)*
American comedian

Am I like the optimist who, while falling ten stories from a building, says at each story, I'm all right so far?
Gretel Ehrlich *(1946-)*
American travel writer

It is characteristic of genius to be hopeful and aspiring.
Harriet Martineau *(1802-1876)*
English social theorist

If we can recognize that change and uncertainty are basic principles, we can greet the future and the transformation we are undergoing with the understanding that we do not know enough to be pessimistic.
Hazel Henderson *(1933-)*
English futurist

Keep your face to the sunshine and you cannot see the shadows.
Helen Keller *(1880-1968)*
American author, educator

You have to count on living every single day in a way you believe will make you feel good about your life – so that if it were over tomorrow you'd be content with yourself.
Jane Seymour *(1508-1537)*
English, Queen consort

I guess I just prefer to see the dark side of things. The glass is always half empty. And cracked. And I just cut my lip on it. And chipped a tooth.
Janeane Garofalo *(1964-)*
American comedian

Hope is the feeling you have that the feeling you have isn't permanent.
Jean Kerr *(1923-2003)*
American author

I am an extreme optimist, while my husband likes to play the devil's advocate. He wants to know the worst thing that can happen. I don't even want to think about the worst case. I provide the discipline and stick-to-it-iveness.
Jenny Craig *(1932-)*
American entrepreneur

What else are we gonna live by if not dreams? We need to believe in something. What would really drive us crazy is to believe this reality we run into every day is all there is. If I don't believe that there's a happy ending out there – that will-you-marry-me in the sky – I can't keep working today.
Jill Robinson *(1955-)*
English activist

We were that generation called silent, but we were silent neither, as some thought, because we shared the period's official optimism nor, as others thought, because we feared its official repression. We were silent because the exhilaration of social action seemed to many of us just one more way of escaping the personal, of masking for a while that dread of the meaningless which was everyone's fate.
Joan Didion *(1934-)*
American writer

I have become my own version of an optimist. If I can't make it through one door, I'll go through another door – or I'll make a door. Something terrific will come no matter how dark the present.
Joan Rivers *(1933-)*
American comedian

Sometimes I found that in my happy moments I could not believe that I had ever been miserable.
Joanna Field *(1900-1998)*
British psychoanalyst

Hope ... is not a feeling; it is something you do.
Katherine Paterson *(1932-)*
China-born author of children's books

If I hear the word 'perky' again, I'll puke.
Katie Couric *(1957-)*
American journalist

We have no more right to steal the brightness out of the day for our own family than we have to steal the purse of a stranger.
Laura Ingalls Wilder *(1867-1957)*
American writer

I want no part of making any contribution whatsoever to the despair which eventually follows downbeat thinking.
Loretta Young *(1913-2000)*
American actress

One of the things I learned the hard way was that it doesn't pay to get discouraged. Keeping busy and making optimism a way of life can restore your faith in yourself.
Lucille Ball *(1911-1989)*
American comedian, actress

That is one good thing about this world... there are always sure to be more springs.
Lucy Maud Montgomery *(1874-1942)*
Canadian writer

You find yourself refreshed in the presence of cheerful people. Why not make an honest effort to confer that pleasure on others? Half the battle is gained if you never allow yourself to say anything gloomy.
Lydia M. Child *(1802-1880)*
American activist

Happiness is not a state to arrive at but a manner of traveling.
Margaret Lee Runbeck *(1905-1956)*
American author

After all, tomorrow is another day.
Margaret Mitchell *(1900-1949)*
American novelist

The optimism of a healthy mind is indefatigable.
Margery Allingham *(1904-1966)*
English crime writer

At first, I only laughed at myself. Then I noticed that life itself is amusing. I've been in a generally good mood ever since.
Marilyn vos Savant *(1946-)*
American writer

Misery is a communicable disease.
Martha Graham *(1894-1991)*
American dancer, choreographer

Every day I live I am more convinced that the waste of life lies in the love we have not given, the powers we have not used, the selfish prudence that will risk nothing and which, shirking pain, misses happiness as well.
Mary Cholmondeley *(1859-1925)*
English novelist

Instant gratification is not soon enough.
Meryl Streep *(1949-   )*
American actress

*I've been through some dark times but I've experienced
joy too. Now that joy can't be suppressed.*
Michelle Shocked *(1962-   )*
American musician

Hope is the feeling we have that the feeling we have is not permanent.
Mignon McLaughlin *(1913-1983)*
American journalist

*I'm not sure what the future holds but I do know that I'm going to be positive
and not wake up feeling desperate. As my dad said Nic, it is what it is, it's
not what it should have been, not what it could have been, it is what it is.*
Nicole Kidman *(1967-   )*
Australian actress

*It struck me that the movies had spent more than half a century
saying, "They lived happily ever after" and the following quarter-
century warning that they'll be lucky to make it through the weekend.
Possibly now we are now entering a third era in which the movies will be
sounding a note of cautious optimism: You know it just might work.*
Nora Ephron *(1941-   )*
American director, screenwriter

*Please understand there is no depression in this house and we are
not interested in the possibilities of defeat. They do not exist.*
Queen Victoria *(1819-1901)*
English royalty

*To stand at the edge of the sea, to sense the ebb and flow of the tides,
to feel the breath of a mist moving over a great salt marsh, to watch
the flight of shore birds that have swept up and down the surf lines
of the continents for untold thousands of year, to see the running
of the old eels and the young shad to the sea, is to have knowledge
of things that are as nearly eternal as any earthly life can be.*
Rachel Carson *(1907-1964)*
American environmentalist

Taking joy in life is a woman's best cosmetic.
Rosalind Russell *(1907-1976)*
American actress

Dwelling on the negative simply contributes to its power.
Shirley MacLaine *(1934-)*
American actress

Hope costs nothing.
Sidonie-Gabrielle Colette *(1873-1954)*
French novelist

Optimism with some experience behind it is much more energizing than plain old experience with a certain degree of cynicism.
Twyla Tharp *(1941-)*
American dancer

What sane person could live in this world and not be crazy?
Ursula K. LeGuin *(1929-)*
American novelist

When accused of being an unrealistic optimist,
say the sun never stops shining.
Vanna Bonta *(1958-)*
American novelist, poet

These are the soul's changes. I don't believe in aging. I believe in forever altering one's aspect to the sun. Hence my optimism.
Virginia Woolf *(1882-1941)*
English author

Never explain, never complain.
Wallis Simpson *(1895-1986)*
American royalty

When the sun is shining I can do anything; no mountain is too high, no trouble too difficult to overcome.
Wilma Rudolph *(1940-1994)*
American Olympic runner

Patience

I do not believe that sheer suffering teaches. If suffering alone taught, all the world would be wise, since everyone suffers. To suffering must be added mourning, understanding, patience, love, openness and the willingness to remain vulnerable.
Anne Morrow Lindbergh *(1906-2001)*
American aviator, author

The sea does not reward those who are too anxious, too greedy, or too impatient. To dig for treasures shows not only impatience and greed, but lack of faith. Patience, patience, patience, is what the sea teaches. Patience and faith. One should lie empty, open, choiceless as a beach – waiting for a gift from the sea.
Anne Morrow Lindbergh *(1906-2001)*
American aviator, author

Patience is the ability to idle your motor when you feel like stripping your gears.
Barbara Johnson *(1947-2009)*
American literary critic

You philosophers are lucky men. You write on paper, which is patient. Unfortunate Empress that I am, I write on the susceptible skins of living beings.
Catherine the Great *(1729-1796)*
Russian royalty

There was a time when Patience ceased to be a virtue. It was long ago.
Charlotte Perkins Gilman *(1860-1935)*
American sociologist, novelist

Faith is not simply a patience that passively suffers until the storm is past. Rather, it is a spirit that bears things – with resignations, yes, but above all, with blazing, serene hope.
Corazon Aquino *(1933-2009)*
Philippine president

People don't realize how difficult it is to win. Winning is a learned behavior. That's what I did today. I relied on my experience and my patience and I was able to hang on.
Cristie Kerr *(1977-)*
American golfer

I am patient with stupidity but not with those who are proud of it.
Edith Sitwell *(1887-1964)*
British poet, critic

Experience, like a pale musician, holds a dulcimer of patience in their hand.
Elizabeth Barrett Browning *(1806-1861)*
English poet

The days of our lives, for all of us, are numbered. We know that. And,
yes, there are certainly times when we aren't able to muster as much
strength and patience as we would like. It's called being human.
Elizabeth Edwards *(1949-2010)*
American activist, author

I endeavor to be wise when I cannot be merry, easy when I cannot be glad,
content with what cannot be mended and patient when there is no redress.
Elizabeth Montagu *(1718-1800)*
British social reformer

It is very strange that the years teach us patience – that the
shorter our time, the greater our capacity for waiting.
Elizabeth Taylor *(1932-2011)*
British-born actress

The key to everything is patience. You get the chicken
by hatching the egg – not by smashing it.
Ellen Glasgow *(1873-1945)*
American novelist

My worst quality is impatience.
Emma Thompson *(1959-)*
British actress

I don't sleep a whole lot – four hours a night – I'm very quick
as well. I'm not talking about intellectually quick. Everything
I do is quick. I'm fairly impatient. There's some element
of stress in that, but you also just get things done.
Gail Kelly *(1956-)*
American, CEO Westpac

I have declared that patience is never more than patient. I too
have declared, that I who am not patient am patient.
Gertrude Stein *(1874-1946)*
American writer

Patience! Patience! Patience is the invention of dullards and sluggards. In a well-regulated world there should be no need of such a thing as patience.
Grace King *(1852-1932)*
American author

Every great dream begins with a dreamer. Always remember, you have within you the strength, the patience, and the passion to reach for the stars to change the world.
Harriet Tubman *(1913-)*
American abolitionist

We would never learn to be brave and patient if there were only joy in the world.
Helen Keller *(1880-1968)*
American author, educator

That I did not fail was due in part to patience....
Jane Goodall *(1934-)*
English, chimpanzee researcher

You can't have genius without patience.
Margaret Deland *(1857-1945)*
American short story writer

I am extraordinarily patient, provided I get my own way in the end.
Margaret Thatcher *(1925-)*
English Prime Minister

Impatience is the mark of independence, not of bondage.
Marianne Moore *(1887-1972)*
American poet, writer

Patient endurance attends to all things.
Teresa of Avila *(1515-1582)*
Spanish Roman Catholic nun, saint

People Skills

It is not necessary to deny another's reality in order to affirm your own.
Anne Wilson Schaef *(1947-)*
American psychotherapist

People, even more than things, have to be restored, renewed, revived, reclaimed, and redeemed; never throw out anyone.
Audrey Hepburn *(1929-1993)*
Belgian-born actress

Show me someone who never gossips and I'll show you someone who isn't interested in people.
Barbara Walters *(1929-)*
American broadcast journalist, author

Life is a matter of dealing with other people, in little matters and cataclysmic ones, and that means a series of conversations.
Deborah Tannen *(1945-)*
American academic, linguist

There is entirely too much charm around, and something must be done to stop it.
Dorothy Parker *(1893-1967)*
American writer, satirist

The problem with people who have no vices is that generally you can be pretty sure they're going to have some pretty annoying virtues.
Elizabeth Taylor *(1932-2011)*
British-born actress

It is awfully important to know what is and what is not your business.
Gertrude Stein *(1874-1946)*
American writer

I suppose leadership at one time meant muscles; but today it means getting along with people.
Indira Gandhi *(1917-1984)*
Indian Prime Minister

I do not want people to be agreeable, as it saves me the trouble of liking them.
Jane Austen *(1775-1817)*
English novelist

The easiest kind of relationship for me is with ten thousand people. The hardest is with one.
Joan Baez *(1941-)*
American folksinger, songwriter

*Charm is the ability to make someone else think
that both of you are pretty wonderful.*
Kathleen Winsor *(1919-2003)*
American author

*Society is like a large piece of frozen water; and
skating well is the great art o social life.*
Letitia Landon *(1802-1838)*
English poet, novelist

*It's important that someone celebrate our existence... People are the only
mirror we have to see ourselves in. The domain of all meaning. All virtue,
all evil, are contained only in people. There is none in the universe at
large. Solitary confinement is a punishment in every human culture.*
Lois McMaster Bujold *(1949-)*
American author

I hate people. People make me pro-nuclear.
Margaret Chase Smith *(1897-1995)*
American politician

Praise is the only gift for which people are really grateful.
Marguerite Blessington *(1789-1849)*
Irish-born English writer

*Whenever I meet someone, I try to imagine them wearing an
invisible sign that says: Make me feel important! I respond
to this sign immediately, and it works wonders.*
Mary Kay Ash *(1918-2001)*
American entrepreneur

*I've learned that people will forget what you said, people will forget
what you did, but people will never forget how you made them feel.*
Maya Angelou *(1928-)*
American poet, memoirist

*Never give up. Get the knack of getting people to help you and
also pitch in yourself. A little money helps, but what really gets
it right is to never under any conditions face the facts.*
Ruth Gordon *(1896-1985)*
American actress, writer

Performance

We have too many high sounding words and too few actions that correspond with them.
Abigail Adams *(1744-1818)*
American First Lady

Let your performance do the thinking.
Charlotte Bronte *(1816-1855)*
English novelist

What happens is, when I perform, I'm somewhere else. I go back in time and get in touch with who I really am. I forget my troubles, my worries.
Etta James *(1938-)*
American musician

It's more than assembling a great team; it's raising the bar on performance. We laid out higher expectations for our people, and some under-performers were let go. It's incredibly difficult but liberating for the rest of the organization to understand we were truly walking our talk. It created a sense of optimism, not fear.
Irene Rosenfeld *(1953-)*
American, CEO Kraft Foods

The best thing about the term 'performance artist' is that it includes just about everything you might want to do.
Laurie Anderson *(1947-)*
American performance artist

Every society honors its live conformists and its dead troublemakers.
Mignon McLaughlin *(1913-1983)*
American journalist

At the Olympics, you are there to do a job. I feel you should take it seriously. You should be respectful. You are putting on the red-white-and-blue and going out there to perform for your country.
Shannon Miller *(1977-)*
American gymnast

We only do well the things we like doing.
Sidonie-Gabrielle Colette *(1873-1954)*
French novelist

The height of mediocrity is still low.
Vanna Bonta *(1958-)*
American novelist, poet

Perseverance

Living is a form of not being sure, not knowing what next or how...
We guess. We may be wrong, but we take leap after leap in the dark.
Agnes De Mille *(1905-1993)*
American dancer

In soloing – as in other activities – it is far easier
to start something than it is to finish it.
Amelia Earhart *(1897-1937)*
American aviator

Folks differs, dearie. They differs a lot. Some can stand things that others
can't. There's never no way of knowin' how much they can stand.
Ann Petry *(1908-1997)*
American author

There are two ways of attaining an important end, force and perseverance;
the silent power of the latter grows irresistible with time.
Anne Sophie Swetchine *(1752-1857)*
Russian mystic

No matter what happens, keep on beginning and failing. Each
time you fail, start all over again, and you will grow stronger until
you find that you have accomplished a purpose – not the one you
began with perhaps, but one you will be glad to remember.
Anne Sullivan Macy *(1866-1936)*
American teacher, companion Helen Keller

Aim at a high mark and you'll hit it. No, not the first time, nor
the second time. Maybe not the third. But keep on aiming and
keep on shooting for only practice will make you perfect.
Annie Oakley *(1860-1926)*
American sharpshooter

Keep trying. Take care of the small circle around you. When you have
succeeded with them then move outwards one small step at a time.
Audrey Hepburn *(1929-1993)*
Belgian-born actress

The question isn't who is going to let me; it's who is going to stop me.
Ayn Rand *(1905-1982)*
Russian-American novelist

Over and over I'm on the point of giving it up.
Beatrice Wood *(1893-1998)*
American artist

To gain that which is worth having, it may be necessary to lose everything else.
Bernadette Devlin *(1947-)*
Irish, member of Parliament

Champions keep playing until they get it right.
Billie Jean King *(1934-)*
American tennis player

You have to go through the falling down in order to learn to walk. It helps to know that you can survive it. That's an education in itself.
Carol Burnett *(1933-)*
American actress, comedian

It's not the failure that holds us back but the reluctance to begin over again that causes us to stagnate.
Clarissa Pinkola Estés *(1945-)*
American poet, psychoanalyst

Refuse to fall down. If you cannot refuse to fall down, refuse to stay down.
Clarissa Pinkola Estés *(1945-)*
American poet, psychoanalyst

You do not have to be superhuman to do what you believe in.
Debbi Fields *(1956-)*
American entrepreneur

I am willing to put myself through anything; temporary pain or discomfort means nothing to me as long as I can see that the experience will take me to a new level. I am interested in the unknown and the only path to the unknown is through breaking barriers – an often painful process.
Diana Nyad *(1949-)*
American distance swimmer

Storms make trees take deeper roots.
Dolly Parton *(1946-)*
American singer-songwriter

It's not the tragedies that kill us, it's the messes.
Dorothy Parker *(1893-1967)*
American writer, satirist

Oh! Much may be done by defying The ghosts of Despair and Dismay, And much may be gained by relying On 'Where there's a Will There's a Way.'
Eliza Cook *(1818-1889)*
English author, poet

I think the main thing, don't you, is to keep the show on the road.
Elizabeth Bowen *(1899-1973)*
Irish novelist

We don't get offered crises, they arrive.
Elizabeth Janeway *(1913-2005)*
American author, critic

What everyone in the astronaut corps shares in common is not gender or ethnic background, but motivation, perseverance, and desire – the desire to participate in a voyage of discovery.
Ellen Ochoa *(1958-)*
American astronaut

Always give them the old fire, even when you feel like a squashed cake of ice.
Ethel Merman *(1908-1984)*
American singer

Every minute you are thinking of evil, you might have been thinking of good instead. Refuse to pander to a morbid interest in your own misdeeds. Pick yourself up, be sorry, shake yourself, and go on again.
Evelyn Underhill *(1875-1941)*
English writer

I am convinced that there are times in everybody's experience when there is so much to be done that the only way to do it is to sit down and do nothing.
Fanny Fern *(1811-1872)*
American writer

Failure after long perseverance is much grander than never to have a striving good enough to be called a failure.
George Eliot *(1819-1880)*
English novelist

If someone asked you, Can you swim a mile? you'd say, Nah. But if you found yourself dumped out at sea, you'd swim the mile. You'd make it.
Gertrude Boyle *(1925-)*
German-born, American entrepreneur

You must never feel that you have failed. You can always come back to something later on when you have more knowledge or better equipment and try again.
Gertrude Elion *(1954-)*
American, Nobel prize winning biochemist

Just remember, you can do anything you set your mind to, but it takes action, perseverance, and facing your fears.
Gillian Anderson *(1968-)*
American actress

Try not to do too many things at once. Know what you want, the number one thing today and tomorrow. Persevere and get it done.
Gracie Allen *(1906-1964)*
American actress, comedian

When you get in a tight place and everything goes against you till it seems as though you could not hold on a minute longer, never give up then, for that is just the time and the place the tide will turn.
Harriet Beecher Stowe *(1811-1896)*
American writer

Nothing could be worse than the fear that one had given up too soon, and left one unexpended effort that might have saved the world.
Jane Addams *(1860-1935)*
American activist

Roots creep under the ground to make a firm foundation. Shoots seems new and small, but to reach the light they can break through brick walls.
Jane Goodall *(1934-)*
English, chimpanzee researcher

The great thing and the hard thing is to stick to a thing when you have outlived the first interest and not yet the second which comes with a sort of mastery.
Janet Erskine Stuart *(1857-1914)*
English, Roman Catholic nun

Until the day I die, or until the day I can't think anymore, I
want to be involved in the issues that I care about.
Janet Reno *(1938-)*
American Attorney General

She who limps is still walking.
Joan Rivers *(1933-)*
American comedian

Studies indicate that the one quality all successful people have is
persistence. They're willing to spend more time accomplishing a
task and to persevere in the face of many difficult odds. There's a
very positive relationship between people's ability to accomplish
any task and the time they're willing to spend on it.
Joyce Brothers *(1927-)*
American psychologist

If you are never scared, embarrassed, or hurt,
it means you never take chances.
Julia Soul *(1958-)*
Chinese actress

Perseverance is failing nineteen times and succeeding the twentieth.
Julie Andrews *(1935-)*
British film, stage actress

Without discipline, there is no life at all.
Katharine Hepburn *(1907-2003)*
American actress

Go within every day and find the inner strength so
that the world will not blow your candle out.
Katherine Dunham *(1912-2006)*
American actress

If enough people think of a thing and work hard enough at it, I guess
it's pretty nearly bound to happen, wind and weather permitting.
Laura Ingalls Wilder *(1867-1957)*
American writer

I've lost track of the number of people who want to be writers but never
actually write anything. Talking about writing, dreaming about writing
can be very fun, but it won't get a book written. You've got to write.
Laurell K. Hamilton *(1963-)*
American writer

It's not the load that breaks you down, it's the way you carry it.
Lena Horne *(1917-2010)*
American singer, actress

Whoever said anybody has a right to give up?
Marian Wright Edelman *(1939-   )*
American, founder Children's Defense Fund

Being defeated is often a temporary condition.
Giving up is what makes it permanent.
Marilyn vos Savant *(1946-   )*
American writer

Mr. or Mrs. Meant-to has a friend, their name is Didn't-Do. Have
you met them? They live together in a house called Never-Win. And
I am told that it is haunted by the Ghost of Might-have-Been.
Marva Collins *(1936-   )*
American educator

When you reach an obstacle, turn it into an opportunity. You have the
choice. You can overcome and be a winner, or you can allow it to overcome
you and be a loser. The choice is yours and yours alone. Refuse to throw
in the towel. Go that extra mile that failures refuse to travel. It is far
better to be exhausted from success than to be rested from failure.
Mary Kay Ash *(1918-2001)*
American entrepreneur

The vision of a champion is bent over, drenched in sweat, at
the point of exhaustion, when nobody else is looking.
Mia Hamm *(1972-   )*
American soccer player

What you can't get out of... Get into wholeheartedly.
Mignon McLaughlin *(1913-1983)*
American journalist

Three failures denotes uncommon strength. A
weakling had not enough grit to fail thrice.
Minna Thomas Antrim *(1861-1950)*
American writer

The thought that we are enduring the unendurable
is one of the things that keep us going.
Molly Haskell *(1939-   )*
American film critic

Any road is bound to arrive somewhere if you follow it far enough.
Patricia Wentworth *(1878-1961)*
British crime fiction writer

Keep the faith, don't lose your perseverance
and always trust your gut instinct.
Paula Abdul *(1962-)*
American singer, songwriter

The stubbornness I had as a child has been transmitted into perseverance. I
can let go but I don't give up. I don't beat myself up about negative things.
Phylicia Rashad *(1948-)*
American actress

I'm not stopping. My dream has come true, and I'm staying.
Rita Coolidge *(1944-)*
American musician

Too many people let others stand in their way
and don't go back for one more try.
Rosabeth Moss Kanter *(1943-)*
American academic, author

Often we can achieve an even better result when we stumble yet are
willing to start over, when we don't give up after a mistake, when
something doesn't come easily but we throw ourselves into trying,
when we're not afraid to appear less than perfectly polished.
Sharon Salzberg *(1952-)*
American author

I do not know the word 'quit.' Either I never did, or I have abolished it.
Susan Butcher *(1954-2006)*
American Iditerod winner

Impossible' is not a scientific term.
Vanna Bonta *(1958-)*
American novelist, poet

Believe me, the reward is not so great without the struggle.
Wilma Rudolph *(1940-1994)*
American Olympic runner

Spring passes and one remembers one's innocence. Summer passes and one remembers one's exuberance. Autumn passes and one remembers one's reverence. Winter passes and one remembers one's perseverance.

Yoko Ono *(1933-)*
Japanese artist, musician

Personal Growth

Don't wait around for other people to be happy for you. Any happiness you get you've got to make yourself.

Alice Walker *(1944-)*
American writer

There were always in me, two women at least, one woman desperate and bewildered, who felt she was drowning and another who would leap into a scene, as upon a stage, conceal her true emotions because they were weaknesses, helplessness, despair, and present to the world only a smile, an eagerness, curiosity, enthusiasm, interest.

Anais Nin *(1902-1977)*
French author, diarist

We do not grow absolutely, chronologically. We grow sometimes in one dimension, and not in another; unevenly. We grow partially. We are relative. We are mature in one realm, childish in another. The past, present, and future mingle and pull us backward, forward, or fix us in the present. We are made up of layers, cells, constellations.

Anais Nin *(1902-1977)*
French author, diarist

Where there is age there is evolution, where there is life there is growth.

Anjelica Huston *(1951-)*
American actress

I read and walked for miles at night along the beach, writing bad blank verse and searching endlessly for someone wonderful who would step out of the darkness and change my life. It never crossed my mind that that person could be me.

Anna Quindlen *(1952-)*
American journalist

Only in growth, reform, and change, paradoxically enough, is true security to be found.
Anne Morrow Lindbergh *(1906-2001)*
American aviator, author

Your regrets aren't what you did, but what you didn't do. So I take every opportunity.
Cameron Diaz *(1972-)*
American actress

I have never savored life with such gusto as I do now.
Candace Bergen *(1946-)*
American actress

I always think it's interesting to dig a little bit deeper every time you go to someplace that seems like a revelation or a strong connection to an emotional truth.
Carly Simon *(1945-)*
American singer, songwriter

Only I can change my life. No one can do it for me.
Carol Burnett *(1933-)*
American actress, comedian

Better to be without logic than without feeling.
Charlotte Bronte *(1816-1855)*
English novelist

I was very, very shy as a younger girl, just petrified of people. Tennis helped give me an identity and made me feel like somebody.
Chris Evert *(1954-)*
American tennis player

Others are writing my biography, and let it rest as they elect to make it. I have lived my life, well and ill, always less well than I wanted it to be but it is, as it is, and as it has been; so small a thing, to have had so much about it!
Clara Barton *(1821-1912)*
American nurse

I don't want to be a passenger in my own life.
Diane Ackerman *(1948-)*
American poet, naturalist

*It is wonderful how quickly you get used to
things, even the most astonishing.*
Edith Nesbitt *(1858-1924)*
English poet, author

If only we'd stop trying to be happy we could have a pretty good time.
Edith Wharton *(1862-1937)*
American novelist

*The wideness of the horizon has to be inside us, cannot be anywhere but
inside us, otherwise what we speak about is geographic distances.*
Ella Maillart *(1903-1997)*
Swiss writer

*Anyway, I believe you don't fix the inside by
putting something on the outside.*
Elle Macpherson *(1964-)*
Australian model

Laugh at yourself first, before anyone else can.
Elsa Maxwell *(1883-1963)*
American gossip columnist

*I'll walk where my own nature would be leading;
it vexes me to choose another guide.*
Emily Brontë *(1818-1848)*
English author

*The history of human growth is at the same time the history of every
new idea heralding the approach of a brighter dawn and the brighter
dawn has always been considered illegal outside of the law.*
Emma Goldman *(1869-1940)*
Russian-born, American activist

*If you've got to my age, you've probably had your heart broken
many times. So it's not that difficult to unpack a bit of grief
from some little corner of your heart and cry over it.*
Emma Thompson *(1959-)*
British actress

You grow up the day you have your first real laugh – at yourself.
Ethel Barrymore *(1879-1959)*
American actress

The loneliest period for a musician is immediately after a concert.
Evelyn Glennie *(1965-)*
Scottish deaf percussionist

*Five years from now I'm probably going to look
back on the things I'm doing and cringe.*
Fiona Apple *(1977-)*
American musician

*Changes are not only possible and predictable, but to deny them
is to be an accomplice to one's own unnecessary vegetation.*
Gail Sheehy *(1937-)*
American writer, lecturer

Growth demands a temporary surrender of security.
Gail Sheehy *(1937-)*
American writer, lecturer

*There is only one failure in life possible, and that
is not to be true to the best one knows.*
George Eliot *(1819-1880)*
English novelist

Human beings have an inalienable right to invent themselves.
Germaine Greer *(1939-)*
Australian-born writer

*My life comes down to three moments: the death of my father,
meeting my husband, and the birth of my daughter. Everything I
did previous to that just doesn't seem to add up to very much.*
Gwyneth Paltrow *(1972-)*
American actress

*In grief we know the worst of what we feel. But
who can tell the end of what we fear?*
Hannah More *(1745-1833)*
English writer, philanthropist

*I have not been that wise. Health I have taken for granted. Love
I have demanded, perhaps too much and too often. As for money,
I have only realized its true worth when I didn't have it.*
Hedy Lamarr *(1914-2000)*
Austrian actress

The mystery of language was revealed to me. I knew then that 'w-a-t-e-r' meant the wonderful cool something that was flowing over my hand. That living word awakened my soul, gave it light, joy, set it free!
Helen Keller *(1880-1968)*
American author, educator

The real questions are the ones that obtrude upon your consciousness whether you like it or not, the ones that make your mind start vibrating like a jackhammer, the ones that you come to terms with only to discover that they are still there. The real questions refuse to be placated. They barge into your life at the times when it seems most important for them to stay away. They are the questions asked most frequently and answered most inadequately, the ones that reveal their true natures slowly, reluctantly, most often against your will.
Ingrid Benqis *(1944-)*
American essayist

Getting sober just exploded my life. Now I have a much clearer sense of myself and what I can and can't do. I am more successful than I have ever been. I feel very positive where I never did before, and I think that's all a direct result of getting sober.
Jamie Lee Curtis *(1958-)*
American actress

People assume I'm out there having this great life, but money doesn't erase the pain. When you're young you barrel through life, making choices without thinking of repercussions. A few years down the line, you wake up in a certain place and wonder how the hell you got there.
Jennifer Lopez *(1970-)*
American musician

You get what you give. What you put into things is what you get out of them.
Jennifer Lopez *(1970-)*
American musician

We are well advised to keep on nodding terms with the people we used to be, whether we find them attractive company or not. Otherwise they turn up unannounced and surprise us, come hammering on the mind's door at 4:00 a.m. of a bad night and demand to know who is going to make amends.
Joan Didion *(1934-)*
American writer

We all have our own closets to come out of.
Judith Light *(1949-)*
American actress

Be a first rate version of yourself, not a second rate version of someone else.
Judy Garland *(1922-1969)*
American actress, singer

*Growth is an erratic forward movement: two steps forward, one
step back. Remember that and be very gentle with yourself.*
Julia Cameron *(1948-)*
American teacher, author

*You do not create a style. You work, and develop yourself;
your style is an emanation from your own being.*
Katherine Anne Porter *(1890-1980)*
American journalist

You either mellow at 30, or your head explodes – take your choice.
Laurell K. Hamilton *(1963-)*
American writer

*But pain... seems to me an insufficient reason not to embrace life. Being dead
is quite painless. Pain, like time, is going to come on regardless. Question
is, what glorious moments can you win from life in addition to the pain.*
Lois McMaster Bujold *(1949-)*
American author

Do the best you can with yourself and hope for the best.
Loretta Lynn *(1935-)*
American musician

It's a helluva start, being able to recognize what makes you happy.
Lucille Ball *(1911-1989)*
American comedian, actress

*Those who can soar to the highest heights can also plunge
to the deepest depths, and the natures which enjoy most
keenly are those which also suffer most sharply.*
Lucy Maud Montgomery *(1874-1942)*
Canadian writer

*We are all born with wonderful gifts. We use these gifts to express
ourselves, to amuse, to strengthen, and to communicate. We begin
as children to explore and develop our talents, often unaware that
we are unique, that not everyone can do what we're doing!*
Lynn Johnston *(1947-)*
Canadian cartoonist

Very early, I knew that the only object in life was to grow.
Margaret Fuller *(1810-1850)*
American journalist, author

My work is the only ground I've ever had to stand on. I seem to have a whole superstructure with no foundation but I'm working on the foundation.
Marilyn Monroe *(1926-1962)*
American actress

I really do think that any deep crisis is an opportunity to make your life extraordinary in some way.
Martha Beck *(1962-)*
American author

I hope, when I stop, people will think that somehow I mattered.
Martina Navratilova *(1956-)*
Czech American tennis player

Trust yourself. Think for yourself. Act for yourself. Speak for yourself. Be yourself. Imitation is suicide.
Marva Collins *(1936-)*
American educator

I want to feel my life while I'm in it.
Meryl Streep *(1949-)*
American actress

I accepted a change in my life. I didn't choose that change and those are the best changes to make.
Michelle Shocked *(1962-)*
American musician

My mother wanted us to understand that the tragedies of your life one day have the potential to be comic stories the next.
Nora Ephron *(1941-)*
American director, screenwriter

I always introduce myself as an encyclopedia of defects which I do not deny. Why should I? It took me a whole life to build myself as I am.
Oriana Fallaci *(1929-2006)*
Italian journalist, writer

*The older I get, the more I see that there really aren't huge
zeniths of happiness or a huge abyss of darkness as much
as there used to be. I tend to walk a middle ground.*
Paula Cole *(1968-)*
American musician

*Being true to yourself really means being true to
all the complexities of the human spirit.*
Rita Dove *(1952-)*
American poet

The reward for conformity was that everyone liked you except yourself.
Rita Mae Brown *(1944-)*
American novelist

*I don't spend a lot of time thinking about regrets
because there's nothing I can do.*
Sheryl Crow *(1962-)*
American musician

*If neurotic is wanting two mutually exclusive things at one and the same
time, then I'm neurotic as hell. I'll be flying back and forth between
one mutually exclusive thing and another for the rest of my days.*
Sylvia Plath *(1932-1963)*
American writer

Nobody can be exactly like me. Even I have trouble doing it.
Tallulah Bankhead *(1902-1968)*
American actress

*The only thing that makes life possible is permanent
intolerable uncertainty, not knowing what comes next.*
Ursula K. LeGuin *(1929-)*
American novelist

*There came a moment in my life when I realized I had stepped into another
part of my life. I used to walk into a room full of people and think, do
they like me? And one day I walk in and I thought, do I like them?*
Victoria Principal *(1946-)*
American actress

You can not gain peace by avoiding life.
Virginia Woolf *(1882-1941)*
English author

I've learned to take time for myself and to treat myself with a great deal of love and respect 'cause I like me.... I think I'm kind of cool.
Whoopi Goldberg *(1955-)*
American actress, comedian

I've learned lately that no one is going to hand me a permission slip and tell me to take time out for me.
Wynonna Judd *(1964-)*
American musician

Perspective

In the perspective of every person lies a lens through which we may better understand ourselves.
Ellen J. Langer *(1947-)*
American academic

Not only do we as individuals get locked into single-minded views, but we also reinforce these views for each other until the culture itself suffers the same mindlessness.
Ellen J. Langer *(1947-)*
American academic

When a small thing upset someone my grandmother used to say, Nonsense! That would never be noticed from a trotting horse.
Emily Kimbrough *(1899-1989)*
American journalist

Promises are the uniquely human way of ordering the future, making it predictable and reliable to the extent that this is humanly possible.
Hannah Arendt *(1906-1975)*
German philosopher

That's what makes a character interesting from an actor's perspective – the more screwed up, the better.
Jeri Ryan *(1968-)*
American actress

Perspective is the most important thing to have in life.
Lauren Graham *(1967-)*
American actress

Once you have been confronted with a life-and-death situation,
trivia no longer matters. Your perspective grows and you
live at a deeper level. There's no time for pettiness.
Margaretta (Happy) Rockefeller *(1926-)*
American socialite

There's an easygoing nature that comes with a perspective of
things that aren't as important as we make them sometimes.
Marguerite Moreau *(1977-)*
American actress

Most people see what they want to, or at least what they expect to.
Martha Grimes *(1931-)*
American author detective fiction

There is a law which decrees that two objects may not occupy the same
place at the same time—result: two people cannot see things from the same
point of view, and the slightest difference in angle changes the thing seen.
Mildred Aldrich *(1928-)*
American journalist

Space is as infinite as we can imagine, and expanding this
perspective is what adjusts humankind's focus on conquering our
true enemies, the formidable foes: ignorance and limitation.
Vanna Bonta *(1958-)*
American novelist, poet

It takes as much energy to wish as it does to plan.
Eleanor Roosevelt *(1884 - 1962)*
American First Lady

Power

The most common way people give up their power
is by thinking they don't have any.
Alice Walker *(1944-)*
American writer

I personally believe that those who are leaders with political
power over the world will be forced some day, sooner or later,
to give way to common sense and the will of the people.
Alva Myrdal *(1902-1986)*
Swedish diplomat

*You see what power is – holding someone else's fear
in your hand and showing it to them!*
Amy Tan *(1952-)*
American writer (Chinese descent)

*Today the real test of power is not capacity to
make war but the capacity to prevent it.*
Anne O'Hare McCormick *(1882-1954)*
American news correspondent

*When I dare to be powerful – to use my strength in the service of my
vision, then it becomes less and less important whether I am afraid.*
Audre Lorde *(1934-1992)*
Caribbean-American writer

Power is the ability to do good things for others.
Brooke Astor *(1902-2007)*
American philanthropist

*Power is at the root of the human experience. Our attitudes and beliefs
positive or negative are all extensions of how we define and use power.*
Caroline Myss *(1952-)*
American medical mystic, author

Power consists to a large extent in deciding what stories will be told.
Carolyn Heilbrun *(1926-2003)*
American academic, author

Power without a nation's confidence is nothing.
Catherine the Great *(1729-1796)*
Russian royalty

*Power, when invested in the hands of knaves or
fools, generally is the source of tyranny.*
Charlotte Charke *(1713-1760)*
English actress

*Without the strength to endure the crisis, one will not see the opportunity
within. It is within the process of endurance that opportunity reveals itself.*
Chin-Ning Chu *(1947-2009)*
Chinese business author

As I came to power peacefully, so shall I keep it.
Corazon Aquino *(1933-2009)*
Philippine president

Each underestimates their own power and overestimates the other's.
Deborah Tannen *(1945-)*
American academic, linguist

I think a responsibility comes with notoriety, but I never think of
it as power. It's more like something you hold, like grains of sand.
If you keep your hand closed, you can have it and possess it, but if
you open your fingers in any way, you can lose it just as quickly.
Diana Ross *(1944-)*
American singer, actress

Never allow a person to tell you no who doesn't have the power to say yes.
Eleanor Roosevelt *(1884 - 1962)*
American First Lady

Power is the ability not to have to please.
Elizabeth Janeway *(1913-2005)*
American author, critic

What an immense power over the life is the power of possessing
distinct aims. The voice, the dress, the look, the very motions of a
person, define and alter when he or she begins to live for a reason.
Elizabeth Stuart Phelps *(1844-1911)*
American author

Knowledge is power, if you know the right person.
Ethel Watts Mumford *(1876-1940)*
American author

The trouble in corporate America is that too many people
with too much power live in a box (their home), then travel
the same road every day to another box (their office).
Faith Popcorn *(1948-)*
American advertising executive

Our parents had us so convinced we were precious that by the time I found
out I was nothing, it was already too late – I knew I was something.
Florynce Kennedy *(1916-2000)*
American activist, lawyer

Energy is the power that drives every human being. It
is not lost by exertion but maintained by it.
Germaine Greer *(1939-)*
Australian-born writer

*Power can be taken, but not given. The process of
the taking is empowerment in itself.*
Gloria Steinem *(1934-)*
American activist, writer, publisher

*After 16 years in pictures I could not be intimidated easily,
because I knew where all the skeletons were buried.*
Gloria Swanson *(1899-1983)*
American actress

*We only want that which is given naturally to all peoples
of the world, to be masters of our own fate, not of others,
and in cooperation and friendship with others.*
Golda Meir *(1898-1978)*
Ukrainian-born Israeli leader

*Power and violence are opposites; where the one rules absolutely,
the other is absent. Violence appears where power is in jeopardy,
but left to its own course it ends in power's disappearance.*
Hannah Arendt *(1906-1975)*
German philosopher

*Freedom is actually a bigger game than power. Power is about
what you can control. Freedom is about what you can unleash.*
Harriet Rubin *(1927-2011)*
American author

You can have your titular recognition. I'll take money and power.
Helen Gurley Brown *(1922-)*
American author, publisher

*...I command you to let me know as soon as you are aware of
the arrival of Fastolf; because if he should pass without my
knowledge, I promise you that I will have [your] head removed.*
Joan of Arc *(1412-1431)*
French heroine

I think every woman should have a blowtorch.
Julia Child *(1912-2004)*
American cookbook author

To deny we need and want power is to deny that we hope to be effective.
Liz Smith *(1923-)*
American gossip columnist

Power, like fear, had a taste. But power tasted better.
Lois Wyse *(1926-2007)*
American advertising executive

Genius hath electric power which earth can never tame.
Lydia M. Child *(1802-1880)*
American abolitionist, journalist

Scientific progress makes moral progress a necessity; for if a person's power is increased, the checks that restrain them from abusing it must be strengthened.
Madame de Stael *(1766-1817)*
French writer

Power should not be concentrated in the hands of so few, and powerlessness in the hands of so many.
Maggie Kuhn *(1905-1995)*
American activist

A word after a word after a word is power.
Margaret Atwood *(1939-)*
Canadian poet, novelist

Privacy and security are those things you give up when you show the world what makes you extraordinary.
Margaret Cho *(1968-)*
American comedian, actress

Being powerful is like being a lady. If you have to tell people you are, you aren't.
Margaret Thatcher *(1925-)*
English Prime Minister

We cannot create observers by saying 'observe,' but by giving them the power and the means for this observation and these means are procured through education of the senses.
Maria Montessori *(1870-1952)*
Italian educator

In every community, there is work to be done. In every nation, there are wounds to heal. In every heart, there is the power to do it.
Marianne Williamson *(1952-)*
American author

Fortune is always on the side of the big battalions.
Mariede Rabutin-Chantal *(1626-1696)*
French aristocrat

It's because it was at a time when women didn't have any
power. It was so unusual for a young woman in her 20s to have
power that I seized the power but tried not to flaunt it.
Marlo Thomas *(1937-)*
American actress

The abuse of greatness is when it disjoins remorse from power.
Mary Bertone *(1869-1935)*
American writer

We live in a world which respects power above all things.
Power, intelligently directed, can lead to more freedom.
Mary McLeod Bethune *(1875-1955)*
American educator

Coercive power is the curse of the universe; coactive power,
the enrichment and advancement of every human soul.
Mary Parker Follett *(1868-1933)*
American management consultant

The power of the mind is an incredible thing, one
that can never be underestimated.
Mia Hamm *(1972-)*
American soccer player

Power is something of which I am convinced there
is no innocence this side of the womb.
Nadine Gordimer *(1923-)*
South African novelist, activist

Anybody who's ever dealt with me knows not to mess with me.
Nancy Pelosi *(1940-)*
American politician

I don't keep a dog and bark myself.
Queen Elizabeth I *(1553-1603)*
English royalty

*I know I have the body of a weak and feeble woman, but I have
the heart and stomach of a king, and of a king of England,
too; and think foul scorn that Parma or Spain, or any prince of
Europe, should dare to invade the borders of my realm.*
Queen Elizabeth I *(1553-1603)*
English royalty

Power is the ability to get things done.
Rosabeth Moss Kanter *(1943-)*
American academic, author

All power in human hands is liable to be abused.
Sarah Bernhardt *(1844-1923)*
French actress

Next to genius is the power of feeling where true genius lies.
Sarah Josepha Hale *(1788-1879)*
American nursery rhyme writer

*Evil when we are in its power is not felt as evil
but as a necessity, or even a duty.*
Simone Weil *(1909-1943)*
French philosopher

Beware of trying to accomplish anything by force.
Sister Angela Merici *(1913-2005)*
Italian founder of Ursuline nuns

*The older I get, the greater power I seem to have to help the world;
I am like a snowball – the further I am rolled the more I gain.*
Susan B. Anthony *(1820-1906)*
American activist

*I believe we have a higher level of mentality within us,
but we have to use the power in the right way.*
Tina Turner *(1939-)*
American singer

Problem solving

I don't go to church regular. But I pray for answers to my problems.
Loretta Lynn *(1935-)*
American musician

Whatever reason you have for not being somebody, there's somebody who had that same problem and overcame it.
Barbara Reynolds *(1914-)*
English scholar, lexicographer

We cannot direct the wind, but we can adjust the sails.
Bertha Calloway *(1925-)*
American activist

There's no use talking about the problem unless you talk about the solution.
Betty Williams *(1943-)*
Irish, Nobel Peace Prize recipient

If you really want something you can figure out how to make it happen.
Cher *(1946-)*
American recording artist, actress

Work, community, your own life – these have to be tied together. If you don't bring your whole self to a problem, then you're not going to be much of a problem solver, because you're not going to be giving the best parts of your mind to thinking.
Dorothy Brunson *(1939-2011)*
American broadcaster

We would like to believe that we are not in the business of surviving but in being good, and we do not like to admit to ourselves that we are good in order to survive.
Dorothy Rowe *(1930-)*
Austrian psychologist

Procrastination isn't the problem, it's the solution. So procrastinate now, don't put it off.
Ellen DeGeneres *(1958-)*
American comedian, television host

The way I see it... If you need both of your hands for whatever it is you're doing, then your brain should probably be in on it too.
Ellen DeGeneres *(1958-)*
American comedian, television host

I think that little by little I'll be able to solve my problems and survive.
Frida Kahlo *(1907-1954)*
Mexican artist

There ain't no answer. There ain't gonna be any answer.
There never has been an answer. That's the answer.
Gertrude Stein *(1874-1946)*
American writer

Some people have such a talent for making the best of a bad situation that
they go around creating bad situations so they can make the best of them.
Jean Kerr *(1923-2003)*
American author

Walk away from it until you're stronger. All your problems will
be there when you get back, but you'll be better able to cope.
Lady Bird Johnson *(1912-2007)*
American First Lady

Art does not solve problems but makes us aware of their
existence. It opens our eyes to see and our brain to imagine.
Magdalena Abakanowicz *(1930-)*
Polish sculptor

Too many problem-solving sessions become battlegrounds where
decisions are made based on power rather than intelligence.
Margaret J. Wheatley *(1934-)*
American organization expert

Yet we act as if simple cause and effect is at work. We push to find
the one simple reason things have gone wrong. We look for the one
action, or the one person, that created this mess. As soon as we
find someone to blame, we act as if we've solved the problem.
Margaret J. Wheatley *(1934-)*
American organization expert

There are two ways of meeting difficulties: You alter the
difficulties or you alter yourself to meet them.
Phyllis Bottome *(1884-1963)*
British novelist

Your first big trouble can be a bonanza if you live through it. Get through
the first trouble and you'll probably make it through the next one.
Ruth Gordon *(1896-1985)*
American actress, writer

In the face of an obstacle which is impossible to
overcome, stubbornness is stupid.
Simone de Beauvoir *(1908-1986)*
French writer, philosopher

Never answer a question, other than an offer of marriage, by yes or no.
Susan Chitty *(1916-1971)*
British writer

I've always felt that my part of the job was to analyze and criticize in
the hope that other people might use my work to forge solutions.
Wendy Kaminer *(1949-)*
American writer, social critic

When you collaborate with other people, you tend to regard
your own individual contribution as the most important.
Yang Jiang *(1911-)*
Chinese writer

A problem clearly stated is a problem half solved.
Dorothea Brande *(1893-1948)*
American writer, editor

The trouble with life isn't that there is no answer,
it's that there are so many answers.
Ruth Benedict *(1887-1948)*
American scientist

In the past, I always used to be looking for answers. Today,
I know there are only questions. So I just live.
Sarah Brightman *(1960-)*
English actress

We are looking for innovative ways to work with different
people globally to help solve these problems ... We are looking for
opportunities that are sustainable and that we think will make a
difference for organizations and for people across the world.
Sheryl Sandberg *(1969-)*
American, Google VP of Sales

Some people always assume that if you mention a problem, you caused it.
Sonia Johnson *(1936-)*
American activist, writer

Quotations

The point of quotations is that one can use another's words to be insulting.
Amanda Cross *(1926-)*
American critic, writer

Quoting, like smoking, is a dirty habit to which I am devoted.
Carolyn Heilbrun *(1926-2003)*
American academic, author

I always have a quotation for everything – it saves original thinking.
Dorothy L. Sayers *(1893-1957)*
English crime writer

*How do people go to sleep? I'm afraid I've lost the knack. I might try
busting myself smartly over the temple with the nightlight. I might
repeat to myself, slowly and soothingly, a list of quotations beautiful
from minds profound; if I can remember any of the damn things.*
Dorothy Parker *(1893-1967)*
American writer, satirist

An apt quotation is like a lamp which flings its light over the whole sentence.
Letitia Landon *(1802-1838)*
English poet, novelist

I'd lived by quotations, practically all my life.
Loretta Young *(1913-2000)*
American actress

*Quotations (such as have point and lack triteness) from the great
old authors are an act of reverence on the part of the quoter,
and a blessing to a public grown superficial and external.*
Louise Imogen Guiney *(1884-1879)*
American poet

The everlasting quotation-lover dotes on the husks of learning.
Maria Edgeworth *(1768-1849)*
Anglo-Irish writer

*I love quotations because it is a joy to find thoughts one
might have, beautifully expressed with much authority
by someone recognized wiser than oneself.*
Marlene Dietrich *(1901-1992)*
German-born actress

The taste for quotations (and for the juxtaposition of incongruous quotations) is a Surrealist taste.
Susan Sontag *(1933-2004)*
American activist, writer

Most of the time I quote myself. It's not arrogance, it's a writer's job.
Vanna Bonta *(1958-)*
American novelist, poet

One has to secrete a jelly in which to slip quotations down people's throats – and one always secretes too much jelly.
Virginia Woolf *(1882-1941)*
English author

Regret

Never be afraid to sit awhile and think.
Lorraine Hansberry *(1930-1965)*
American playwright

The only causes of regret are laziness, outbursts of temper, hurting others, prejudice, jealousy and envy.
Germaine Greer *(1939-)*
Australian-born writer

Respect

If I respect myself and believe in what I'm doing, no one can touch me.
Fiona Apple *(1977-)*
American musician

In my day, we didn't have self-esteem, we had self-respect, and no more of it than we had earned.
Jane Haddam *(1951-)*
American mystery writer

The willingness to accept responsibility for one's own life is the source from which self-respect springs.
Joan Didion *(1934-)*
American writer

*I have a respect for manners as such, they are a way of
dealing with people you don't agree with or like.*
Margaret Mead *(1901-1978)*
American cultural anthropologist

*Let us forever forget that every station in life is necessarily that
each deserves our respect; that not the station itself; but the
worthy fulfillment of its duties does honor the person.*
Mary Lyon *(1797-1849)*
American educator

If we lose love and self respect for each other, this is how we finally die.
Maya Angelou *(1928-)*
American poet, memoirist

*Someday I want to be rich. Some people get so rich they lose
all respect for humanity. That's how rich I want to be.*
Rita Rudner *(1953-)*
American comedian

Risk

*Of course I realized there was a measure of danger. Obviously I faced
the possibility of not returning when first I considered going. Once
faced and settled there really wasn't any good reason to refer to it.*
Amelia Earhart *(1897-1937)*
American aviator

*And the day came when the risk to remain tight in a bud
was more painful than the risk it took to blossom.*
Anais Nin *(1902-1977)*
French author, diarist

*I don't think I'm a risk-taker. I don't think any entrepreneur is. I think
that's one of those myths of commerce. The new entrepreneur is more
values-led: you do what looks risky to other people because that's
what your convictions tell you to do. Other companies would say I'm
taking risks, but that's my path – it doesn't feel like risk to me.*
Anita Roddick *(1942-2007)*
English entrepreneur

*I don't view this as an extreme kind of activity, but it's
very hard to convince people that this isn't reckless.*
Ann Bancroft *(1955-)*
American adventurer

*I can say, I am terribly frightened and fear is terrible and awful
and it makes me uncomfortable, so I won't do that because
it makes me uncomfortable. Or I could say get used to being
uncomfortable. It is uncomfortable doing something that's risky.
But so what? Do you want to stagnate and just be comfortable?*
Barbara Streisand *(1942-)*
American singer, actor, producer

*Be bold. If you're going to make an error, make a
doozy, and don't be afraid to hit the ball.*
Billie Jean King *(1934-)*
American tennis player

*Everything's a risk, by the way, these days. Every film
you make is a risk. There's no guarantee.*
Cameron Diaz *(1972-)*
American actress

Throw caution to the wind and just do it.
Carrie Underwood *(1983-)*
American singer, musician

*The door that nobody else will go in at, seems
always to swing open widely for me.*
Clara Barton *(1821-1912)*
American nurse

*Every problem in your life goes away in front of a bull. Because this
problem, the bull, is bigger than all other problems. Of course, I have fear,
but it is fear that I will fail the responsibility I have taken on in front of
all those people – not fear of the bull. Death becomes unimportant when
I am in front of him. I feel so good, it does not matter if he kills me.*
Cristina Sanchez *(1972-)*
Spanish bullfighter

*I'll always push the envelope. To me the ultimate sin
in life is to be boring. I don't play it safe.*
Cybill Shepherd *(1950-)*
American actress, former model

*You're at risk being in your own house. There is a risk of cancer with
every breath you take. There is a chance for tragedy every second.*
Danica Patrick *(1982-)*
American race car driver

*The important thing is to not be afraid to take a chance.
Remember, the greatest failure is to not try. Once you find
something you love to do, be the best at doing it.*
Debbi Fields *(1956-)*
American entrepreneur

Life is a risk.
Diane Von Furstenberg *(1946-)*
Belgian-born fashion designer

*There's something liberating about not pretending.
Dare to embarrass yourself. Risk.*
Drew Barrymore *(1975-)*
American actress

The fullness of life is in the hazards of life.
Edith Hamilton *(1867-1963)*
American educator

*You can feel as brave as Columbus starting for the unknown the first
time you enter a Chinese lane full of boys laughing at you, or when
you risk climbing down in a Tibetan pub for a meal of rotten meat.*
Ella Maillart *(1903-1997)*
Swiss writer

And the trouble is, if you don't risk anything, you risk even more.
Erica Jong *(1942-)*
American writer

*I've always said life is sweetened by risk. Sometimes I succeed, and
sometimes I fail, and sometimes I get criticized for my actions.
But I do things that challenge me, that let me stretch.*
Farrah Fawcett *(1947-2009)*
American actress

Sweetie, if you're not living on the edge, then you're taking up space.
Florynce Kennedy *(1916-2000)*
American activist, lawyer

If you risk nothing, then you risk everything.
Geena Davis *(1956-)*
American actress

I would not creep along the coast, but steer out
in mid-sea, by guidance of the stars.
George Eliot *(1819-1880)*
English novelist

Considering how dangerous everything is, nothing is really very frightening.
Gertrude Stein *(1874-1946)*
American writer

If it's a good idea, go ahead and do it. It's much easier
to apologize than it is to get permission.
Grace Murray Hopper *(1906-1992)*
American Rear Admiral, U.S. Navy

All my life I have gone out on a limb, but I have turned the limb
into a bridge, and there is cool, clear water flowing under.
Holly Near *(1949-)*
American singer, songwriter

You must take the risk to disclose yourself in order to become
more real, more human. And even if the price is high.
Isabelle Adjani *(1955-)*
French actress

Anything's possible if you've got enough nerve.
J. K. Rowling *(1965-)*
English writer

To live without risk for me would be tantamount to death.
Jacqueline Cochran *(1910-1980)*
American aviator

If I hold back, I'm no good. I'm no good. I'd rather be
good sometimes, than holding back all the time.
Janis Joplin *(1943-1970)*
American singer

To me, life, for all its privations, is a luminous thing. You have to risk it.
Jeanette Winterson *(1959-)*
British novelist

What you risk reveals what you value.
Jeanette Winterson *(1959-)*
British novelist

I've got nothing left to lose at this point. The work I've done is out there.
Jessica Lange *(1949-)*
American actress

*So I, with eager voice and news-flushed face, cry to those caught
in comas, stupors, sleeping: come, everything is running, flying,
leaping, hurtling through time! And we are in this race.*
Jessica Powers *(1913-1985)*
American poet

All serious daring starts from within.
Joan Baez *(1941-)*
American folksinger, songwriter

*One life is all we have and we live it as we believe in
living it. But to sacrifice what you are and to live without
belief, that is a fate more terrible than dying.*
Joan of Arc *(1412-1431)*
French heroine

*Accept that all of us can be hurt, that all of us can – and
surely will at times – fail. I think we should follow a simple
rule: if we can take the worst, take the risk.*
Joyce Brothers *(1927-)*
American psychologist

*The more I do, the more frightened I get. But that is
essential. Otherwise why would I go on doing it?*
Judi Dench *(1934-)*
English actress

Leap, and the net will appear.
Julia Cameron *(1948-)*
American teacher, author

*I live for the present always. I accept this risk. I
don't deny the past, but it's a page to turn.*
Juliette Binoche *(1964-)*
French actress

If you let fear of consequence prevent you from following your deepest instinct then your life will be safe, expedient and thin.
Katharine Butler Hathaway *(1890-1942)*
American writer

Risk! Risk anything. Care no more for the opinions of others, for those voices. Do the hardest thing on earth for you. Act for yourself. Face the truth.
Katherine Mansfield *(1888-1923)*
New Zealand-born writer

I don't think about risks much. I just do what I want to do. If you gotta go you gotta go.
Lillian Carter *(1898-1983)*
American activist

It was a risk. ...But I don't look at risk the way other people do. When you're an entrepreneur, you have to go in feeling like you're going to be successful.
Lillian Vernon *(1929-)*
German entrepreneur

Never flinch – make up your own mind and do it.
Margaret Thatcher *(1925-)*
English Prime Minister

The minute a person whose word means a great deal to others dares to take the open-hearted and courageous way, many others follow.
Marian Anderson *(1897-1993)*
American singer

Nothing in life is to be feared. It is only to be understood.
Marie Curie *(1897-1966)*
Polish-French physicist

Risk always brings its own rewards: the exhilaration of breaking through, of getting to the other side; the relief of a conflict healed; the clarity when a paradox dissolves.
Marilyn Ferguson *(1938-2008)*
American author

If I'd observed all the rules, I'd never have got anywhere.
Marilyn Monroe *(1926-1962)*
American actress

*No one else can take risks for us, or face our losses on our behalf,
or give us self-esteem. No one can spare us from life's slings
and arrows, and when death comes, we meet it alone.*
Martha Beck *(1962-)*
American author

*The jump is so frightening between where I am and where I want to
be...because of all I may become I will close my eyes and leap!*
Mary Anne Radmacher *(1957-)*
American writer

*Every day I live I am more convinced that the waste of life lies in the love
we have not given, the powers we have not used, the selfish prudence that
will risk nothing and which, shirking pain, misses happiness as well.*
Mary Cholmondeley *(1859-1925)*
British writer

*Take chances, make mistakes. That's how you grow. Pain nourishes
your courage. You have to fail in order to practice being brave.*
Mary Tyler Moore *(1936-)*
American actress

The distance is nothing; it is only the first step that is difficult.
Mme. Du Deffand *(1697-1780)*
French patron of the arts

*Leaps over walls – especially when taken late in life – can be extremely
perilous. To leap successfully, you need a sense of humor, the spirit of
adventure and an unshakable conviction that what you are leaping
over is an obstacle upon which you would otherwise fall down.*
Monica Baldwin *(1893-1975)*
British nun

A fool without fear is sometimes wiser than an angel with fear.
Nancy Astor *(1879-1964)*
American born, British politician

*Even from a very early age, I knew I didn't want to miss out on anything
life had to offer just because it might be considered dangerous.*
Nicole Kidman *(1967-)*
Australian actress

I believe that one of life's greatest risks is never daring to risk.
Oprah Winfrey *(1954-)*
American media mogul

Luck enters into every contingency. You are a fool if you forget it – and a greater fool if you count upon it.
Phyllis Bottome *(1884-1963)*
British novelist

Too often, the opportunity knocks, but by the time you push back the chain, push back the bolt, unhook the two locks and shut off the burglar alarm, it's too late.
Rita Coolidge *(1944-)*
American musician

You must accept that you might fail, then, if you do your best and still don't win, at least you can be satisfied that you've tried. If you don't accept failure as a possibility, you don't set high goals, you don't branch out, you don't try – you don't take the risk.
Rosalynn Carter *(1927-)*
American First Lady

You have to reach a level of comfort with that risk.
Sally Ride *(1951-)*
American astronaut

I don't judge others. I say if you feel good with what you're doing, let your freak flag fly.
Sarah Jessica Parker *(1965-)*
American actress

I'm in love with the potential of miracles. For me the safest place is out on a limb.
Shirley MacLaine *(1934-)*
American actress

You will do foolish things but do them with enthusiasm.
Sidonie-Gabrielle Colette *(1873-1954)*
French novelist

Sometimes I think we can tell how important it is to risk by how dangerous it is to do so.
Sonia Johnson *(1936-)*
American activist, writer

It's a funny thing, the less people have to live for, the less nerve they have to risk losing nothing.
Zora Neale Hurston *(1891-1960)*
American dramatist

Self-awareness

It is not easy to find happiness in ourselves, and
it is not possible to find it elsewhere.
Agnes Repplier *(1855-1950)*
American essayist

I can spot empty flattery and know exactly where I stand. In the end
it's really only my own approval or disapproval that means anything.
Agnetha Faltskog *(1950-)*
Swedish musician

I just want to live each moment, but it's kind of hard to do
that when you are asked to analyze yourself constantly.
Alexis Bledel *(1981-)*
American actress

And I love kick boxing. It's a lot of fun. It gives you a lot of
confidence when you can kick somebody in the head.
Alicia Keys *(1981-)*
American singer, songwriter

When it's open and honest, that's when the real nature of who
you are as a vocalist or as a performer, all of that stuff can finally
start to become what it's supposed to be. Like a settling into
yourself. It's not even a musical thing, it's a whole mindset, a whole
acceptance of who you were supposed to be. Life sounds good.
Alison Krauss *(1971-)*
American musician

I want the public to remember me as they knew me:
athletic, smart, and healthy.... Remember me strong
and tough and quick, fleet of foot and tenacious.
Althea Gibson *(1927-2003)*
American tennis player

Odd, the years it took to learn one simple fact – that the prize just
ahead, the next job, publication, love affair, marriage always seemed
to hold the key to satisfaction but never, in the longer run, sufficed.
Amanda Cross *(1926-)*
American critic, writer

I did not lose myself all at once. I rubbed out my face over the years washing away my pain the same way carvings on stone are worn down by water.

Amy Tan *(1952-)*
American writer (Chinese descent)

We don't see things as they are. We see them as we are.

Anais Nin *(1902-1977)*
French author, diarist

I don't carry any early childhood trauma around with me, if that's what you're hinting at. The story of the bicycles – and there were three of them which were stolen from me – I've dealt with it well.

Angela Merkel *(1954-)*
German Chancellor

I just started to see the world as it really is and it completely shocked me and changed my opinion on everything... on life and my values and certainly my own sense of self.

Angelina Jolie *(1975-)*
American actress

Don't accept your dog's admiration as conclusive evidence that you are wonderful.

Ann Landers *(1918-2002)*
American advice columnist

It was as if I had worked for years on the wrong side of a tapestry, learning accurately all its lines and figures, yet always missing its color and sheen.

Anna Louise Strong *(1885-1970)*
American journalist, activist

Figuring out who you are is the whole point of the human experience.

Anna Quindlen *(1952-)*
American journalist

Oh, honey, I'm from Oklahoma! This is who I am – middle-class all the way!

Annette Bening *(1958-)*
American actress

I am a frayed and nibbled survivor in a fallen world, and I am getting along. I am aging and eaten and have done my share of eating too. I am not washed and beautiful, in control of a shining world in which everything fits, but instead am wondering awed about on a splintered wreck I've come to care for, whose gnawed trees breathe a delicate air, whose bloodied and scarred creatures are my dearest companions, and whose beauty bats and shines not in its imperfections but overwhelmingly in spite of them...

Annie Dillard *(1945-)*
American author

I break up through the skin of awareness a thousand times a day, as dolphins burst through seas, and dive again, and rise, and dive.

Annie Dillard *(1945-)*
American author

Only by learning to live in harmony with your contradictions can you keep it all afloat.

Audre Lorde *(1934-1992)*
Caribbean-American writer

I am simple complex generous selfish unattractive beautiful lazy and driven.

Barbara Streisand *(1942-)*
American singer, actor, producer

You have got to discover you, what you do, and trust it.

Barbara Streisand *(1942-)*
American singer, actor, producer

Trust your gut.

Barbara Walters *(1929-)*
American broadcast journalist, author

I'm not playing a role. I'm being myself, whatever the hell that is.

Bea Arthur *(1923-2009)*
American actress

You can live a lifetime and, at the end of it, know more about other people than you know about yourself.

Beryl Markham *(1874-1946)*
English-born Kenyan pilot

I didn't belong as a kid, and that always bothered me. If only I'd known that one day my differentness would be an asset, then my early life would have been much easier.
Bette Midler *(1945-)*
American actress

I never hurt nobody but myself and that's nobody's business but my own.
Billie Holiday *(1915-1959)*
American jazz singer

I think self-awareness is probably the most important thing towards becoming a champion.
Billie Jean King *(1934-)*
American tennis player

I have been very happy, very rich, very beautiful, much adulated, very famous and very unhappy.
Brigitte Bardot *(1934-)*
French actress

In bullfighting there is a term called querencia. The querencia is the spot in the ring to which the bull returns. Each bull has a different querencia, but as the bullfight continues, and the animal becomes more threatened, it returns more and more often to his spot. As he returns to his querencia, he becomes more predictable. And so, in the end, the matador is able to kill the bull because instead of trying something new, the bull returns to what is familiar. His comfort zone.
Carly Fiorina *(1954-)*
American, Former HP CEO

As a singer I tried on all these hats, these voices, these clothes, and eventually out came me.
Carly Simon *(1945-)*
American singer, songwriter

I liked myself better when I wasn't me.
Carol Burnett *(1933-)*
American actress, comedian

I am a spy in the house of me. I report back from the front lines of the battle that is me. I am somewhat nonplused by the event that is my life.
Carrie Fisher *(1956-)*
American actress

I'm the female equivalent of a counterfeit $20 bill. Half of what you see is a pretty good reproduction, the rest is fraud.
Cher *(1946-)*
American recording artist, actress

A successful life is one that is lived through understanding and pursuing one's own path, not chasing after the dreams of others.
Chin-Ning Chu *(1947-2009)*
Chinese business author

You get labeled. People tell me every day how great I am, and they don't know me. I'm no angel. I'm a control freak – on and off the court.
Chris Evert *(1954-)*
American tennis player

I used to have a sign on my desk at Columbia that said, Breathe. So whenever there was one of those moments where I was faced with bad news or somebody was screaming at me – which happened more often than I can possibly tell you – I took deep breaths a lot.
Dawn Steel *(1946-1997)*
American movie executive

I'm not really on a mission to tell anybody anything. I'd rather be figured out.
Diana Krall *(1964-)*
Canadian jazz pianist, singer

I work from awkwardness. By that I mean I don't like to arrange things. If I stand in front of something, instead of arranging it, I arrange myself.
Diane Arbus *(1923-1971)*
American photographer

At a certain point, you start to think about your legacy … If you're lucky enough that someone's listening in 100 years, you want 'em to have all the pieces.
Dolly Parton *(1946-)*
American singer-songwriter

The past is not simply the past, but a prism through which the subject filters their own changing self-image.
Doris Kearns Goodwin *(1943-)*
American historian

Sometimes I think we're all tightrope walkers suspended on a wire two thousand feet in the air, and as long as we never look down we're okay, but some of us lose momentum and look down for a second and are never quite the same again; we know.
Dorothy Gilman *(1923-)*
American mystery writer

I shall stay the way I am because I do not give a damn.
Dorothy Parker *(1893-1967)*
American writer, satirist

I am not an eccentric. It's just that I am more alive than most people. I am an unpopular electric eel set in a pond of goldfish.
Edith Sitwell *(1902-1986)*
British poet, critic

After all, one knows one's weak points so well that it's rather bewildering to have the critics overlook them and invent others.
Edith Wharton *(1862-1937)*
American novelist

It is only when we truly know and understand that we have a limited time on earth, and that we have no way of knowing when our time is up, that we will begin to live each day to the fullest; as if it was the only one we had.
Elisabeth Kübler-Ross *(1926-2004)*
Swiss psychiatrist

There is a solitude which each and every one of us has always carried within. More inaccessible than the ice-cold mountains more profound than the midnight sea: the solitude of self.
Elizabeth Cady Stanton *(1815-1902)*
American reformist, writer

During much of my life I was anxious to be what someone else wanted me to be. Now I have given up that struggle. I am what I am.
Elizabeth Coatsworth *(1893-1986)*
American poet

It is always our own self that we find at the end of the journey. The sooner we face that self, the better.
Ella Maillart *(1903-1997)*
Swiss writer

For me, it's that I contributed ... That I'm on this planet doing
some good and making people happy. That's to me the most
important thing, that my hour of television is positive and upbeat
and an antidote for all the negative stuff going on in life.
Ellen DeGeneres *(1958-)*
American comedian, television host

Believing in our hearts that who we are is enough is
the key to a more satisfying and balanced life.
Ellen Sue Stern *(1943-1976)*
American political activist

My life is increasingly an inner one and the
outer setting matters less and less.
Esther Etty Hillesum *(1914-1943)*
Netherlands, Jewish prisoner at Auschwitz

The greatest possession is self-possession.
Ethel Watts Mumford *(1876-1940)*
American author

When I'm performing for the people, I am me, then. I am that little
girl who, when she was five years old, used to sing at church. Or I'm
that 15-year-old young lady who wanted to be grown and wanted
to sing and couldn't wait to be smoking' a cigarette, you know?
Etta James *(1938-)*
American musician

It is those who have a deep and real inner life who are best
able to deal with the irritating details of outer life.
Evelyn Underhill *(1875-1941)*
English writer

I'm just a loud-mouthed middle-aged colored lady with a fused spine
and three feet of intestines missing and a lot of people think I'm crazy.
Maybe you do too, but I never stop to wonder why I'm not like other
people. The mystery to me is why more people aren't like me.
Florynce Kennedy *(1916-2000)*
American activist, lawyer

I paint self-portraits because I am so often alone,
because I am the person I know best.
Frida Kahlo *(1907-1954)*
Mexican artist

I believe that dreams transport us through the underside of our days and that if we wish to become acquainted with the dark side of what we are, the signposts are there waiting for us to translate them.
Gail Godwin *(1937-)*
American short story writer

Would that there were an award for people who come to understand the concept of enough. Good enough. Successful enough. Thin enough. Rich enough. Socially responsible enough. When you have self-respect, you have enough.
Gail Sheehy *(1937-)*
American writer, lecturer

I do not like the idea of happiness – it is too momentary. I would say that I was always busy and interested in something – interest has more meaning than happiness.
Georgia O'Keeffe *(1887-1986)*
American artist

I know now that most people are so closely concerned with themselves that they are not aware of their own individuality. I can see myself, and it has helped me to say what I want to say ... in paint.
Georgia O'Keeffe *(1887-1986)*
American artist

Nobody knows what I am trying to do but I do and I know when I succeed.
Gertrude Stein *(1874-1946)*
American writer

Don't be afraid your life will end; be afraid that it will never begin.
Grace Hansen *(1818-1889)*
American dance director

Life has been difficult for me. You must realize I am a sad person; I am a misfit in life.
Greta Garbo *(1905-1990)*
Swedish-born actress

It changed me more than anything else. You don't want to get to that place where you're the adult and you're palpably in the next generation. And, this shoved me into that.
Gwyneth Paltrow *(1972-)*
American actress

The sad truth is that most evil is done by people who never make up their minds to be either good or evil.
Hannah Arendt *(1906-1975)*
German philosopher

There are certain sacred things in my life that I would never talk about. Because they are clear in my head, I can walk freely around the opposite side. I keep them completely separate in my mind.
Heather Armstrong *(1975-)*
American blogger

I was once the typical daughter then the easily recognizable wife and then the quintessential mother. I seem always to have reminded people of someone in their family. Perhaps I am just the triumph of Plain Jane.
Helen Hayes *(1900-1993)*
American actress

Yes, I have doubted. I have wandered off the path, but I always return. It is intuitive, an intrinsic, built-in sense of direction. I seem always to find my way home.
Helen Hayes *(1900-1993)*
American actress

I have to struggle to change people's perceptions of me. I grew very frustrated with the perception that I'm this shy, retiring, inhibited aristocratic creature when I'm absolutely not like that at all.
Helena Bonham Carter *(1966-)*
British actress

I remember one day sitting at the pool and suddenly the tears were streaming down my cheeks. Why was I so unhappy? I had success. I had security. But it wasn't enough. I was exploding inside.
Ingrid Bergman *(1915-1982)*
Swedish-born, American actress

Even though people may be well known, they hold in their hearts the emotions of a simple person for the moments that are the most important of those we know on earth: birth, marriage and death.
Jacqueline Kennedy Onassis *(1929-1994)*
American First Lady

I have been a selfish being all my life, in practice, though not in principle.
Jane Austen *(1775-1817)*
English novelist

Whenever at an accusation blind rage burns up within us, the reason is that some arrow has pierced the joints of our harness. Behind our shining armor of righteous indignation lurks a convicted and only half-repentant sinner ... [and] we may be almost sure some sharp and bitter grain of truth lurks within it and the wound is best probed.
Jane Harrison *(1850-1928)*
British classical scholar

I was a woman in a man's world. I was a Democrat in a Republican administration. I was an intellectual in a world of bureaucrats. I talked differently. This may have made me a bit like an ink blot.
Jeane Kirkpatrick *(1926-2006)*
American ambassador

I think people deceive themselves about themselves, particularly as they get older.
Jeanette Winterson *(1959-)*
British novelist

If I had my life to live over, I would do it all again, but this time I would be nastier.
Jeannette Rankin *(1880-1973)*
American politician

Once you figure out who you are and what you love about yourself, I think it all kinda falls into place.
Jennifer Aniston *(1969-)*
American actress

To have that sense of one's intrinsic worth... is potentially to have everything.
Joan Didion *(1934-)*
American writer

It's where we go, and what we do when we get there, that tells us who we are.
Joyce Carol Oates *(1938-)*
American writer

I think you've got to have your feet planted firmly on the ground, especially in this business, and you must not believe things that are said or written about you, because everything gets out of proportion one way or the other.
Judi Dench *(1934-)*
English actress

It is far more impressive when others discover
your good qualities without your help.
Judith Martin *(1938-)*
American etiquette author

If I'm such a legend, then why am I so lonely? If I'm a legend, then
why do I sit at home for hours staring at the damned phone?
Judy Garland *(1922-1969)*
American actress, singer

Self-determination has to mean that the leader is your individual
gut, and heart, and mind or we're talking about power, again, and
its rather well-known impurities. Who is really going to care whether
you live or die and who is going to know the most intimate motivation
for your laughter and your tears is the only person to be trusted
to speak for yo u and to decide what you will or will not do.
June Jordan *(1936-2002)*
American writer

The most comprehensive formulation of therapeutic goals is the striving for
wholeheartedness: to be without pretense, to be emotionally sincere, to be
able to put the whole of oneself into one's feelings, one's work, one's beliefs.
Karen Horney *(1885-1952)*
American psychologist

It is only by following your deepest instinct that you can lead a rich life.
Katharine Butler Hathaway *(1890-1942)*
American writer

Life is to be lived. If you have to support yourself, you had bloody
well better find some way that is going to be interesting. And you
don't do that by sitting around wondering about yourself.
Katharine Hepburn *(1907-2003)*
American actress

I want, by understanding myself, to understand others.
I want to be all that I am capable of becoming.
Katherine Mansfield *(1888 - 1923)*
New Zealand-born writer

When you are unhappy, is there anything more maddening than
to be told that you should be contented with your lot?
Kathleen Norris *(1880-1966)*
American poet, novelist

I always ask the question 'Is this what I want in my life?'
Kathy Ireland *(1963-)*
American entrepreneur

I feel like a human piñata. The disappointing thing is, no candy is going to spill out.
Katie Couric *(1957-)*
American journalist

Don't you ever let a soul in the world tell you that you can't be exactly who you are.
Lady Gaga *(1986-)*
American performance artist

If you don't have any shadows you're not in the light.
Lady Gaga *(1986-)*
American performance artist

It is a sad day when you find out that it's not accident or time or fortune but just yourself that kept things from you.
Lillian Hellman *(1905-1984)*
American playwright

I am who I choose to be. I always have been what I chose though not always what I pleased.
Lois McMaster Bujold *(1949-)*
American author

Life isn't one straight line. Most of us have to be transplanted, like a tree, before we blossom.
Louise Nevelson *(1899-1988)*
American sculptor, painter

I would rather regret the things that I have done than the things that I have not.
Lucille Ball *(1911-1989)*
American comedian, actress

I'm not a bit changed – not really. I'm only just pruned down and branched out. The real ME – back here – is just the same.
Lucy Maud Montgomery *(1874-1942)*
Canadian writer

Many people see Eva Peron as either a saint or the incarnation
of Satan. That means I can definitely identify with her.
Madonna Ciccone *(1958-)*
American recording artist

Be good to yourself. Listen to your body, to your heart.
We're very hard on ourselves, and we're always feeling like
we're not doing enough. It's a terribly hard job.
Marcia Wallace *(1942-)*
American actress

Until you've lost your reputation, you never realize what a burden it was.
Margaret Mitchell *(1900-1949)*
American novelist

The one important thing I have learned over the years is the
difference between taking one's work seriously and taking one's self
seriously. The first is imperative and the second is disastrous.
Margot Fonteyn *(1919-1991)*
English ballerina

The best that can be said of my life so far is that it has
been industrious, and the best that can be said of me is
that I have not pretended to what I was not.
Maria Mitchell *(1818-1889)*
American scientist

I suppose I might insist on making issues of things. But that is not my
nature, and I always bear in mind that my mission is to leave behind me
the kind of impression that will make it easier for those who follow.
Marian Anderson *(1897-1993)*
American singer

I'd discovered you never know yourself until you're tested and that
you don't even know you're being tested until afterwards, and
that in fact there isn't anyone giving the test except yourself.
Marilyn French *(1929-2009)*
American author

Being a sex symbol is a heavy load to carry, especially
when one is tired, hurt and bewildered.
Marilyn Monroe *(1926-1962)*
American actress

I was raised almost entirely on turnips and potatoes, but I think that the turnips had more to do with the effect than the potatoes.
Marlene Dietrich *(1901-1992)*
German-born actress

I find that balancing my life with my work with the kids at St. Jude, working on books, working on my career as an actor and taking time out for my husband and family helps to cushion a lot of the blows.
Marlo Thomas *(1937-)*
American actress

I did not want to be a tree, a flower or a wave. In a dancer's body, we as audience must see ourselves, not the imitated behavior of everyday actions, not the phenomenon of nature, not exotic creatures from another planet, but something of the miracle that is a human being.
Martha Graham *(1894-1991)*
American dancer, choreographer

I live in a kind of controlled awareness. I wouldn't call it fear, but it's an awareness. I know I have a responsibility to behave in a certain way. I'm able to do that.
Mary Tyler Moore *(1936-)*
American actress

The great omission in American life is solitude. . . that zone of time and space, free from the outside pressures, which is the incinerator of the spirit.
Marya Mannes *(1904-1990)*
American author, critic

I have always regarded myself as the pillar of my life.
Meryl Streep *(1949-)*
American actress

My vigor, vitality, and cheek repel me. I am the kind of woman I would run from.
Nancy Astor *(1879-1964)*
American born, British politician

Doubt yourself and you doubt everything you see. Judge yourself and you see judges everywhere. But if you listen to the sound of your own voice, you can rise above doubt and judgment. And you can see forever.
Nancy Kerrigan *(1969-)*
American Olympic skater

*Two thirds of the public have absolutely no idea
who I am. I see that as a strength.*
Nancy Pelosi *(1940-)*
American politician

If you don't understand yourself you don't understand anybody else.
Nikki Giovanni *(1943-)*
American poet, author

*I didn't want to say No because I didn't want people to think
I'm not nice. And that, to me, has been the greatest lesson of
my life: to recognize that I am solely responsible for it, and not
trying to please other people, and not living my life to please
other people, but doing what my heart says all the time.*
Oprah Winfrey *(1954-)*
American media mogul

*Though I am grateful for the blessings of wealth, it hasn't changed who
I am. My feet are still on the ground. I'm just wearing better shoes.*
Oprah Winfrey *(1954-)*
American media mogul

*There's a period of life when we swallow a knowledge of
ourselves and it becomes either good or sour inside.*
Pearl Bailey *(1918-1990)*
American entertainer

*I'm one Pia Zadora, the same way all the time. That's why I'm happy. It
took me a long time to get to the point where I could be myself all the time.*
Pia Zadora *(1953-)*
American actress

*I'd like to be a queen in people's hearts but I don't
see myself being Queen of this country.*
Princess Diana *(1961-1997)*
British princess

*I would rather go to any extreme than suffer anything that
is unworthy of my reputation, or of that of my crown.*
Queen Elizabeth 1 *(1553-1603)*
English royalty

It is the soul's duty to be loyal to its own desires.
Rebecca West *(1892-1983)*
Irish-born, British writer

All of us have moments in our childhood where we come alive for the first time. And we go back to those moments and think, This is when I became myself.
Rita Dove *(1952-)*
American poet

The statistics on sanity are that one out of every four Americans is suffering from some form of mental illness. Think of your three best friends. If they're okay, then it's you.
Rita Mae Brown *(1944-)*
American novelist

I had already learned from more than a decade of political life that I was going to be criticized no matter what I did, so I might as well be criticized for something I wanted to do.
Rosalynn Carter *(1927-)*
American First Lady

Nothing perhaps is strange once you have accepted life itself – the great strange business which includes all lesser strangeness.
Rose Macaulay *(1881-1958)*
British writer

I used to think I was an interesting person, but I must tell you how sobering a thought it is to realize your life's story fills about thirty-five pages and you have, actually, not much to say.
Roseanne Arnold *(1953-)*
American actress, comedian

I need people's good opinion. This is something in myself I dislike because I even need the good opinion of people who I don't admire. I am afraid of what they will say to me. I am afraid of their tongues and their indifference.
Ruth Rendell *(1930-)*
English writer, detective fiction

But there isn't any second half of myself waiting to plug in and make me whole. It's there. I'm already whole.
Sally Field *(1946-)*
American actress

I make the most of all that comes and the least of all that goes.
Sara Teasdale *(1884-1933)*
American poet

I think I've probably re-invented myself three or
four times now, if that's what one calls it.
Sarah Brightman *(1960-)*
English actress

I've learned to trust myself, to listen to truth, to not
be afraid of it and to not try and hide it.
Sarah McLachlan *(1968-)*
Canadian singer, songwriter

If I could know me I could know the universe.
Shirley MacLaine *(1934-)*
American actress

I stopped believing in Santa Claus at age six when my mother
took me to see him in a store and he asked for my autograph.
Shirley Temple Black *(1928-)*
American actress

It is a fault to wish to be understood before we
have made ourselves clear to ourselves.
Simone Weil *(1909-1943)*
French philosopher

I've never tried to block out the memories of the past, even though
some are painful. I don't understand people who hide from their past.
Everything you live through helps to make you the person you are now.
Sophia Loren *(1934-)*
Italian actress

The world is made for people who aren't cursed with self-awareness.
Susan Sarandon *(1946-)*
American actress

I'm as pure as the driven slush.
Tallulah Bankhead *(1902-1968)*
American actress

Learn to self-conquest, persevere thus for a time, and you will
perceive very clearly the advantage which you gain from it.
Teresa of Avila *(1515-1582)*
Spanish Roman Catholic nun, saint

*Especially in the entertainment industry, because you have
to focus on yourself and your career every day, it's really
important to do things that remind you that it's not just
about you; things that really take you back to reality.*
Trisha Yearwood *(1959-)*
American musician

*If people don't like me for whatever I do, for being me, then that's too bad. I
don't want to change to be something that I'm not for other people to like me.*
Vanessa Hudgens *(1988-)*
American actress

*I would rather have an inferiority complex and be pleasantly surprised,
than have a superiority complex and be rudely awakened.*
Vanna Bonta *(1958-)*
American novelist, poet

*You can't be responsible for the way people respond
to you. You're only responsible for yourself.*
Victoria Principal *(1946-)*
American actress

*Each has their past shut in them like the leaves of a book known
to them by heart and their friends can only read the title.*
Virginia Woolf *(1882-1941)*
English author

I believe in me more than anything in this world.
Wilma Rudolph *(1940-1994)*
American Olympic runner

*It's very expressive of myself. I just lump everything in a great
heap which I have labeled the past, and, having thus emptied this
deep reservoir that was once myself, I am ready to continue.*
Zelda Fitzgerald *(1900-1948)*
American artist, writer

*I love myself when I am laughing. And then again
when I am looking mean and impressive.*
Zora Neale Hurston *(1891-1960)*
American dramatist

Success

If you want a place in the sun, you've got to put up with a few blisters.
Abigail Van Buren *(1918-2002)*
American advice columnist

Most successes are unhappy. That's why they are successes
– they have to reassure themselves about themselves by
achieving something that the world will notice.
Agatha Christie *(1890-1976)*
English detective novelist

When I'm living in the world of luxury and celebrity, which is where I found
myself for a large part of my life, it's a walk-on part. Not a vital necessity,
like it is for so many people. I enjoy it but I can see right through it!
Agnetha Faltskog *(1950-)*
Swedish musician

But once I acclimated and really used fame for what it was
offering me as a tool to serve my life purpose of inspiring
and contributing, then it started to get fun again.
Alanis Morisette *(1974-)*
Canadian singer

I don't get recognized in London or at home either – very seldom
anyway. Either that or I look so crazy no one wants to come up to me.
Alison Krauss *(1971-)*
American musician

Most of the time it's the parents who recognize me. They try to tell
their kids, 'Look, it's Giselle,' and I say, 'No, no, no, don't ruin this
for them,' because I'm usually standing there with my hair sideways
and no make-up on. And the kid is saying, 'That is not Giselle. No
way. That is some worn-out girl who really needs a bath.'
Amy Adams *(1974-)*
American actress

I have always found that my view of success has been iconoclastic: success to
me is not about money or status or fame, it's about finding a livelihood that
brings me joy and self-sufficiency and a sense of contributing to the world.
Anita Roddick *(1942-2007)*
English entrepreneur

If you have a good name, if you are right more often than you are wrong, if your children respect you, if your grandchildren are glad to see you, if your friends can count on you and you can count on them in time of trouble, if you can face your God and say I have done my best, then you are a success.

Ann Landers *(1918-2002)*
American advice columnist

Whatever success I may have attained is due to the fact that since I was old enough to work at all, my ambition has never deserted me.

Anna Held *(1872-1918)*
Polish-born stage performer

If your success is not on your own terms, if it looks good to the world but does not feel good in your heart, it is not success at all.

Anna Quindlen *(1952-)*
American journalist

There's a will to ensure that our company not only survives but has an opportunity to become great again.

Anne Mulcahy *(1952-)*
American, former CEO Xerox

People seldom see the halting and painful steps by which the most significant success is achieved.

Anne Sullivan Macy *(1866-1936)*
American teacher, companion Helen Keller

Getting to the top isn't bad, and it's probably best done as an afterthought.

Anne Wilson Schaef *(1947-)*
American psychotherapist

Success is like reaching an important birthday and finding you're exactly the same.

Audrey Hepburn *(1929-1993)*
Belgian-born actress

The formula for success is simple: practice and concentration then more practice and more concentration.

Babe Didrikson Zaharias *(1911-1956)*
American golfer

The secret of the truly successful, I believe, is that they learned very early in life how not to be busy. They saw through that adage, repeated to me so often in childhood, that anything worth doing is worth doing well. The truth is, many things are worth doing only in the most slovenly, halfhearted fashion possible, and many other things are not worth doing at all.
Barbara Ehrenreich *(1941-)*
American writer

Success can make you go one of two ways. It can make you a prima donna or it can smooth the edges, take away the insecurities, let the nice things come out.
Barbara Walters *(1929-)*
American broadcast journalist, author

Success breeds confidence.
Beryl Markham *(1874-1946)*
English-born Kenyan pilot

Being called very, very difficult is the beginning of success. Until you're called very, very difficult you're really nobody at all.
Bette Davis *(1908-1989)*
American actress

The worst part of success is to try and find someone who is happy for you.
Bette Midler *(1945-)*
American actress

I lived through the garbage. I might as well dine on the caviar.
Beverly Sills *(1929-2007)*
American operatic soprano

Being Number One isn't everything to me, but for those few hours on the court it's way ahead of whatever's in second place.
Billie Jean King *(1934-)*
American tennis player

I like being famous when it's convenient for me and completely anonymous when it's not.
Catherine Deneuve *(1943-)*
French actress

Success is often achieved by those who don't know that failure is inevitable.
Coco Chanel *(1883-1971)*
French fashion designer

What I wanted was to be allowed to do the thing in the world
I did best-which I believed then and believe now is the greatest
privilege there is. When I did that success found me.
Debbi Fields *(1956-)*
American entrepreneur

Whatever you want in life other people are going to want it too. Believe
in yourself enough to accept the idea that you have an equal right to it.
Diane Sawyer *(1945-)*
American broadcast journalist

Sometimes you can do all the right things and not
succeed. And that's a hard lesson of reality.
Donna Tartt *(1963-)*
American novelist

I'm never going to be famous. My name will never be writ large on the
roster of Those Who Do Things. I don't do any thing. Not one single
thing. I used to bite my nails, but I don't even do that any more.
Dorothy Parker *(1893-1967)*
American writer, satirist

Success is a great deodorant.
Elizabeth Taylor *(1932-2011)*
British-born actress

When I was younger I thought success was something different. I thought,
When I grow up, I want to be famous. I want to be a star. I want to be in
movies. When I grow up I want to see the world, drive nice cars. I want to
have groupies. But my idea of success is different today. For me, the most
important thing in your life is to live your life with integrity and not to
give into peer pressure, to try to be something that you're not. To live your
life as an honest and compassionate person. To contribute in some way.
Ellen DeGeneres *(1958-)*
American comedian, television host

Success is counted sweetest by those who never succeed.
Emily Dickinson *(1830-1886)*
American poet

I never dreamed about success. I worked for it.
Estee Lauder *(1906-2004)*
American cosmetics entrepreneur

For an actress to be a success she must have the face of Venus,
the brains of Minerva, the grace of Terpsichore, the memory of
Macaulay, the figure of Juno, and the hide of a rhinoceros.
Ethel Barrymore *(1879-1959)*
American actress

What does so-called success or failure matter if only you have succeeded
in doing the thing you set out to do? The doing is all that really counts.
Eva Le Gallienne *(1899-1991)*
English-American actress, director

The quick success was a bit strange to get used to.
Fiona Apple *(1977-)*
American musician

I attribute my success to this: I never gave or took an excuse.
Florence Nightingale *(1820-1910)*
English nurse, writer

If a person asks for success and prepares for failure, they
will get the situation they have prepared for.
Florence Scovel Shinn *(1871-1940)*
American artist, book illustrator

Success didn't spoil me; I've always been insufferable.
Fran Lebowitz *(1950-)*
American writer

This seems to be the law of progress in everything we do; it moves along a
spiral rather than a perpendicular; we seem to be actually going out of the
way, and yet it turns out that we were really moving upward all the time.
Frances E. Willard *(1839-1898)*
American educator, suffragist

None of us suddenly becomes something overnight. The
preparations have been in the making for a lifetime.
Gail Godwin *(1937-)*
American short story writer

I do want to get rich but I never want to do what there is to do to get rich.
Gertrude Stein *(1874-1946)*
American writer

*Fame was thrilling only until it became grueling. Money
was fun only until you ran out of things to buy.*
Gloria Swanson *(1899-1983)*
American actress

*I can honestly say that I was never affected by the question of
the success of an undertaking. If I felt it was the right thing
to do, I was for it regardless of the possible outcome.*
Golda Meir *(1898-1978)*
Ukrainian-born Israeli leader

*The ladder of success in Hollywood is usually a press agent,
actor, director, producer, leading man; and you are a star if you
sleep with each of them in that order. Crude, but true.*
Hedy Lamarr *(1914-2000)*
Austrian actress

*My mother drew the distinction between achievement and success.
She said that achievement is the knowledge that you have studied
and worked hard and done the best that is in you. Success is being
praised by others, and that's nice, too, but not as important or
satisfying. Always aim for achievement and forget about success.*
Helen Hayes *(1900-1993)*
American actress

*Sometimes I wonder whether I've given up too much for
the theatre, but I have one big consolation – money.*
Hermione Gingold *(1897-1987)*
British actress

*Success and failure are both greatly overrated but
failure gives you a whole lot more to talk about.*
Hildegard Knef *(1925-2002)*
German actress, singer

*I've never sought success in order to get fame and money;
it's the talent and the passion that count in success.*
Ingrid Bergman *(1915-1982)*
Swedish-born, American actress

*Success as a woman has changed me. That's what I feel is the first thing.
When I feel like a successful woman as a rounded human being, then
it feeds my work in a broader way so it becomes more interesting.*
Jacqueline Bisset *(1944-)*
English actress

Success supposes endeavor.
Jane Austen *(1775-1817)*
English novelist

*My private measure of success is daily. If this were to be the last
day of my life would I be content with it? To live in a harmonious
balance of commitments and pleasures is what I strive for.*
Jane Rule *(1931-2007)*
Canadian writer

*All my life, I always wanted to be somebody. Now I
see that I should have been more specific.*
Jane Wagner *(1935-)*
American writer, director

Now that I'm here where am I?
Janis Joplin *(1943-1970)*
American singer

*I worked half my life to be an overnight success,
and still it took me by surprise.*
Jessica Savitch *(1947-1983)*
American journalist

*When you feel so strongly about something and other people feel equally
strongly, you have to feel stronger about it in order to succeed.*
Joan Chen *(1961-)*
Chinese actress

*I wish I could tell you that the Children's Television Workshop and
Sesame Street were thanks to my genius but it really was a lucky break.*
Joan Ganz Cooney *(1929-)*
American television producer

I succeeded by saying what everyone else is thinking.
Joan Rivers *(1933-)*
American comedian

It is weak and despicable to go on wanting things and not trying to get them.
Joanna Field *(1900-1998)*
British psychoanalyst

*The person interested in success has to learn to view failure as a
healthy, inevitable part of the process of getting to the top.*
Joyce Brothers *(1927-)*
American psychologist

My husband was actually very keen that I would become a Bond girl.
Judi Dench *(1934-)*
English actress

When I did have a little bit of commercial success, it really didn't suit my temperament at all. I'm a terrible public person.
Juliana Hatfield *(1967-)*
American musician

To be an artist includes much; one must possess many gifts - absolute gifts - which have not been acquired by one's own effort. And, moreover, to succeed, the artist much possess the courageous soul.
Kate Chopin *(1851-1904)*
American author, poet

When you are young you are surprised if everything isn't a success, and when you get older you're mildly surprised if anything is.
Kathleen Norris *(1880-1966)*
American poet, novelist

I've always been famous, it's just no one knew it yet.
Lady Gaga *(1986-)*
American performance artist

Self-trust, we know, is the first secret of success.
Lady Wilde *(1821-1896)*
Irish poet

Success isn't everything but it makes a person stand straight.
Lillian Hellman *(1905-1984)*
American playwright

If I had known what it would be like to have it all, I might have been willing to settle for less.
Lily Tomlin *(1939-)*
American actress, comedian

Sometimes I worry about being a success in a mediocre world.
Lily Tomlin *(1939-)*
American actress, comedian

I don't get out of bed for less than $10,000 a day.
Linda Evangelista *(1965-)*
Canadian supermodel

*The best thing that can come with success is the
knowledge that it is nothing to long for.*
Liv Ullmann *(1938-)*
Norwegian actress, director

If you want a place in the sun, you have to expect a few blisters.
Loretta Young *(1913-2000)*
American actress

*We must have ideals and try to live up to them, even if
we never quite succeed. Life would be a sorry business
without them. With them it's grand and great.*
Lucy Maud Montgomery *(1874-1942)*
Canadian writer

*Belief in oneself is one of the most important bricks
in building any successful venture.*
Lydia M. Child *(1802-1880)*
American activist

*I am a woman who came from the cotton fields of the South.
From there I was promoted to the washtub. From there I was
promoted to the cook kitchen. And from there I promoted
myself into the business of manufacturing hair goods and
preparations...I have built my own factory on my own ground.*
Madame C. J. Walker *(1867-1919)*
American entrepreneur

*Success is meaningless if you can't sleep at night because of harsh
things said, petty secrets sharpened against hard and stony regret,
just waiting to be plunged into the soft underbelly of a 'friendship.'*
Margaret Cho *(1968-)*
American comedian, actress

*I personally measure success in terms of the contributions an
individual makes to her or his fellow human beings.*
Margaret Mead *(1901-1978)*
American cultural anthropologist

*Success is having a flair for the thing that you are doing, knowing that is
not enough, that you have got to have hard work and a sense of purpose.*
Margaret Thatcher *(1925-)*
English Prime Minister

Winning the prize [1963 Nobel Prize in physics] wasn't
half as exciting as doing the work itself.
Maria Goeppert Mayer *(1906-1972)*
German-born theoretical physicist

Every performance of Marie Lloyd is a performance
by command of the British public.
Marie Lloyd *(1870-1922)*
English entertainer

It isn't success after all, is it, if it isn't an expression of your deepest energies?
Marilyn French *(1929-2009)*
American author

There was my name up in lights. I said, 'God, somebody's made
a mistake.' But there it was, in lights. And I sat there and said,
'Remember, you're not a star.' Yet there it was up in lights.
Marilyn Monroe *(1926-1962)*
American actress

Fame lost its appeal for me when I went into a public restroom and an
autograph seeker handed me a pen and paper under the stall door.
Marlo Thomas *(1937-)*
American actress

Success doesn't come to you… you go to it.
Marva Collins *(1936-)*
American educator

To be a celebrity in America is to be forgiven everything.
Mary McGrory *(1918-2003)*
American journalist

To me success means effectiveness in the world, that I am able to carry my
ideas and values into the world – that I am able to change it in positive ways.
Maxine Hong Kingston *(1940-)*
Chinese-American author

Success is liking yourself, liking what you do, and liking how you do it.
Maya Angelou *(1928-)*
American poet, memoirist

No-one gets an iron-clad guarantee of success. Certainly, factors like opportunity, luck and timing are important. But the backbone of success is usually found in old-fashioned, basic concepts like hard work, determination, good planning and perseverance.

Mia Hamm *(1972-)*
American soccer player

Youth is not enough. And love is not enough. And success is not enough. And, if we could achieve it, enough would not be enough.

Mignon McLaughlin *(1913-1983)*
American journalist

The penalty for success is to be bored by the people who used to snub you.

Nancy Astor *(1879-1964)*
American born, British politician

For you to be successful, sacrifices must be made. It's better that they are made by others but failing that, you'll have to make them yourself.

Rita Mae Brown *(1944-)*
American novelist

Success is a public affair. Failure is a private funeral.

Rosalind Russell *(1907-1976)*
American actress

Success is important only to the extent that it puts one in a position to do more things one likes to do.

Sarah Caldwell *(1924-2006)*
American opera conductor

I don't think you ever think that you have made it but I did take a look at myself one day and think back to when I was a little girl and it was nice to know that I had at least made it this far.

Sharon Stone *(1958-)*
American actress

If you don't quit, and don't cheat, and don't run home when trouble arrives, you can only win.

Shelley Long *(1949-)*
American actress

342

After I won the Oscar, my salary doubled, my friends tripled, my children became more popular at school, my butcher made a pass at me, and my maid hit me up for a raise.
Shirley Jones *(1933-)*
American actress

Success ... depends on your ability to make and keep friends.
Sophie Tucker *(1886-1996)*
Russian/Ukranian born entertainer

Success is completion. Success is being able to complete what we set out to do – each individual action, each specific step, each desired experience whether a big project or a very small errand.
Susan Collins *(1952-)*
American politician

People I know who succeed don't mind working. Those who are competent seem to like doing things well – not stopping because they haven't accomplished what they wanted to on the first go-round. They're willing to do it twenty times, if necessary. There's an illusion that the good people can easily do something, and it's not necessarily true. They're just determined to do it right.
Sylvia A. Earle *(1935-)*
American oceanographer

I never thought I'd be successful. It seems in my own mind that in everything I've undertaken I've never quite made the mark. But I've always been able to put disappointments aside. Success isn't about the end result; it's about what you learn along the way.
Vera Wang *(1949-)*
American designer

Success doesn't mean that you are healthy, success doesn't mean that you're happy, success doesn't mean that you're rested. Success really doesn't mean that you look good, or feel good, or are good.
Victoria Principal *(1946-)*
American actress

You always feel you are not deserving. People who are successful at what they do know what kind of work goes with it, so they are surprised at the praise.
Virginia Hamilton *(1936-2002)*
American author, children's books

If people are highly successful in their professions they lose their senses. Sight goes. They have no time to look at pictures. Sound goes. They have no time to listen to music. Speech goes. They have no time for conversation. They lose their sense of proportion – the relations between one thing and another. Humanity goes.
Virginia Woolf *(1882-1941)*
English author

No matter how successful I become as a playwright, my mother would be thrilled to hear me tell her that I'd just lost twenty pounds, gotten married and become a lawyer.
Wendy Wasserstein *(1969-)*
American playwright

The secret of our success is that we never, never give up.
Wilma Pearl Mankiller *(1945-2010)*
American Cherokee leader

If I can make a connection, one connection, to any one listener in the world, I consider that successful.
Wynonna Judd *(1964-)*
American musician

My story of success and failure is not just about music and being famous. It's about living and loving and trying to find purpose in this crazy world.
Wynonna Judd *(1964-)*
American musician

We haven't really gotten the credit for what we have done.
Nancy Pelosi *(1940-)*
American politician

Talent

The distinction between talent and genius is definite. Talent combines and uses; genius combines and creates.
Anna Jameson *(1794-1860)*
British writer

No one can arrive from being talented alone, work transforms talent into genius.
Anna Pavlova *(1881-1931)*
Russian ballerina

All our talents increase in the using and every faculty
both good and bad strengthens by exercise.
Anne Bronte *(1820-1849)*
British novelist, poet

After my screen test, the director clapped his hands gleefully
and yelled, She can't talk! She can't act! She's sensational!
Ava Gardner *(1922-1990)*
American actress

This is what I learned: that everybody is talented,
original and has something important to say.
Brenda Ueland *(1891-1985)*
American journalist

Hire the best people and then delegate.
Carol A. Taber *(1917-2010)*
American magazine publisher

The only thing that happens overnight is recognition. Not talent.
Carol Haney *(1924-1964)*
American dancer

Keep your talent in the dark and you'll never be insulted.
Elsa Maxwell *(1883-1963)*
American gossip columnist

When I stand before God at the end of my life, I would hope that I would not
have a single bit of talent left, and could say, 'I used everything you gave me.'
Erma Bombeck *(1927-1996)*
American writer, humorist

I'll pat myself on the back and admit I have talent. Beyond that,
I just happened to be in the right place at the right time.
Ethel Merman *(1908-1984)*
American singer

There's a very simple strategy that we're running here that really says if you
seek to engage people, people are willing, people are positive... people who
like people, people who care, people who are energetic, people who want to
try, people who aren't cynical, who aren't arrogant, who aren't self-serving.
Gail Kelly *(1956-)*
American, CEO Westpac

Talent is the infinite capacity for taking pains. Genius is the infinite capacity for achievement without taking any pains at all.
Helene Hanff *(1916-1997)*
American writer

*I think the most important thing a woman can have –
next to talent, of course – is her hairdresser.*
Joan Crawford *(1905-1977)*
American actress

I do not want to die. . . until I have faithfully made the most of my talent and cultivated the seed that was placed in me until the last small twig has grown.
Kathe Kollwitz *(1867-1945)*
German sculptor

Always hire people who are better than you. Hiring dummies is shortsighted. You can't move up the ladder until everyone is comfortable with your replacement.
Lois Wyse *(1926-2007)*
American advertising executive

We can't take credit for our talents. It's how we use them that counts.
Madeleine L'Engle *(1918-)*
American novelist

There are some people that you cannot change, you must either swallow them whole or leave them alone. You can do something with talent, but nothing with genius.
Margot Asquith *(1864-1945)*
Anglo-Scottish socialite

Genius is the gold in the mine, talent is the miner who works and brings it out.
Marguerite Blessington *(1789-1849)*
Irish-born English writer

There are two kinds of talents, man-made talent and God-given talent. With man-made talent you have to work very hard. With God-given talent, you just touch it up once in a while.
Pearl Bailey *(1918-1990)*
American entertainer

One can present people with opportunities. One cannot make them equal to them.
Rosamond Lehmann *(1901-1990)*
Brtitish novelist

You have to have a talent for having talent.
Ruth Gordon *(1896-1985)*
American actress, writer

Things happen to you out of luck, and if you get to stick around it's because you're talented.
Whoopi Goldberg *(1955-)*
American actress, comedian

Those that don't got it, can't show it. Those that got it, can't hide it.
Zora Neale Hurston *(1891-1960)*
American dramatist

Everyone has talent. What is rare is the courage to follow the talent to the dark places where it leads.
Erica Jong *(1942-)*
American writer

Teamwork

There are three ways of dealing with difference: domination, compromise and integration. By domination only one side gets what it wants; by compromise neither side gets what it wants; by integration we find a way by which both sides may get what they wish.
Mary Parker Follett *(1868-1933)*
American management consultant

I am a member of a team, and I rely on the team, I defer to it and sacrifice for it, because the team, not the individual, is the ultimate champion.
Mia Hamm *(1972-)*
American soccer player

We don't accomplish anything in this world alone… and whatever happens is the result of the whole tapestry of one's life and all the weavings of individual threads form one to another that creates something.
Sandra Day O'Connor *(1930-)*
American Supreme Court Justice

People will support that which they help to create.
Mary Kay Ash *(1918-2001)*
American entrepreneur

At the end of the day government is about teamwork and partnership and we will be proving that by working together.
Julia Gillard *(1961-)*
Welsh-born, Australian politician

Overall, do we have a good team? Yeah. Are we all on the same page at all times? Absolutely not. It's just a matter of trying to pull it together, trying to get chemistry.
Lisa Leslie *(1972-)*
American basketball player

Time

We must go fast, because the race is against time.
Anna Held *(1872-1918)*
Polish-born stage performer

A schedule defends from chaos and whim. It is a net for catching days. It is a scaffolding on which a worker can stand and labor with both hands at sections of time.
Annie Dillard *(1945-)*
American author

Have you ever noticed that life consists mostly of interruptions, with occasional spells of rush work in between?
Buwei Yang Chao *(1889-1981)*
American Chinese physician

Great artists treasure their time with a bitter and snarling miserliness.
Catherine Bowen *(1897-1973)*
American writer

It's not so much how busy you are, but why you are busy. The bee is praised, the mosquito is swatted.
Catherine O'Hara *(1954-)*
Canadian-American actress

If something anticipated arrives too late it finds us numb, wrung out from waiting, and we feel – nothing at all. The best things arrive on time.
Dorothy Gilman *(1923-)*
American mystery writer

When people ask for time, it's always for time to say no. Yes has one more letter in it, but it doesn't take half as long to say.
Edith Wharton *(1862-1937)*
American novelist

First of my own personal requirements is inner calm. This, I think, is an essential. One of the secrets of using your time well is to gain a certain ability to maintain peace within yourself so that much can go on around you and you can stay calm inside.
Eleanor Roosevelt *(1884 - 1962)*
American First Lady

The timelessness of a concept has to be woven into the running warp of dying time, vertical power has to be wedded to the horizontal earth.
Ella Maillart *(1903-1997)*
Swiss writer

I am a member of a small, nearly extinct minority group, a kind of urban lost tribe who insist, in the face of all evidence to the contrary, on the sanctity of being on time. Which is to say that we On-timers are compulsively, unfashionably prompt, that there are only handfuls of us in any given city and, unfortunately, we never seem to have appointments with each other.
Ellen Goodman *(1950-)*
American journalist

Time is my greatest enemy.
Evita Peron *(1895-1974)*
Argentina First Lady

Time is a dressmaker specializing in alterations.
Faith Baldwin *(1893-1978)*
American author

Time is the sea in which people grow, are born, or die.
Freya Stark *(1893-1993)*
French-born travel writer, explorer

I'm always aware that I risk being taken for a neurasthenic prima donna when I explain to someone who wants just a little of my time that five minutes of the wrong kind of distraction can ruin a working day.
Gail Godwin *(1937-)*
American short story writer

Time is always wanting to me, and I cannot meet with a single day when I am not hurried along, driven to my wits' end by urgent work, business to attend to, or some service to render.
George Sand *(1804-)*
French novelist, memoirist

I must govern the clock, not be governed by it.
Golda Meir *(1898-1978)*
Ukrainian-born Israeli leader

I have been five minutes too late all my life-time!
Hannah Cowley *(1743-1809)*
English dramatist, poet

Time seems to stop in certain places.
Jacqueline Bisset *(1944-)*
English actress

Oh! do not attack me with your watch. A watch is always too fast or too slow. I cannot be dictated to by a watch!
Jane Austen *(1775-1817)*
English novelist

If you realize too acutely how valuable time is, you are too paralyzed to do anything.
Katharine Butler Hathaway *(1890-1942)*
American writer

Why should we need extra time in which to enjoy ourselves? If we expect to enjoy our life, we will have to learn to be joyful in all of it, not just at stated intervals when we can get time or when we have nothing else to do.
Laura Ingalls Wilder *(1867-1957)*
American writer

Just as you began to feel that you could make good use of time, there was no time left to you.
Lisa Alther *(1944-)*
American author

Time is compressed like the fist I close on my knee ... I hold inside it the clues and solutions and the power for what I must do now.
Margaret Atwood *(1939-)*
Canadian poet, novelist

The best way to fill time is to waste it.
Marguerite Duras *(1914-1996)*
French writer

Peace is when time doesn't matter as it passes by.
Maria Schell *(1926-2005)*
Austrian/Swiss actress

Even a stopped clock is right twice a day.
Marie von Ebner-Eschenbach *(1830-1916)*
Austrian writer

I've been on a calendar, but I've never been on time.
Marilyn Monroe *(1926-1962)*
American actress

There is no pleasure in having nothing to do; the fun is in having lots to do and not doing it.
Mary Wilson Little *(1944-)*
American writer

It is privilege of living to be ... acutely agonizingly conscious of the moment that is always present and always passing.
Marya Mannes *(1904-1990)*
American author, critic

We have as much time as we need.
Melody Beattie *(1948-)*
American author

I don't know why I don't watch a lot of movies; I can barely keep up with the things my friends are in. There isn't enough time in life.
Meryl Streep *(1949-)*
American actress

Time is change; we measure its passing by how much things alter.
Nadine Gordimer *(1923-)*
South African novelist, activist

All my possessions for a moment of time.
Queen Elizabeth I *(1533-1603)*
English royalty

*At the end of every year, I add up the time that I have spent on
the phone on hold and subtract it from my age. I don't count
that time as really living. I spend more and more time on hold
each year. By the time I die, I'm going to be quite young.*
Rita Rudner *(1953-)*
American comedian

And when is there time to remember, to sift, to weigh, to estimate, to total?
Tillie Olsen *(1913-2007)*
American novelist

Patience is being friends with Time.
Vanna Bonta *(1958-)*
American novelist, poet

Trust

Where large sums of money are concerned, it is advisable to trust nobody.
Agatha Christie *(1890-1976)*
English detective novelist

*Trust is to human relationships what faith is to gospel
living. It is the beginning place, the foundation upon which
more can be built. Where trust is, love can flourish.*
Barbara Smith *(1946-)*
American writer

*Acting is also working with people who invite you into their
dreams and trust you with their innermost being.*
Catherine Deneuve *(1943-)*
French actress

Who would not rather trust and be deceived?
Eliza Cook *(1818-1889)*
English author, poet

*No soul is desolate as long as there is a human being
for whom it can feel trust and reverence.*
George Eliot *(1819-1880)*
English novelist

In almost every profession – whether it's law or journalism, finance or medicine or academia or running a small business – people rely on confidential communications to do their jobs. We count on the space of trust that confidentiality provides. When someone breaches that trust, we are all worse off for it.

Hillary Rodham Clinton *(1947-)*
American, Secretary of State

Today I trust my instinct, I trust myself. Finally.

Isabelle Adjani *(1955-)*
French actress

Never trust anything that can think for itself if you can't see where it keeps its brain.

J. K. Rowling *(1965-)*
English writer

I work in a strange business, and trust is a word that's not even in the vocabulary.

Kim Basinger *(1953-)*
American actress

Repeat nothing – absolutely nothing – that is told you in confidence. There is no such thing as telling just one person.

Lois Wyse *(1926-2007)*
American advertising executive

As contagion of sickness makes sickness, contagion of trust can make trust.

Marianne Moore *(1887-1972)*
American poet, writer

I do not trust people who don't love themselves and yet tell me, 'I love you.' There is an African saying which is: Be careful when a naked person offers you a shirt.

Maya Angelou *(1928-)*
American poet, memoirist

I have in sincerity pledged myself to your service, as so many of you are pledged to mine. Throughout all my life and with all my heart I shall strive to be worthy of your trust.

Queen Elizabeth II *(1926-)*
English royalty

Everyone realizes that one can believe little of what people say about each other. But it is not so widely realized that even less can one trust what people say about themselves.
Rebecca West *(1892-1983)*
Irish-born, British writer

If we really want to be full and generous in spirit, we have no choice but to trust at some level.
Rita Dove *(1952-)*
American poet

Not everyone can be trusted. I think we all have to be very selective about the people we trust.
Shelley Long *(1949-)*
American actress

We must trust our own thinking. Trust where we're going. And get the job done.
Wilma Pearl Mankiller *(1945-2010)*
American Cherokee leader

Truth

There are few nudities so objectionable as the naked truth.
Agnes Repplier *(1855-1950)*
American essayist

Truth is simply whatever you can bring yourself to believe.
Alice Childress *(1920-1994)*
American playwright, author

Truth can be outraged by silence quite as cruelly as by speech.
Amelia E. Barr *(1831-1919)*
British novelist

I don't tell the truth any more to those who can't make use of it. I tell it mostly to myself, because it always changes me.
Anais Nin *(1902-1977)*
French author, diarist

No blame should attach to telling the truth.
Anita Brookner *(1938-)*
English historian

The naked truth is always better than the best-dressed lie.
Ann Landers *(1918-2002)*
American advice columnist

There are new words now that excuse everybody. Give me the good old days of heroes and villains. The people you can bravo or hiss. There was a truth to them that all the slick credulity of today cannot touch.
Bette Davis *(1908-1989)*
American actress

I never know how much of what I say is true. If I did, I'd bore myself to death.
Bette Midler *(1945-)*
American actress

Keep the other person's well being in mind when you feel an attack of soul-purging truth coming on.
Betty White *(1922-)*
American actress, comedian

I speak truth, not so much as I would, but as much as I dare; and I dare a little more, as I have grown older.
Catherine Bowen *(1897-1973)*
American writer

Are we to go out with trumpets and tell everything we know, just because it is true? Is there not such a thing as egotistical truthfulness?
Constance Fenimore Woolson *(1840-1894)*
American novelist

Nothing is easier than self-deceit. For what someone wishes, that they also believe to be true.
Diane Arbus *(1923-1971)*
American photographer

It is terrible to destroy a person's picture of themselves in the interest of truth or some other abstraction.
Doris Lessing *(1919-)*
Persian-born British writer

The great advantage about telling the truth is that nobody ever believes it.
Dorothy L. Sayers *(1893-1957)*
English crime writer

I don't care what is written about me so long as it isn't true.
Dorothy Parker *(1893-1967)*
American writer, satirist

Mind and spirit together make up that which separates us from the rest of the animal world, that which enables a person to know the truth and that which enables them to die for the truth.
Edith Hamilton *(1867-1963)*
American educator

The public will believe anything, so long as it is not founded on truth.
Edith Sitwell *(1887-1964)*
British poet, critic

If I ever said in grief or pride, I tired of honest things, I lied.
Edna Saint Vincent Millay *(1892-1950)*
American poet, playwright

Nobody speaks the truth when there's something they must have.
Elizabeth Bowen *(1899-1973)*
Irish novelist

Truth is the only safe ground to stand upon.
Elizabeth Cady Stanton *(1815-1902)*
American reformist, writer

Most of the basic truths of life sound absurd at first hearing.
Elizabeth Goudge *(1900-1984)*
English novelist

Much sheer effort goes into avoiding truth: left to itself, it sweeps in like the tide.
Fay Weldon *(1931-)*
English author

The truth does not change according to our ability to stomach it.
Flannery O'Connor *(1925-1964)*
American writer

The mode of delivering a truth makes, for the most part, as much impression on the mind of the listener as the truth itself.
Frances Wright *(1795-1852)*
Scottish-born writer

The truth will set you free. But first, it will piss you off.
Gloria Steinem *(1934-)*
American activist, writer, publisher

I am interested in telling my particular truth as I have seen it.
Gwendolyn Brooks *(1917-2000)*
American poet

The trouble with lying and deceiving is that their efficiency depends entirely upon a clear notion of the truth that the liar and deceiver wishes to hide.
Hannah Arendt *(1906-1975)*
German philosopher

Truth has as many coats as an onion...and each one of them hollow when you peel it off.
HelenWaddell *(1889-1965)*
Irish poet

The truth. It is a beautiful and terrible thing, and should therefore be treated with great caution.
J. K. Rowling *(1965-)*
English writer

Seldom, very seldom, does complete truth belong to any human disclosure; seldom can it happen that something is not a little disguised, or a little mistaken.
Jane Austen *(1775-1817)*
English novelist

I am the only real truth I know.
Jean Rhys *(1890-1979)*
British novelist

No matter who the characters are, you can strip them down and find small universal truths.
Jena Malone *(1984-)*
American actress

Children say that people are hung sometimes for speaking the truth.
Joan of Arc *(1412-1431)*
French heroine

Art, whose honesty must work through artifice, cannot avoid cheating truth.
Laura Riding *(1901-1991)*
American poet

Cynicism is an unpleasant way of telling the truth.
Lillian Hellman *(1905-1984)*
American playwright

Truth made you a traitor as it often does in a time of scoundrels.
Lillian Hellman *(1905-1984)*
American playwright

What a word is truth. Slippery, tricky, unreliable.
Lillian Hellman *(1905-1984)*
American playwright

There has never been a useful thought or a profound truth
that has not found its century and admirers.
Madame de Stael *(1766-1817)*
French writer

Truth is eternal, knowledge is changeable. It is disastrous to confuse them.
Madeleine L'Engle *(1918-)*
American novelist

Every new truth begins in a shocking heresy.
Margaret Deland *(1857-1945)*
American short story writer

There is no power on earth more formidable than the truth.
Margaret Lee Runbeck *(1905-1956)*
American author

Of course it's the same old story. Truth usually is the same old story.
Margaret Thatcher *(1925-)*
English Prime Minister

Truthfulness with me is hardly a virtue. I cannot discriminate
between truths that need and those that need not be told.
Margot Asquith *(1864-1945)*
Anglo-Scottish socialite

The simplest and most familiar truth seems new and wonderful
the instant we ourselves experience it for the first time.
Marie von Ebner-Eschenbach *(1830-1916)*
Austrian writer

People do think that if they avoid the truth, it might change
to something better before they have to hear it.
Marsha Norman *(1947-)*
American playwright

Gradually I came to realize that people will more readily swallow lies than truth, as if the taste of lies was homey, appetizing: a habit.
Martha Gellhorn *(1908-1998)*
American journalist

Truth is strong, and sometime or other will prevail.
Mary Astell *(1666-1731)*
English writer

What a weak barrier is truth when it stands in the way of an hypothesis!
Mary Wollstonecraft *(1759-1797)*
British philosopher

A politician should be able to look anyone in the eye and say: 'Sorry, I can't do that.'
Millicent Fenwick *(1910-   )*
American politician

I believe that ignorance is the root of all evil. And that no one knows the truth.
Molly Ivens *(1944-2007)*
American political commentator

I am not afraid of the pen, or the scaffold, or the sword. I will tell the truth wherever I please.
Mother Jones *(1830-1930)*
American activist

Truth isn't always beauty, but the hunger for it is.
Nadine Gordimer *(1923-   )*
South African novelist, activist

If now isn't a good time for the truth I don't see when we'll get to it.
Nikki Giovanni *(1943-   )*
American poet, author

You never find yourself until you face the truth.
Pearl Bailey *(1918-1990)*
American entertainer

Truth is always exciting. Speak it, then; life is dull without it.
Pearl S. Buck *(1892-1973)*
American writer

Many people choose, early on, their own truths from the large smorgasbord available. And once they've chosen them, for good reason or no reason, they proceed rather selectively, wisely gathering whatever will bolster them or at least carry out the color scheme.

Peg Bracken *(1918-2007)*
American humorist, author

The truth you believe and cling to makes you unavailable to hear anything new.

Pema Chodron *(1936-)*
Tibetan Buddhist teacher

Truth, though it has many disadvantages, is at least changeless. You can always find it where you left it.

Phyllis Bottome *(1884-1963)*
British novelist

So often the truth is told with hate, and lies are told with love.

Rita Mae Brown *(1944-)*
American novelist

Sometimes, surely, truth is closer to imagination or to intelligence, to love than to fact? To be accurate is not to be right.

Shirley Hazzard *(1931-)*
Australian novelist

Defending the truth is not something one does out of a sense of duty or to allay guilt complexes, but is a reward in itself.

Simone de Beauvoir *(1908-1986)*
French writer, philosopher

I tore myself away from the safe comfort of certainties through my love for the truth and truth rewarded me.

Simone de Beauvoir *(1908-1986)*
French writer, philosopher

The truth is balance, but the opposite of truth, which is unbalance, may not be a lie.

Susan Sontag *(1933-2004)*
American activist, writer

It takes two to tell the truth...one to tell, one to hear. A speaker and a receiver. To tell the truth about any complex situation requires a certain attitude in the receiver.
Sybille Bedford *(1911-2006)*
German writer

Truth has beauty, power and necessity.
Sylvia Ashton-Warner *(1908-1984)*
New Zealand writer, poet

There is at least one thing more brutal than the truth, and that is the consequence of saying less than the truth.
Ti-Grace Atkinson *(1938-)*
American author

It is in our idleness, in our dreams, that the submerged truth sometimes comes to the top.
Virginia Woolf *(1882-1941)*
English author

Artistic growth is, more than it is anything else, a refining of the sense of truthfulness. The stupid believe that to be truthful is easy; only the artist, the great artist, knows how difficult it is.
Willa Cather *(1873-1947)*
American writer

Understanding

Everything in moderation, including moderation.
Julia Child *(1912-2004)*
American cookbook author

I believe in practicing prudence at least once every two or three years.
Molly Ivens *(1944-2007)*
American political commentator

I like trees because they seem more resigned to the way they have to live than other things do.
Willa Cather *(1873-1947)*
American writer

Vision

I learned that one can never go back, that one should not ever try to go back
– that the essence of life is going forward. Life is really a one way street.
Agatha Christie *(1890-1976)*
English detective novelist

Anything I do has to be directly related to my music.
If it isn't, I don't really see a point to it.
Alanis Morisette *(1974-)*
Canadian singer

Forethought spares afterthought.
Amelia E. Barr *(1831-1919)*
British novelist

If people want the future, we have made them an offer.
Angela Merkel *(1954-)*
German Chancellor

The here and now is all we have, and if we play it right it's all we'll need.
Ann Richards *(1933-2006)*
American politician

Every time you spend money, you're casting a
vote for the kind of world you want.
Anna Lappe *(1973-)*
American author

The future is built on brains, not prom court, as most people
can tell you after attending their high school reunion. But you'd
never know it by talking to kids or listening to the messages
they get from the culture and even from their schools.
Anna Quindlen *(1952-)*
American journalist

It's utterly impossible for me to build my life on a foundation of chaos,
suffering and death. I see the world being slowly transformed into a
wilderness, I hear the approaching thunder that, one day, will destroy
us too. I feel the suffering of millions. And yet, when I look up at the
sky, I somehow feel that everything will change for the better, that this
cruelty too shall end, that peace and tranquility will return once more.
Anne Frank *(1929-1945)*
German writer, holocaust victim

The wave of the future is coming and there is no fighting it.
Anne Morrow Lindbergh *(1906-2001)*
American aviator, author

To profit, you have to know what value to create.
Anne Mulcahy *(1952-)*
American, former CEO Xerox

In the age in which we live, the impossible is every day losing ground.
Anne Sophie Swetchine *(1752-1857)*
Russian mystic

Some of our finest moments come in our darkest hour.
Anne Sweeney *(1957-)*
American, Co-Chair Disney Media Networks

Throughout the centuries there were people who took first steps, down new roads, armed with nothing but their own vision.
Ayn Rand *(1905-1982)*
Russian-American novelist

You can avoid reality, but you cannot avoid the consequences of avoiding reality.
Ayn Rand *(1905-1982)*
Russian-American novelist

Without wonder and insight, acting is just a trade. With it, it becomes creation.
Bette Davis *(1908-1989)*
American actress

What that says to me is that you have to have strategic vision and peripheral vision. Strategic vision is the ability to look ahead and peripheral vision is the ability to look around, and both are important.
Carly Fiorina *(1954-)*
American, Former HP CEO

When a just cause reaches its flood-tide, as ours has done in that country, whatever stands in the way must fall before its overwhelming power.
Carrie Chapman Catt *(1859-1947)*
American activist

*If you've lost focus, just sit down and be still. Take the idea
and rock it to and fro. Keep some of it and throw some
away, and it will renew itself. You need do no more.*
Clarissa Pinkola Estés *(1945-)*
American poet, psychoanalyst

*A painting is a symbol for the universe. Inside it, each piece
relates to the other. Each piece is only answerable to the rest of
that little world. So, probably in the total universe, there is that
kind of total harmony, but we get only little tastes of it.*
Corita Kent *(1918-1986)*
American, Roman Catholic nun, artist

I really believe there are things nobody would see if I didn't photograph them.
Diane Arbus *(1923-1971)*
American photographer

*If you're not out front defining your vision, your opponent
will spend gobs of money to define it for you.*
Donna Brazile *(1959-)*
American politician

*But romantic vision can also lead one away from certain very
hard, ugly truths about life that are important to know.*
Donna Tartt *(1963-)*
American novelist

Envisioning the end is enough to put the means in motion.
Dorothea Brande *(1893-1948)*
American writer, editor

*Nobody can take away your future. Nobody can
take away something you don't have yet.*
Dorothy B. Hughes *(1904-1993)*
American crime writer

People need dreams; there's as much nourishment in 'em as food.
Dorothy Gilman *(1923-)*
American mystery writer

*While time lasts there will always be a future, and that future will hold
both good and evil, since the world is made to that mingled pattern.*
Dorothy L. Sayers *(1893-1957)*
English crime writer

I can't imagine going on when there are no more expectations.
Edith Evans *(1888-1976)*
English actress

True originality consists not in a new manner but in a new vision.
Edith Wharton *(1862-1937)*
American novelist

How do geese know when to fly to the sun? Who tells them the seasons?
How do we humans know when it is time to move on? As with the
migrant birds, so surely with us, there is a voice within if only we would
listen to it, that tells us certainly when to go forth into the unknown.
Elisabeth Kübler-Ross *(1926-2004)*
Swiss psychiatrist

I only want people around me who can do the impossible.
Elizabeth Arden *(1884-1966)*
Canadian-American entrepreneur

The future bears a great resemblance to the past, only more so.
Faith Popcorn *(1948-)*
American advertising executive

Were there none who were discontented with what they
have, the world would never reach anything better.
Florence Nightingale *(1820-1910)*
English nurse, writer

Every great work, every great accomplishment, has been brought into
manifestation through holding to the vision, and often just before
the big achievement comes apparent failure and discouragement.
Florence Scovel Shinn *(1871-1940)*
American artist, book illustrator

I knew I could not cope with the future unless
I was able to rediscover the past.
Gene Tierney *(1920-1991)*
American actress

Your world is as big as you make it.
Georgia Douglas Johnson *(1880-1966)*
American poet

It is a terrible thing to see and have no vision.
Helen Keller *(1880-1968)*
American author, educator

I have always believed that business could be a force for good. Today, I know it is. As a global food company, we can help raise people up – out of hunger, out of poverty, toward healthier lifestyles – through what we make and how we make it. And millions of times a day, in ways big and small around the world, we're doing just that. We're seeking solutions that, by design, benefit our business and our society and by doing so, we're helping tackle some the toughest challenges facing the world today.
Irene Rosenfeld *(1953-)*
American, CEO Kraft Foods

While you are experimenting, do not remain content with the surface of things. Don't become a mere recorder of facts, but try to penetrate the mystery of their origin.
Isabel Allende *(1942-)*
Chilean writer

So this is my effort – to bring back the hope that we must have if we are to change direction. . . . I think to be fully human, we need to have meaning in our lives, and that's what I am trying to help these young people to find.
Jane Goodall *(1934-)*
English, chimpanzee researcher

Normal is not something to aspire to, it's something to get away from.
Jodie Foster *(1962-)*
American actress

Those who have been required to memorize the world as it is will never create the world as it might be.
Judith Groch *(1952-)*
American writer

Life itself is the proper binge.
Julia Child *(1912-2004)*
American cookbook author

If you stick with a vision, it might not all work, but some of it will be absolute genius.
Kim Cattrall *(1956-)*
American actress

Anyone who limits her vision to memories of yesterday is already dead.
Lillie Langtry *(1853-1929)*
British actress

Things are going to get a lot worse before they get worse.
Lily Tomlin *(1939-)*
American actress, comedian

I never was able to believe in the existence of next
year except as in a metaphysical notion.
Madame de Stael *(1766-1817)*
French writer

To look backward for a while is to refresh the eye, to restore it, and
to render it the more fit for its prime function of looking forward.
Margaret Fairless Barber *(1869-1901)*
English author

I hadn't set out to change the world in any way. Whatever I am,
it is a culmination of the goodwill of people who, regardless of
anything else, saw me as I am, and not as somebody else.
Marian Anderson *(1897-1993)*
American singer

Humanity needs practical people, who get the most out of their work, and,
without forgetting the general good, safeguard their own interests. But
humanity also needs dreamers, for whom the disinterested development
of an enterprise is so captivating that it becomes impossible for them to
devote their care to their own material profit. A well-organized society
should assure to such workers the efficient means of accomplishing their
task, in a life freed from material care and freely consecrated to research
Marie Curie *(1897-1966)*
Polish-French physicist

I'm not a big believer in a thing called luck. I believe it has a lot to do with
fate and just really having a vision of the way you would see your life.
Marla Maples *(1963-)*
American actress

Practice means to perform, over and over again in the
face of all obstacles, some act of vision, of faith, of desire.
Practice is a means of inviting the perfection desired.
Martha Graham *(1894-1991)*
American dancer, choreographer

A false vision was better than none.
Martha Ostenso *(1900-1963)*
Canadian novelist

*What would it be like to have not only color vision but culture
vision, the ability to see the multiple worlds of others.*
Mary Catherine Bateson *(1939-)*
American anthropologist

*The most successful leader of all is one who sees
another picture not yet actualized.*
Mary Parker Follett *(1868-1933)*
American management consultant

*I learned to make my mind large, as the universe is
large, so that there is room for paradoxes.*
Maxine Hong Bottome *(1940-)*
Chinese-American author

It is well that the earth is round that we do not see too far ahead.
Meryl Streep *(1949-)*
American actress

*The future comes quickly. Before you know it,
you turn around and it's tomorrow.*
Pia Zadora *(1953-)*
American actress

*One way to open your eyes is to ask yourself, 'What if I had never
seen this before? What if I knew I would never see it again?'*
Rachel Carson *(1907-1964)*
American environmentalist

*Those who foresee the future and recognize it as tragic are often
seized by a madness which forces them to commit the very acts
which makes it certain that what they dread shall happen.*
Rebecca West *(1892-1983)*
Irish-born, British writer

*A vision is not just a picture of what could be; it is an appeal
to our better selves, a call to become something more.*
Rosabeth Moss Kanter *(1943-)*
American academic, author

Our faith in the present dies out long before our faith in the future.
Ruth Benedict *(1887-1948)*
American scientist

If you have enough fantasies, you're ready, in
the event that something happens.
Sheila Ballantyne *(1933-2007)*
American novelist

I am incapable of conceiving infinity, and yet I do not accept finity.
Simone de Beauvoir *(1908-1986)*
French writer, philosopher

As you enter positions of trust and power, dream a little before you think.
Toni Morrison *(1931-)*
American novelist

I see the dream and I see the nightmare, and I believe you
can't have the dream without the nightmare.
Tori Amos *(1963-)*
American singer, songwriter

I didn't have a Barbie doll, so I played with eternity.
Vanna Bonta *(1958-)*
American novelist, poet

Not seeing is half-believing.
Vita Sackville-West *(1892-1962)*
English author

By the time a person has achieved years adequate for
choosing a direction, the die is cast and the moment has
long since passed which determined the future.
Zelda Fitzgerald *(1900-1948)*
American artist, writer

Winning

In sports, you simply aren't considered a real champion until
you have defended your title successfully. Winning it once can
be a fluke; winning it twice proves you are the best.
Althea Gibson *(1927-2003)*
American tennis player

In real life, it is the hare who wins. Every time. Look around you. And in any case it is my contention that Aesop was writing for the tortoise market. Hares have no time to read. They are too busy winning the game.
Anita Brookner *(1938-)*
English historian

You can't win them all – but you can try.
Babe Didrikson Zaharias *(1911-1956)*
American golfer

It's all about us having that focus and being together even when we hit adversity. We just have to keep banding together and fighting to come out with a win.
Barbara Turner *(1934-)*
American actress, screenwriter

A champion is afraid of losing. Everyone else is afraid of winning.
Billie Jean King *(1934-)*
American tennis player

Winning doesn't always mean being first. Winning means you're doing better than you've ever done before.
Bonnie Blair *(1964-)*
American Olympic speed skater

Every time, all the time, I'm a perfectionist. I feel I should never lose.
Chris Evert *(1954-)*
American tennis player

Winning may not be everything, but losing has little to recommend it.
Dianne Feinstein *(1933-)*
American politician

People don't pay attention to you when you are second best. I wanted to see what it felt like to be number one.
Florence Griffith Joyner *(1959-1998)*
American track and field star

You've got to rattle your cage door. You've got to let them know that you're in there, and that you want out. Make noise. Cause trouble. You may not win right away, but you'll sure have a lot more fun.
Florynce Kennedy *(1916-2000)*
American activist, lawyer

I've done the calculation and your chances of winning the lottery are identical whether you play or not.
Fran Lebowitz *(1950-)*
American writer

When I was a kid, my mother told me that if you could not be a good loser, then there's no way you could be a good winner.
Halle Berry *(1968-)*
American actress

You will never win if you never begin.
Helen Rowland *(1875-1950)*
American writer

You play. You win. You play. You lose. You play.
Jeanette Winterson *(1959-)*
British novelist

The problem with winning the rat race is you're still a rat.
Lily Tomlin *(1939-)*
American actress, comedian

You may have to fight a battle more than once to win it.
Margaret Thatcher *(1925-)*
English Prime Minister

The person that said winning isn't everything, never won anything.
Mia Hamm *(1972-)*
American soccer player

Part of being a champ is acting like a champ. You have to learn how to win and not run away when you lose.
Nancy Kerrigan *(1969-)*
American Olympic skater

One shouldn't be afraid to lose; this is sport. One day you win; another day you lose. Of course, everyone wants to be the best. This is normal. This is what sport is about. This is why I love it.
Oksana Baiul *(1977-)*
Ukrainian Olympic skater

What does it take to be a champion? Desire, dedication, determination, concentration and the will to win.
Patty Berg *(1918-2006)*
American golfer

I've found that small wins, small projects, small differences often make huge differences.
Rosabeth Moss Kanter *(1943-)*
American academic, author

The one who cares the most wins…That's how I knew I'd end up with everyone else waving the white flags and not me. That's how I knew I'd be the last person standing when it was all over…I cared the most.
Roseanne Arnold *(1953-)*
American actress, comedian

When you lose a couple of times, it makes you realize how difficult it is to win.
Steffi Graf *(1969-)*
German tennis player

I think sportsmanship is knowing that it is a game, that we are only as a good as our opponents, and whether you win or lose, to always give 100 percent.
Sue Wicks *(1966-)*
American basketball player

Winning is great, sure, but if you are really going to do something in life, the secret is learning how to lose. Nobody goes undefeated all the time. If you can pick up after a crushing defeat, and go on to win again, you are going to be a champion someday.
Wilma Rudolph *(1940-1994)*
American Olympic runner

Work ethic

You shouldn't have to justify your work.
Judy Chicago *(1939-)*
American historian

I went back to being an amateur, in the sense of somebody who loves what she is doing. If a professional loses the love of work, routine sets in, and that's the death of work and of life.
Ade Bethune *(1914-2002)*
American artist

We gain energy from being free to do those things we chose to do. We never tire when we are working on our projects.
Alexandra Stoddard *(1967-)*
American journalist

Nobody ever drowned in their own sweat.
Ann Landers *(1918-2002)*
American advice columnist

There is no disgrace in working. There was no silver spoon around at the time I was born.
Anna Held *(1872-1918)*
Polish-born stage performer

Work has always been my favorite form of recreation.
Anna Howard Shaw *(1847-1919)*
American suffragist

Work in some form or other is the appointed lot of all.
Anna Jameson *(1794-1860)*
British writer

Success depends in a very large measure upon individual initiative and exertion, and cannot be achieved except by a dint of hard work.
Anna Pavlova *(1881-1931)*
Russian ballerina

You cannot be really first-rate at your work if your work is all you are.
Anna Quindlen *(1952-)*
American journalist

Hope begins in the dark, the stubborn hope that if you just show up and try to do the right thing, the dawn will come. You wait and watch and work: You don't give up.
Anne Lamott *(1954-)*
American novelist

The quickest way to kill the human spirit is to ask someone to do mediocre work.
Ayn Rand *(1905-1982)*
Russian-American novelist

To live exhilaratingly in and for the moment is deadly serious work, fun of the most exhausting sort.
Barbara Grizzuti Harrison *(1934-2002)*
American journalist, essayist

*To fulfill a dream, to be allowed to sweat over lonely labor, to be given a
chance to create, is the meat and potatoes of life. The money is the gravy.*
Bette Davis *(1908-1989)*
American actress

*People are not the best because they work hard.
They work hard because they are the best.*
Bette Midler *(1945-)*
American actress

There are no shortcuts to any place worth going.
Beverly Sills *(1929-2007)*
American operatic soprano

*I think that anything that you do, any accomplishment that you make, you
have to work for. And I've worked very hard in the last ten years of my life,
definitely, and I can tell you that hard work pays off. It's not just a cliché.*
Cameron Diaz *(1972-)*
American actress

Actors have to be there and do the work, and that's enough.
Catherine Deneuve *(1943-)*
French actress

*The first duty of a human being is to assume the right relationship
to society – more briefly, to find your real job, and do it.*
Charlotte Perkins Gilman *(1860-1935)*
American sociologist, novelist

*I realized that with hard work the world was your oyster. You could
do anything you wanted to do. I learned that at a young age.*
Chris Evert *(1954-)*
American tennis player

*In the final analysis there is no other solution to a person's
progress but the day's honest work, the day's honest decision,
the day's generous utterances, and the day's good deed.*
Clare Boothe Luce *(1903-1987)*
American playwright, diplomat

*It's in the preparation, in those dreary pedestrian virtues
they taught you in seventh grade and you didn't believe.
It's making the extra call and caring a lot.*
Diane Sawyer *(1945-)*
American broadcast journalist

If you worry about who is going to get credit, you don't get much work done.
Dorothy Height *(1912-2010)*
American activist

It is not hard work which is dreary; it is superficial work.
Edith Hamilton *(1867-1963)*
American educator

*I am not at all in favor of hard work for its own sake; many
people who work very hard indeed produce terrible things,
and should most certainly not be encouraged.*
Edna Saint Vincent Millay *(1892-1950)*
American poet, playwright

*I would say 'no'! It's such a thankless job. If you do great, nobody
mentions it. If you don't, everyone complains. It's a lot of work.*
Ellen DeGeneres *(1958-)*
American comedian, television host

*Normal is getting dressed in clothes that you buy for work and
driving through traffic in a car that you are still paying for – in order
to get to the job you need to pay for the clothes and the car, and the
house you leave vacant all day so you can afford to live in it.*
Ellen Goodman *(1950-)*
American journalist

*My second favorite household chore is ironing. My first being
hitting my head on the top bunk bed until I faint.*
Erma Bombeck *(1927-1996)*
American writer, humorist

You'll never prove you're too good for a job by not doing your best.
Ethel Merman *(1908-1984)*
American singer

The days you work are the best days.
Georgia O'Keeffe *(1887-1986)*
American painter

There are so many ways of earning a living and most of them are failures.
Gertrude Stein *(1874-1946)*
American writer

Paintin's not important. The important thing is keepin' busy.
Grandma Moses *(1860-1961)*
American folk artist

*Life is a short day; but it is a working day. Activity may
lead to evil, but inactivity cannot lead to good.*
Hannah More *(1745-1833)*
English writer, philanthropist

Happiness consists in the full employment of our faculties in some pursuit.
Harriet Martineau *(1802-1876)*
English social theorist

*The only thing that separates successful people from the ones
who aren't is the willingness to work very very hard.*
Helen Gurley Brown *(1922-)*
American author, publisher

Hard work keeps the wrinkles out of the mind and spirit.
Helena Rubinstein *(1870-1965)*
Polish-American cosmetics industrialist

*Fame is what comes after you're dead. When you're alive it's
notoriety – and an annoyance. I'm just a working woman.*
Imogen Cunningham *(1883-1976)*
American photographer

*My grandfather once told me that there were two kinds of people:
those who do the work and those who take the credit. He told me
to try to be in the first group; there was much less competition.*
Indira Gandhi *(1917-1984)*
Indian Prime Minister

*If you really want something, and really work hard, and take
advantage of opportunities, and never give up, you will find a way.*
Jane Goodall *(1934-)*
English, chimpanzee researcher

*It's a shame to call somebody a 'diva' simply because
they work harder than everybody else.*
Jennifer Lopez *(1970-)*
American musician

*Work is creativity accompanied by the comforting realization that one is
bringing forth something really good and necessary, with the conviction that
a sudden, arbitrary cessation would cause a sensitive void, produce a loss.*
Jenny Heynrichs *(1829-1902)*
German author

*When I am home for like a two-year stretch, I
get antsy, because I want to work.*
Jessica Lange *(1949-)*
American actress

*Never refuse an assignment except when there is a conflict of
interest, a potential of danger to you or your family, or you hold
a strongly biased attitude about the subject under focus.*
Jessica Savitch *(1947-1983)*
American journalist

Never drink black coffee at lunch; it will keep you awake in the afternoon.
Jilly Cooper *(1937-)*
English author

*I think you should take your job seriously, but not
yourself – that is the best combination.*
Judi Dench *(1934-)*
English actress

*The simple idea that everyone needs a reasonable amount of
challenging work in his or her life, and also a personal life, complete
with noncompetitive leisure, has never really taken hold.*
Judith Martin *(1938-)*
American etiquette author

*Of course I work hard. Why shouldn't I? Who am I
to think I should get things the easy way?*
Judy Holliday *(1921-1965)*
American actress

*All I can do is just do good work. As far as selling tickets
is concerned, that's completely out of my hands.*
Julia Roberts *(1967-)*
American actress

Success is a nice by-product but what I really want is work.
Juliette Lewis *(1973-)*
American actress

*I don't think that work ever really destroyed anybody. I think
that lack of work destroys them a hell of a lot more.*
Katharine Hepburn *(1907-2003)*
American actress

The only genius that's worth anything is the genius for hard work.
Kathleen Winsor *(1919-2003)*
American author

I have too much respect for the characters I play to make them anything but as real as they can possibly be. I have a great deal of respect for all of them...And I don't want to screw them by not portraying them honestly.
Kyra Sedgwick *(1965-)*
American actress

I always treated writing as a profession, never as a hobby. If you don't believe in yourself, no one else will.
Laurell K. Hamilton *(1963-)*
American writer

People should tell your children what life is all about – it's about work.
Lauren Bacall *(1924-)*
American actress

I'm nice, and I show up on time.
Lauren Graham *(1967-)*
American actress

Everyone talks about age, but it's not about age. It's about work ethic. Winning never gets old.
Lisa Leslie *(1972-)*
American basketball player

I am so full of my work, I can't stop to eat or sleep, or for anything but a daily run.
Louisa May Alcott *(1832-1888)*
American author

In my studio I'm as happy as a cow in her stall.
Louise Nevelson *(1899-1988)*
American sculptor, painter

Luck? I don't know anything about luck. I've never banked on it and I'm afraid of people who do. Luck to me is something else: hard work – and realizing what is opportunity and what isn't.
Lucille Ball *(1911-1989)*
American comedian, actress

*The thing that I have done throughout my life is to
do the best job that I can and to be me.*
Mae Jemison *(1956-)*
American astronaut

*I do not know anyone who has got to the top without hard work. That is the
recipe. It will not always get you to the top, but should get you pretty near.*
Margaret Thatcher *(1925-)*
English Prime Minister

Take your work seriously, but never yourself.
Margot Fonteyn *(1919-1991)*
English ballerina

*I always feel I work for those people who work hard, who go to the box
office and put down their money and want to be entertained. I always feel
I do it for them. I don't care so much about what the director thinks.*
Marilyn Monroe *(1926-1962)*
American actress

*Yes. I did more research than I ever wanted to and saw some things
I wish I didn't. I went on ride-alongs, spent time with Homicide,
Cold Case, and SVU detectives, hung out in subways learning how
to spot pervs and pick-pockets, viewed an autopsy, went to a police
firing range, and witnessed court cases and I read, read, read.*
Mariska Hargitay *(1964-)*
American actress

Everybody's got a job to do, and I do mine as best I can.
Marlee Matlin *(1965-)*
American actress

*You can have unbelievable intelligence, you can have connections,
you can have opportunities fall out of the sky. But in the end, hard
work is the true, enduring characteristic of successful people.*
Marsha Evans *(1947-)*
American, US Navy Rear Admiral

*Practice means to perform, over and over again in the
face of all obstacles, some act of vision, of faith, of desire.
Practice is a means of inviting the perfection desired.*
Martha Graham *(1894-1991)*
American dancer, choreographer

It is easier to do a job right than to explain why you didn't.
Martina Navratilova *(1956-)*
Czech American tennis player

*I think that if you shake the tree, you ought to be
around when the fruit falls to pick it up.*
Mary Cassatt *(1844-1926)*
American impressionist artist

*Work itself is the reward. If I choose challenging work it will
pay me back with interest. At least I'll be interested even if
nobody else is. And this attempt for excellence is what sustains
the most well lived and satisfying, successful lives.*
Meryl Streep *(1949-)*
American actress

Hard work has made it easy. That is my secret. That is why I win.
Nadia Comaneci *(1961-)*
Romanian Olympic gymnast

*Awards are so unnecessary, because I think we get so much out
of our work just by doing it. The work is a reward in itself.*
Natalie Portman *(1981-)*
American actress

*The ability to take pride in your own work is one of the
hallmarks of sanity. Take away the ability to both work
and be proud of it and you can drive anyone insane.*
Nikki Giovanni *(1943-)*
American poet, author

*The big secret in life is that there is no big secret. Whatever
your goal, you can get there if you're willing to work.*
Oprah Winfrey *(1954-)*
American media mogul

*I don't wait for moods. You accomplish nothing if you do that.
Your mind must know it has got to get down to work.*
Pearl S. Buck *(1892-1973)*
American writer

*I believe you are your work. Don't trade the stuff of your life,
time, for nothing more than dollars. That's a rotten bargain.*
Rita Mae Brown *(1944-)*
American novelist

It seems we always exceed even our own expectations – after a lot of hard work.
Roberta Williams *(1953-)*
American computer game designer

I have the same attitude with work – I like to go to work, I like to work really hard, I like to give everything my all, I like to try things that are new, you know.
Rosie Huntington-Whiteley *(1987-)*
English model

Do the best you can in every task, no matter how unimportant it may seem at the time. No one learns more about a problem than the person at the bottom.
Sandra Day O'Connor *(1930-)*
American Supreme Court Justice

The only thing that ever sat its way to success was a hen.
Sarah Brown *(1963-)*
British executive

I'm of peasant stock. I put my head down and work. Push. Push. Push. Push. There's nothing delicate or dainty about it.
Sharon Stone *(1958-)*
American actress

I worked hard and made my own way, just as my father had. ...I learned, from observing him, the satisfaction that comes from striving and seeing a dream fulfilled.
Sigourney Weaver *(1949-)*
American actress

I like to laugh, but on the court, it is my work. I try to smile, but it is so difficult. I concentrate on the ball, not on my face.
Steffi Graf *(1969-)*
German tennis player

It is only mercenaries who expect to be paid by the day.
Teresa of Avila *(1515-1582)*
Spanish Roman Catholic nun, saint

I never drink, and I have never done drugs, ...All I have ever done is work, work, work.
Tina Turner *(1939-)*
American singer

Pay me for my work but I don't do it for the money.
Vanna Bonta *(1958-)*
American novelist, poet

I am fierce for work. Without work I am nothing.
Winifred Holtby *(1898-1935)*
English novelist

Made in the USA
San Bernardino, CA
12 March 2018